Bitcoin Bros

Bitcoin Bros

Masculinity, Cryptocurrency, and the Future of Men

Dan Cassino

BLOOMSBURY ACADEMIC
LONDON · NEW YORK · OXFORD · NEW DELHI · SYDNEY

BLOOMSBURY ACADEMIC
Bloomsbury Publishing Plc, 50 Bedford Square, London, WC1B 3DP, UK
Bloomsbury Publishing Inc, 1359 Broadway, New York, NY 10018, USA
Bloomsbury Publishing Ireland, 29 Earlsfort Terrace, Dublin 2, D02 AY28, Ireland

BLOOMSBURY, BLOOMSBURY ACADEMIC and the Diana logo are trademarks of
Bloomsbury Publishing Plc

First published in Great Britain 2026

Cover design by Namkwan Cho
Cover image © Shutterstock

A catalogue record for this book is available from the British Library.

Library of Congress Control Number: 2025945462

ISBN: HB: 978-1-3505-0809-5
      PB: 978-1-3505-0808-8
    ePDF: 978-1-3505-0811-8
   eBook: 978-1-3505-0810-1

Typeset by Newgen KnowledgeWorks Pvt. Ltd., Chennai, India
Printed and bound in Great Britain

For product safety related questions contact productsafety@bloomsbury.com.

To find out more about our authors and books visit www.bloomsbury.com
and sign up for our newsletters.

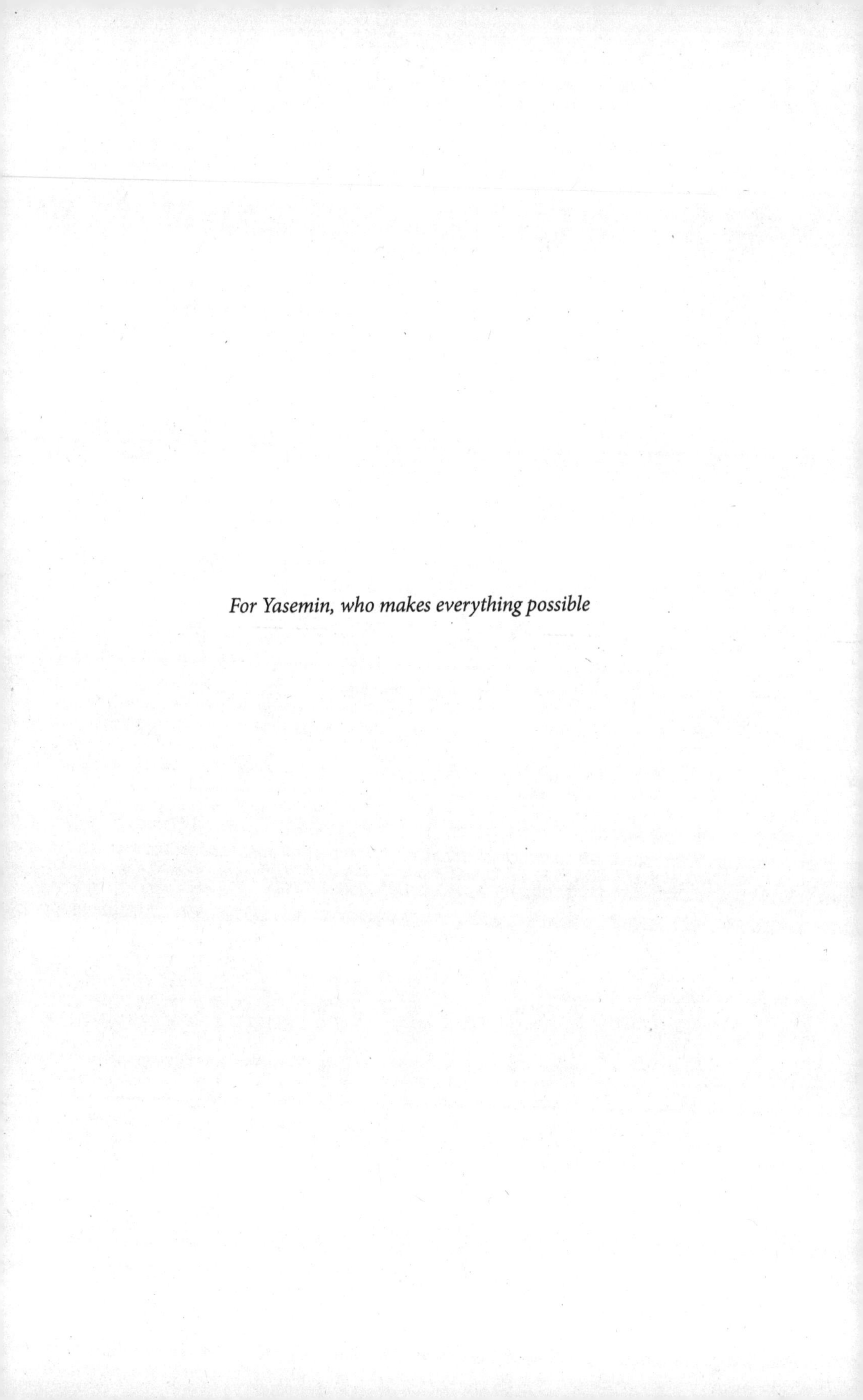

For Yasemin, who makes everything possible

Contents

About the Author

Dan Cassino is Professor of Government and Politics at Fairleigh Dickinson University and the Executive Director of the FDU Poll.

Figures

Tables

"Do you even lift, bro?" Cryptocurrency and Technical Masculinities

In the summer of 2024, news sites writing about cryptocurrencies were abuzz with rapid increases in the price of online masculinity influencer Andrew Tate's DADDY coin, which had achieved market capitalization of more than $100 million—Tate claimed that he would take it to a billion—dropping only slightly as other cryptocurrencies suffered major drop-offs in value.

This increase came despite signs that the value of the coin might have been artificially pumped, with insiders buying up more than a quarter of the supply early, and some apparently cashing out (one suspicious-looking transaction had an early buyer turning $1,950 worth of coins into a bit shy of $1.75 million). Market capitalization in cryptocurrencies is almost definitionally exaggerated, but someone was making real money off the coin.

Tate had been confined to Romania while awaiting trial on criminal charges including human trafficking, but a court ruling that he would be allowed to leave Romania and travel throughout the EU was seen as a boost to the coin's viability, as Tate would be allowed to travel to promote it. That travel would likely not take him to the UK, however, as he faced civil and criminal charges there, as well as a tax investigation. The valuation of his other coin, the name of which includes a racial slur not suitable for print, was also on the rise.

Tate—a former professional kickboxer who first gained wide notoriety when producers removed him from UK reality show "Big Brother" after just six days over a rape investigation—might be an extreme example, but the fact remains that tens of thousands of people have given him money to buy a digital asset that is based on no business, on no revenue, and purely on the expectation that others might want to buy it as well. Defenders of cryptocurrencies will often argue that they are not really that different from stocks, or from the currencies issued by governments, but stocks, in some sense, are tied to the revenues of a corporation and currencies are backed by the full faith and credit of the issuing country. Coins like DADDY are based on nothing, but that hasn't stopped millions of Americans, mostly men, from buying them up. It might be nice to think of this as a marginalized behavior, something for young men who are terminally online, who have been seduced by online shysters and influencers, but it's not. Forty percent of men aged thirty and under in the United States say that they own, or have owned, crypto. One in six voters in US national elections say that they own, or have owned, it. We ignore it, or marginalize it, at our own risk.

When cryptocurrencies were first moving into the mainstream, there were a host of news articles asking why women *weren't* buying them. The real question, though, is why millions of men *are* buying them.

When men buy into cryptocurrencies, or the related phenomenon of meme stocks, they're not buying an asset nearly as much as they're buying into a set of ideas. For the overwhelming majority of buyers, these are not good investments, but it doesn't really matter, as the payoff isn't financial, but emotional, giving the buyer an opportunity to perform a version of masculinity in a world where they find such displays to be increasingly difficult. Cryptocurrencies and meme stocks give young men a chance to show a community—real or imagined—that they have mastered a technical, esoteric, masculinized area of knowledge, that they are rational risk-takers, rebels, loyal, and persevering. The people who sell them these coins prey on these desires, offering them the chance to display these traits along with the promise—however unlikely—that by doing so, by holding on to the asset no matter what, they could become fabulously wealthy. The story of cryptocurrency isn't really about finance and economics. It's about gender, about the ways in which men are looking to perform masculinities in a changing world. It's about how masculinity itself is shifting, and young men's desperate attempts to keep up.

Technical Masculinities

For young men, masculinity has always been a problem. Men benefit from the fact that masculinity is much more valued in our society than femininity is, but the standards of masculinity that men feel that they're supposed to live up to are difficult, or perhaps impossible, for men to achieve. In the construction used by University of South Florida professors Joseph Vandello and Jennifer Bosson, masculinity is both elusive (aspirational, hard to achieve, and not open to everyone) and tenuous, subject to loss at any time (Vandello & Bosson 2013).

To be perceived as masculine, men must perform their gender in ways that are recognizable to the community that they're in, ways that are often tied to wealth, race, ethnicity, body shape, sexuality, or other factors that are out of their control. This is not to say that gay men, trans men, or Black men can't be masculine—only that they're often cut out of certain ways that dominant performances of masculinity are constructed or find that there are much higher barriers to their performance. One of the pillars of modern constructions of masculinity in the United States, for instance, is fatherhood: having and supporting children. Any version of masculinity that stresses the importance of biological children is necessarily going to involve barriers for gay men, just as versions that stress the importance of home ownership are going to present barriers for poor men. To meet the demands of masculinity, men have to both *be* certain things and *do* certain things, while the demands of femininity only require women to be something (Bosson & Vendello 2013).

The tenuous nature of masculinity ensures that even if men feel that they're meeting the demands of masculinity right now, there's no guarantee that they'll continue to do so in the future. The loss of a job, or even of income relative to their spouse, can function as a threat to men's claim on dominant forms of masculinity. And because the standards of masculinity change over time and between communities, men have to be vigilant, looking to see if other men are accepting their current performance of masculinity.

In the past decades, the economic and social reality of what men, and especially young men, can expect to achieve has shifted drastically. In the past, jobs that paid enough to support a single-earner household and didn't require a college degree may not have been common or open to everyone, but they existed for many white men. Houses in suburban neighborhoods with schools that were considered good, in areas that were considered safe, were relatively affordable for those allowed to buy them. Fifty years ago, the median home price in the United States was about 3.75 times the median annual income; today, it's about 7.25 times the median income (LongTermTrends.net 2025). White men were exalted in the workplace, given precedence over female workers, almost without regard to skills or qualifications. Today, a single-earner household isn't a middle-class marker, but a sign of wealth, akin to polo. Housing prices, especially in neighborhoods that are perceived to have good schools, have put the affordable homes of the past out of reach for even many middle-class workers. In a world with increasing economic and social inequality, and one in which women are now more likely to earn college degrees than men, the expectations of masculinity haven't evolved much past *Mad Men*.

When men feel that the expectations of dominant forms of masculinity are just a little out of their reach, when their reach just exceeds their grasp, they often double down in their performance of behaviors or traits that they think will demonstrate their masculinity. They might buy guns to play up their role as a protector (Carlson 2015; Cassino & Besen-Cassino 2020) or buy a big truck or SUV (Munch & Gruys 2018; Nelson 2020). But when they feel that the demands of dominant forms of masculinity are completely unattainable, they're likely to reorient themselves and look for alternative performances of masculinity that they can achieve.

Buying cryptocurrency might not be a marker of currently dominant[1] forms of masculinity, but it can be a way for men to perform technical masculinities. These performances of masculinity—described in greater detail in Chapter 2— rely on men demonstrating knowledge and mastery over masculine-coded areas of expertise. Performing such masculinities requires that men demonstrate technical, hidden, or esoteric knowledge of these fields, leading to sometimes incomprehensibly jargon-filled language, or claims of knowledge that's outside of what the mainstream can understand.

Young men's purchases of cryptocurrencies and similar assets make a lot more sense when put into this context. Many of the men aren't buying them because they're good investments (though they may believe that they are), but as part of a performance of technical masculinities. Buying and trading cryptocurrencies is not an easy or straightforward process: as I'll talk about in Chapter 3, it's a market lousy with pump and dumps, rug pulls[2] and other scams, as well as just straight theft targeting new or unwary investors. That means that merely buying the assets becomes a demonstration of knowledge and mastery of multiple masculine-coded areas: finance, investments, and computers. Knowing which cryptocurrencies to buy—through detailed analysis of price shifts over time, or even based on instinctual vibes—is a further demonstration of that knowledge. Even the constant threat of scams is an opportunity for demonstrating knowledge by being able to spot them.

The assets are also incredibly volatile, which would normally make them bad investments, but that volatility gives these men the opportunity to perform masculine traits like perseverance ("I believe in it, so I'm holding on through the dip") and rationality ("I won't get emotional and be scared off by a temporary drop in price"). A safe asset just doesn't give men the chance at such performances: if a stock is safe, or rising a little bit every month, no one's going to be applauded for holding on to it.

The very characteristics that make cryptocurrency investments generally a bad idea are the characteristics that make them effective as a demonstration of technical masculinities. But if this is a performance, there must be an audience. In this case, the audience for these performances of masculinity is almost entirely online, in the message boards and social media sites where people gather to talk about cryptocurrencies, meme stocks, and the like. From a research perspective, this is a good thing, as looking at what men are saying on these forums provides insight into how men understand these investments. In most other respects, though, the links between these forums, and forums dedicated to much more problematic topics, mean that men become embedded in deeply misogynistic language and ideas.

Gender, Sex, and Sexuality

Before diving into the relationship between cryptocurrency and gender, it's important to define what I mean by "gender" in this context. In everyday conversation, "gender" is frequently used as a euphemism for sex, referring to the mostly biological traits of an individual: gender as male or female.[3] It's also used to denote whether someone is trans or not, or their social presentation of their sex. In many languages, it's a grammatical construction. But as used here, "gender" refers to the attitudes and behaviors that people use in order to assert their claim to a particular sexual identity (as in West & Zimmerman 1987). So, masculinity is what people do in order to be seen (by themselves or others) as being men; femininity is what they do in order to be seen as being women. These behaviors and traits might be socially dependent, or they might be at least in part driven by genes or hormones: where they arise from doesn't matter nearly as much as their function. Much of the influential early theoretical work on the social expression of gender used trans people as case studies: West and Zimmerman (1987), for instance, spend much of their influential piece unpacking the ways in which a trans woman demonstrates feminine traits so that she'll be seen as a woman in social contexts. In some cases, West and Zimmerman argue that she's going a little overboard in the way that she's enacting femininity, to bolster her claim to being seen as a woman. The normal takeaway from this work is that we can understand gender as being a performance, one played out not just by trans people, but by everyone. As with any performance, there are scripts: this is how men talk, and walk, and act; this is how women do so. We label those scripts masculinity and femininity, and someone is masculine or feminine to the extent that they hit their marks and say their lines.

This conceptualization of gender was an enormous advance over the way that gender was previously conceptualized (see, for instance, the measures promulgated in Terman & Miles 1936 or Rosenberg, Sutton-Smith, & Morgan 1961), but is still limited in the way it sees masculinity and femininity as unitary concepts. In all of this work, masculinity and femininity are seen as collections of traits: men are aggressive and emotionally restrained, for example; women are expressive and concerned with other people's emotions. The problem with such a view is that it defines gender without paying attention to gender relations, the ways in which masculinity and femininity structure social interactions.

This aspect of gender was brought into focus by Australian sociologist Raewyn Connell. In her seminal work on masculinity, Connell (1995) argued that masculinity, in particular, was expressed in innumerable ways but that those expressions of masculinity were hierarchical: there isn't one way of being masculine, but a contentious, graduated series of masculinities. At the top of the scale are dominant expressions of masculinity; at the bottom of the scale are the expressions of masculinity that are tied to marginalized groups (especially, in Connell's work, gay men). These masculinities are not set, and are constantly in flux, with masculinities higher on the pecking order borrowing from and modifying innovations pioneered by those lower down. I'll get deeper into these ideas in Chapter 2, but the important thing to understand is that there are many ways in which men can perform masculinity, and that these different performances are jostling for position within a hierarchy. Each of these performances can make use of different traits or behaviors to justify their position in the gender hierarchy, and that hierarchy might vary between social classes and regions. A form of masculinity that values hunting and woodsmanship might be dominant in rural areas, while one based around travel, worldliness, and wealth might be dominant in globalized cities. Cryptocurrency purchases, then, aren't a way of performing masculinity, so much as a way of performing a certain kind of masculinity: one that I'm calling technical masculinity.[4] If this was just a way for men to perform a certain kind of marginalized online masculinity, it would still be interesting, but perhaps not so consequential. However, the men who use technical masculinities to perform their gender don't seem content with a spot low on the hierarchy of masculinities and are making a case for why their version of masculinity should become the dominant form within our society. This leads me to argue that technical masculinities are a form of protest masculinities: gender constructions that are trying to move up the hierarchy of performances.

Understanding cryptocurrency and related assets is also important for understanding how finance and society are changing. Cryptocurrencies are a multibillion-dollar industry; meme stocks have led to millions of Americans buying up stock of (often foundering) companies like GameStop, AMC Theatres, or (the now bankrupt) Bed, Bath and Beyond. Studying why people, almost all of them men, put their money into such ventures is intrinsically important, but it also provides a second case study on how men are using investments and claims of knowledge to perform their gender identities.

Because cryptocurrency has become ubiquitous in the United States in recent years, with ads on the Super Bowl challenging men to be bold, and major financial firms finding ways to move money into them, it's arguably the most visible instantiation of the technical masculinities that these young men are trying to assert. But it isn't the only way, and as problematic as cryptocurrency purchases might be, many of the other ways in which men express technical masculinities are much, much worse, and some of the frankly horrifying ideals of what's called the "manosphere" are packaged along with them.

Technical Masculinities and the Manosphere

The story of gender and cryptocurrency is also the story of the online spaces that shape the narratives around these investments and the communities that serve as the audience for these performances of masculinity. In a 2022 survey of young men (see the Methodological Appendix for a table showing all of the surveys used in the text), I asked respondents who had bought individual stocks or cryptocurrency where they got their information about which assets they should buy: the most popular answer by a wide margin was "online sources, like Reddit or Twitter." A majority of respondents who bought these assets said that they learned about them on web forums; the number two answer was a nebulous response that they "did their own research some other way." Only about 15 percent said that they consulted a financial advisor. These investment decisions, and the way that they're understood and experienced by the people making them are shaped by these web forums, so understanding these decisions means understanding these forums.

Despite attempts to make cryptocurrency investment more mainstream, it's still driven in large part by these online discussion boards speculating about investment strategies and the probable price movements of cryptocurrencies both relatively well known (like Bitcoin or Ethereum) and obscure (most meme coins). At their best, these forums are full of posters providing guidance to new investors, spotting scams, and commiserating over losses.

However, these forums are often not at their best. When they're not, they're rife with posturing and relentless mockery of other users. As with Andrew

Tate's meme coins, there's enormous crossover between forums discussing cryptocurrencies and those discussing other, perhaps more problematic, areas within masculinity. On Reddit, this is clear from the user overlap between subreddits devoted to crypto. Individuals who post on r/cryptocurrency are very likely to also post on other subreddits devoted to crypto topics (they're about twenty-two times as likely as the average Reddit user to post on the subreddit r/bitcoin, for instance), but they're also about three times as likely as the average user to post on forums about poker, or sports betting, or performance enhancing drugs (nootropics or steroids), and twice as likely to post on forums about influencers like Joe Rogan or Jordan Peterson. Reddit users who post on r/bitcoin are 3.5 times as likely as the average Reddit user to have posted on the rabidly misogynistic (and now banned) "Men Going Their Own Way" forum, three times as likely to post on subreddits devoted to masculinity influencers, and twice as likely to post about sports cars or seduction techniques.[5]

In their analysis of one particular subreddit (r/unpopular), Hanson, Pascoe, and Light (2023) find clear evidence of the connections between these seemingly disparate topics. Discussions on that forum of politics, feminism, race, religion, education, and even grammar are linked by the underlying contention that straight white men are the real victims of discrimination, in what they call "bundled grievances." And while there's no obvious connection between them, one of the clusters of discussion topics identified in their analysis includes abortion, education, violence, feminism, sexual assault, relationships, and money. Even if it's just in the minds of the men discussing them, these topics are all linked, so while it's normal to talk about money, finance, and crypto without talking about sex and gender, that's not how they're actually experienced.

The point is that online, in both content and in users, discussions of cryptocurrency (as well as meme stocks[6]) are tightly connected to what researchers have dubbed the "manosphere" (i.e. Ging 2019a), websites that have played a substantial role in shaping how young men experience their gender identity and which shape their views about what it means to be a man. These sites include forums ranging in content from men's rights activism, incel groups, alt-right political groups, pick-up artists, and videogames (as seen most clearly in the "gamergate" harassment campaigns) and have been characterized not just by the extent to which they cater to young men, but by their often deeply misogynistic content.[7] These online sites are important not just because they're relatively popular among young men looking for models of what it means to be a man in modern society, and not just because they give us an insight into how these men are constructing their gender, but because of their transnational nature. Generally, masculinities have been constructed on the local level, with overlapping performances of masculinities within small groups (geographic or social), within communities and countries. These performances spread across areas like all ideas and fashions do, with particularly vivid ways of performing masculinities being attractive to men outside of where they originated and taken up by others. In this way, innovation and globalization of masculinities coexist with local and traditional ways of performing masculinities. However, these online forums serve to homogenize performances of masculinities, creating new categories of transnational masculinities (Ging 2019a) that might once have been limited to the highly mobile vanguard of globalization but can now spread anywhere young men have internet access.

While there has been a great deal of research looking at the content of the online "manosphere," finance-based forums on Reddit (like r/WallStreetBets) or elsewhere (like the Telegram channels for crypto meme coin sites like pump.fun) have not always been included in these analyses. But they should be. While they don't have as much explicit masculinity content, they are very much serving the same functions, giving young men what they see as a path toward the traits, or at least the rewards, of dominant forms of masculinity. These groups teach men that marginal forms of investing—meme stocks, crypto, forex, and the like—are a test of their masculinity, and if they have sufficient knowledge, mastery, and perseverance not only will they inevitably get rich, but they'll be part of a heroic struggle against an ill-defined (but powerful) enemy—this underlying narrative is explored further in Chapters 3 and 4. As with any test, not everyone is going to pass: some men won't "do their own research" and will fall for a scam or be the victim of a rug pull. Some will sell at the wrong time, too early or too late, demonstrating a failure of the mastery that success requires. Some won't be able to tough out losses, because they let emotion overwhelm their rationality, or because they get scared, giving into FUD (fear, uncertainty, and doubt).

Investments in cryptocurrencies, meme stocks, and related assets aren't driven by financial considerations but rather by the desire to assert a masculine gender identity, especially among young men who do not see other paths to do so. They are far from the only way that men make use of technical masculinities, leveraging knowledge over a masculine-coded area to assert their gender identities, but they're a powerful one, because they represent a credible commitment—someone literally putting their money where their mouth is— and because of the heroic narrative that's built around them. As we'll see, these heroic narratives are generally ridiculous from the outside—it's hard to imagine that there's really a Wall Street cabal determined to bankrupt a chain of video game stores—but it doesn't matter. The buying and selling of these assets is often discussed in almost incomprehensible technical jargon; as a completely sincere post about NFTs (a briefly popular form of cryptocurrency that takes the form of digital collectible) that was heavily memed said,

> ape holders can use multiple slurp juices on a single ape
>
> so if you have 1 astro ape and 3 slurp juices you can create 3 new apes
>
> Tonight's slurp juice mint event is essentially a minting event for both Lab Monkes and Special Forces

And even when they're talking about cryptocurrency directly, rather than NFTs, the rhetoric is scarcely more comprehensible.

> Audio Memecoin that Jeribond & Damx launched on the Gas Pump went to the DeDust in only 10 minutes

The fact that such statements are simultaneously incomprehensible to an outsider (is the slurp juice mint flavored?) and make perfect sense to an insider is part of the appeal. If it's not difficult to understand what's going on, then there's no opportunity to show off by understanding it. In the same way that men use understanding of male-coded topics like pop culture properties, or craft beers, to establish hierarchy within a masculine-coded space, they're using knowledge and mastery of fringe financial assets to demonstrate their masculinity.

The network of web forums that discussions of cryptocurrency and related assets are embedded in aren't just a collection of interests but present a unified world view based around the idea that they system (whatever that means) is fixed, and only by operating outside of it, or hacking it in some way can men ever achieve the success that they deserve. If men are falling short of the (impossible) standards that have been set for them, it's not because they're bad—it's the society that makes success by normal means impossible.

University of California-Santa Barbara Sociologist Shawn P. Van Valkenburgh (2021) carried out a content analysis of postings on one of the more prolific of these forums, the subreddit "The Red Pill" (r/theredpill).[8] In this case, the red pill is a reference to the 1999 science fiction film "The Matrix," and while the filmmakers have made clear that the pills in the movie were a metaphor for acceptance of a trans identity (BBC 2020), the users on the forum take it rather more literally, believing that they, having taken the metaphorical red pill, see the world as it truly is and can therefore use that knowledge to bend reality to their wishes.[9] In this case, the "true" state of the world is that feminism is a lie used to disguise female dominance over men, backed up by the state, which uses coercive power to redistribute benefits and money from men to women.

Taking the red pill means seeing through fictions like the oppression of women and using esoteric scientific understanding of evolutionary psychology, biology, and economics to be able to manipulate the system (much as Neo, in the movie, is able to achieve superhuman powers in the Matrix from his understanding that it is not real[10]). The fact that much of the research they draw on might well be seen as pseudoscientific matters little: indeed, the fact that it's rejected by the mainstream scientific community can be seen as a sign that the work is valid (much as in the anti-vax movements that arose during the Covid-19 pandemic). Understanding how claims of knowledge and mastery are used in these forums to supposedly get men what they feel that they deserve—in this case, sex—helps to show how these forums see the world and provide context for their views of finance.

Before posting on r/theredpill, users are instructed to read a set of foundational documents—what Van Valkenburgh refers to as "the sidebar"— that together are about the length of a medium-sized book. While the details of the theories discussed in these documents is beyond the scope of this discussion, the essence of their argument is that women are genetically predisposed to want to reproduce with certain kinds of men (referred to as "alphas") but be in long-term relationships with other kinds of men (betas), a view that they see as driven by research in evolutionary psychology. Combined with work in the economics of dating markets—and the concept of "sexual market value"—these documents argue that women are essentially designed to exploit men, but understanding the means by which women do so allows men to short-circuit the systems and get sexual access to women, turning the tables on them. Any concerns about the morality of such a project—fooling women in order to have sex with them—is waved away by the appeals to the Machiavellian nature of women and the logic of free markets. Ging (2019b, 57) notes that these theories arise largely from the men's rights movement of the 1980s, and aside from justifying misogyny, they also serve as a kind of rhetorical jiu-jitsu: if men's actions are biologically ingrained, feminist demands that men adjust their behavior are an attack on men's existential rights.

All of this is premised on appeals to science, rationality, and positivism. As one of the documents Van Valkenburgh quotes says, "Understanding the facets of this [evolutionary] psychology are key to developing a good sexual strategy." Once someone understands evolutionary psychology, the economics of dating markets and the like, they can learn to assert (or fake) traits that will make them sexually attractive to women: but these are learned skills, and a failure to be sexually attractive is therefore to properly internalize the underlying science (and the often wild conclusions drawn from it).

They start with the assumption that there is a group of men—"Chads," "Alphas," or whatever terminology is in vogue—who are meeting the demands of hegemonic masculinity, and reaping the rewards thereof: financial success, sexual access to women, and so on. However, the content is not marketed to them—they don't need any help!—but rather to the young men who don't meet this (unrealistic, perhaps impossible) standard. What are these men to do? Well, one option is to live life as they have been, "blue-pilled" and pining for success that they'll never have; the best that they can hope for is to marry and support a woman who will inevitably cheat on them. The alternative is knowledge, learning the (pseudo)science that underlies the red pill worldview, internalizing those theories and processes, and using that knowledge to get the benefits that naturally accrue to the alphas. Knowledge—and not just any knowledge, but esoteric, hidden knowledge that's only available to initiates—can serve to either simulate a higher status within the hierarchies of masculinities or even to achieve it.

It's important to note that the understanding of evolutionary psychology posited in these forums isn't generally too far off (see, for instance, Baumeister & Vohs's 2004 piece on "sexual economics"), even if the conclusions users draw from it are.[11] In the views promulgated on these sites, sexual access to women arises from men's understanding of the details of scientific theories, especially those that are outside of the mainstream. The science promulgated in r/theredpill is often referred to as the sorts of things that aren't taught in universities (which have, in this telling, been overrun by feminists, gays, and other groups that are cooperating to oppress men) and requires careful study and understanding. But once it is internalized, it provides the benefits of dominant forms of masculinity— dominance not only over women but also over other men (especially the betas and "cucks" who haven't been red-pilled).

The exact techniques that the self-help guides and forums argue can win sexual access to women are upsetting, eye-rolling, and beside the point. The key is that they argue that seduction is simply a skill that can be mastered through study and the understanding of esoteric or technical knowledge that's not held or understood by most people. Indeed, most men—what these forums refer to as "average frustrated chumps" (Almog & Kaplan 2017)—can't learn these techniques or wouldn't have the perseverance necessary to actually continue engaging in seemingly counterintuitive behaviors like subtly insulting women.[12]

While the guides to these seduction techniques acknowledge that there are some men who are naturally attractive to women (men who already meet the demands of hegemonic masculinities), the audience is assumed to be outside of that category but is assured that they can get the same results through technical knowledge and skill.

All of this may seem very similar to the rhetoric seen in incel ("involuntary celibate") forums, frequented by men who bemoan their lack of sexual access to women, and believe that they will never be able to get such access. While related to these communities, Van Valkenburgh notes that these red-pilled communities differ in that they believe that men can achieve sexual success by following the "scientific" prescriptions of the community. Incel groups are rather more pessimistic, arguing that (often violent) reordering of sex relations is necessary for men to get sexual access to women. Like r/theredpill, the cryptocurrency forums aren't for men who have given up: they're for men who feel shut out of the system and are looking for an alternative way in.

I'll come back to these ideas in Chapter 3, but investments in cryptocurrency are very much the concept of the red pill applied to finance. "They" want men to believe that they can get ahead by working hard and following the rules: get an education and a good job, invest wisely, and save money. In the version of reality promulgated on these forums, though, the system is rigged, and those strategies will never work. In the same way that the only way for (most) men to get sexual access to women is by understanding the system and hacking it, the only way to get ahead financially is by understanding how the system is fixed and finding alternatives, like cryptocurrencies or meme stocks. They also share an underlying narrative about men who have been unfairly treated making use of their mastery of these hidden forms of knowledge to get what they deserve, bringing down their oppressors in the process.

Even the purported rewards of meeting the standards of masculinity are problematic. Chapter 2 will go into more detail, but the men who are embracing technical masculinities see them as a wholesale replacement of currently dominant forms of masculinity. Not only are the means of achieving masculinity different, but so are the rewards for having done so. In this case, the rewards are less about picket fences and a high-paying job than cash and flash. Almog and Kaplan (2017) link these online performances of masculinities to the British concept of "laddism," which combines rampant consumerism—especially with regard to male-coded areas of interest like alcohol, sports, and cars—with sexism and the pervasive objectification of women (in the United States, *Maxim* magazine might be the most familiar example). This version of masculinity may seem to pertain much more to extant dominant performances of masculinity rather than knowledge-based technical masculinities discussed here, but manosphere websites bridge this gap by arguing that social interactions with women are simply a game that can be mastered. The same technical prowess that can get a high score in a videogame or help debug a computer program can be turned to getting sexual access to women (actual long-term relationships are rarely seen as the goal of such interactions).

As the overlap between users of cryptocurrency forums and these other online spaces demonstrate, these are different instantiations of the same underlying grievances and the same knowledge-based performances of masculinity. Cryptocurrency is now much more widespread than most Americans realize, but even if we wanted to dismiss it as some kind of internet fad, the fact that it is tied so closely with all of these other deeply problematic beliefs means that we ignore it at our own peril. And while research on investment decisions has always been dominated by the assumption of rationality, investments in cryptocurrency make for a perfect way to understand young men's masculinities *because* they're irrational. Have some people made money on cryptocurrencies? Sure. But some people also make money off pyramid schemes. The key is that, for most investors, these are not only money-losing assets but *clearly* money-losing assets that violate any rational choice model of investment. Cryptocurrencies are widespread enough today that it's important to understand why people are buying them, and because crypto markets are now interacting with the larger economy, we can't fully understand financial markets without taking them into account. They also give us an entree into how the troubling narratives being built on the internet have shaped the conceptions of masculinity of a generation of young men.

The Masculinity Gap

One of the key concepts in this book is the masculinity gap. This gap arises when there's a disconnect between how much men value masculinity and the extent to which they feel that they're meeting the demands of masculinity. If a man values masculinity and feels like he's meeting that (unrealistic) standard, he's fine (at least on that front). If a man doesn't feel like he's living up to the demands of masculinity, but doesn't value it, he's fine as well. The problem for men arises when they value masculinity but also say that they're not living up to what they think masculinity demands of them. It's those men who are falling into the masculinity gap, and who will be most motivated to find some way to bridge it. This is all, of course, completely subjective: there's no masculinity licensing board going around seeing if a man is sufficiently masculine; they're not explicitly written down anywhere. Boys and men seek out ideas of what constitutes masculine behavior, internalize them, and assess their own behavior by their self-generated benchmark, reinforced with feedback from the media, their peers, and their families.

One way men deal with a disconnect between what they think men should be and do, and what they do themselves is to stress different elements of masculinity, to find a way that they can argue to themselves that they really are meeting the standard (or, at least, a part of it that they'll decide is important to the whole project). This will be discussed later as a strategy of compensatory masculinities. The behaviors being discussed in this book, however, are better understood as a more radical response. Rather than trying to justify their behaviors as being part of existing dominant forms of masculinity, they're looking to reject those forms, and substitute an alternative conception of masculinity, changing the conflict from *within* forms of masculinity to *between* forms of masculinity.

This matters because of the societal value that is placed on masculinity. Masculine traits are valued, but masculinity itself is necessarily elusive and tenuous (DiMuccio & Knowles 2025). Men can never be totally sure that they've met the standards, which are set impossibly high; and even if they have met them, masculinity can be lost in a moment of fear or weakness. If someone says "he's not a real man," we know exactly what they mean. The centrality of gender to the way that we understand and construct our identities means that the tension between what men feel that they should be doing or being, and what they are doing or being has the potential to drive attitudes and behaviors in a way that other social identities (religion, race, ethnicity, and so on) do not.

While a theoretical understanding of technical masculinities, what they consist of, and how they interact with other conceptions of masculinity is an important part of the project of this book, there also has to be data. To identify the men who are most likely to fall into this masculinity gap, I make use of two constructs. The first is based on questions that ask men to rate how masculine they are; the second measures how much men value traditional performances of masculinity using a scale called the Masculine Role Norms Inventory (MRNI). The analyses, in all of the chapters but one (for which MRNI data was not available), look at the interaction of these two variables to see how men who fall into the masculinity gap (high scores on the MRNI, meaning that they value masculinity, and lower scores on their self-assessed masculinity, meaning that they don't think of themselves as being that masculine) differ in behavior from men who do not fall into the gap.

Measuring Masculinity

At the most basic level, this book is looking at the link between men's gender identities and their financial behaviors. The measurement of financial behaviors is easy enough, based on self-reports[13] and survey experiments, but the measurement of men's gender identities is much trickier.

Most of the analyses in this volume measure gender identity by asking men to place themselves on masculinity-femininity scales. Such scales represent a departure from past practice in the social sciences, which have largely relied on trait-based scales like the Bem Sex Role Inventory (BSRI; Bem 1974). Such trait-based scales measure masculinity and femininity by asking men to rate the extent to which they have certain traits that are seen[14] as agentic (masculine) or communal (feminine). Other scales have adopted similar operationalizations of masculinity and femininity, and while it is certainly a very narrow notion of what it means to be masculine or feminine, such measures have the virtue of providing clear, well-validated measures. They might not be measuring all the aspects of masculinity or femininity, but they're measuring something that's a big part of how many people view gender (see Markstedt et al., 2021, for an analysis looking at how individuals define masculinity and femininity) and doing it with reliable measures that have held up reasonably well over time. One of the major virtues of trait-based scales like the BSRI is that they have low levels of reactivity: people taking the scales generally don't realize that the scales are measuring gender. That's normally a good thing: if people think it's desirable to have a particular score on a scale, and they know what the scale is measuring, they may tailor their answers to get the desirable score.

On most of the self-report scales used in this book, respondents place themselves on a scale that runs from "completely masculine" to "completely feminine" or, in some instances, separate masculinity and femininity scales. What's interesting is that when people respond to these self-placements, their responses are pretty close on the main dimension of interest to what we would get from a trait-based scale. When men say how masculine they are, they're assessing themselves pretty much how they would be assessed on masculinity in a trait-based scale, with women doing the same for femininity. Men and women do worse in assessing their levels of the gender not traditionally associated with their sex (i.e., men's self-assessed femininity scores don't align with a trait-based measure), but if we want to find out the extent to which a man has masculine traits, we can get a lot of information just by asking. The fact that these are reactive scales might be an issue, but we can also think of them as being expressive: when a man declares to an interviewer in a telephone survey that he's "completely masculine," he's not just describing himself but doing the thing he's describing. In this way, they're like Jesus in the Sermon on the Mount: saying "blessed are the peacemakers" is not just a statement, but an action, blessing the peacemakers at the same time as the blessing is described (Sims & Cereno 2018), what semioticians refer to as an illocutionary act (Austin 1962). Just so, responding to the question by *saying* "completely masculine" is, itself, a demonstration of that masculinity, so even if such responses weren't accurate descriptions of masculine traits, they would serve as a marker of who feels that it is important to assert a masculine gender identity. The fact that such self-placements reliably predict sociopolitical attitudes, even controlling for other factors, certainly tells us that they're measuring something.

Of course, the biggest reason that self-placement masculinity-femininity scales have come into vogue in social science as a measure of gender is their brevity. Even the short form of a trait-based measure like the BSRI is 20 questions long: self-placement measures are just one or two questions, short enough to include in non-dedicated surveys, even if they do require a bit of an introduction setting up the measure.

On these self-placement scales, most men in the United States place themselves on the extreme masculine side of the scale: if we're looking at a six- or seven-point masculinity-femininity scale, most men pick the most extreme masculine option. If it's a 101-point scale (like the ones used for online studies like the Canadian Election Study, which has included such items for several years now), most men place themselves at ninety or above.

Women place themselves at the extreme end of femininity at about the same rate that men do (and slightly more in some samples, like the August 2024 national poll), but across surveys, women's placements are rather more spread out. Women are much more likely than men, for instance, to place themselves in the masculine categories than men are to place themselves in the feminine categories (about 4 percent in the August 2024 survey, versus about 1 percent for men), but most people still say that they have a gender identity that's "mostly" or "completely" in line with what is traditionally associated with their sex.

While this variable is theoretically varying across six points, as Figure 1.1 makes clear, the real difference is much narrower. There just aren't a

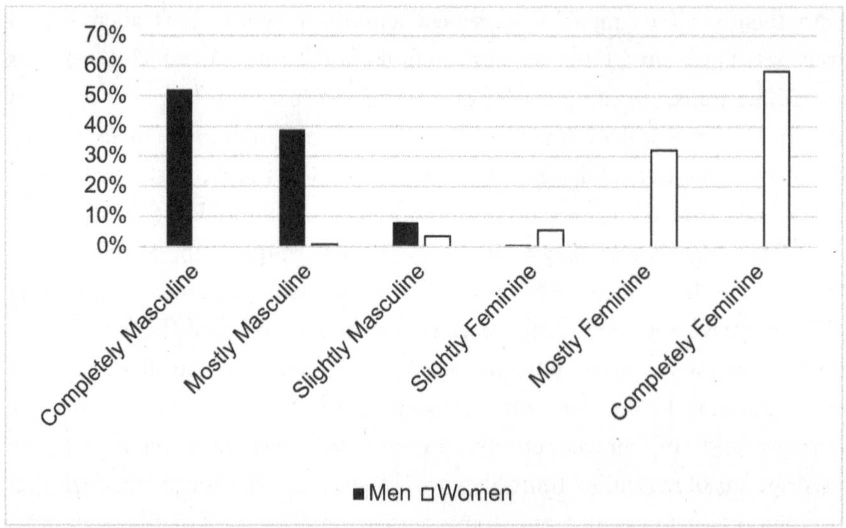

Figure 1.1 Masculinity-femininity self-placement, by sex, August 2024 national poll.

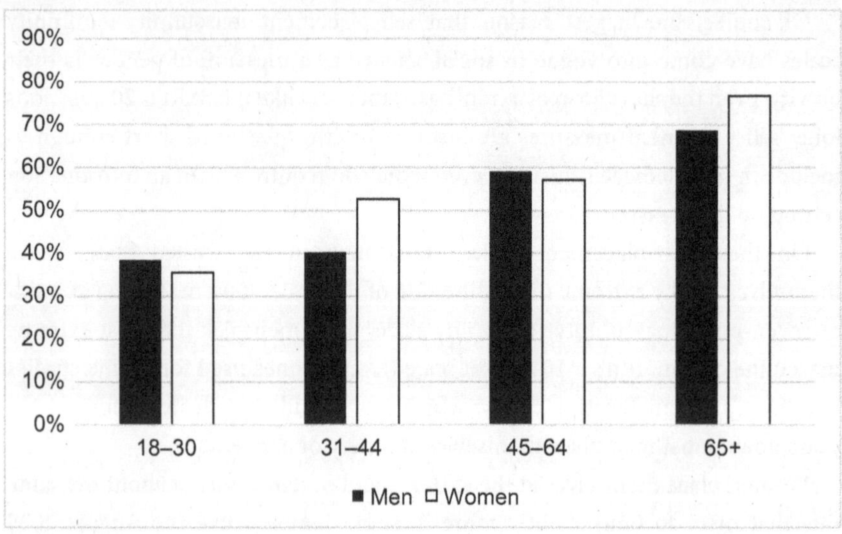

Figure 1.2 Percent "completely" masculine or feminine, by sex and age, August 2024 national poll.

lot of men who describe themselves as "slightly masculine," or at all feminine, so when this variable is used in analyses, I generally break it down into just two categories: "completely masculine" men and everyone else.

As might be expected, the percent of men and women placing themselves in the most traditional gender category—"completely masculine" for men, or "completely feminine" for women—increases with age. As seen in Figure 1.2, fewer than 40 percent of men and women aged thirty and under put themselves into these categories, but more than 70 percent of Americans aged sixty-five and over do.

While there is relatively little data on trans and nonbinary people (as there are relatively few of them in any given sample of the general population), members of sexual orientation and gender identity (SOGI) minority groups seem to be more likely than others to place themselves toward the middle of these scales. It makes sense, then, that in surveys of populations that include more sexuality and gender-diverse individuals (like young people), there are fewer respondents toward the edges of the scales (at the extreme masculine and feminine categories) and more toward the middle.

Relatively few men place themselves on the feminine side of the spectrum—fewer than 3 percent in most surveys using a unidimensional masculine-feminine scale—though numbers are a little higher in the bidimensional scales that let respondents describe their masculinity and femininity separately. Women are more likely to describe themselves as masculine, but even then, it's generally less than 10 percent in a general population sample. The big divide, especially when we're looking at American men as a whole, is really between men who place themselves in the extreme masculine category and men who place themselves anywhere else. The difference between a man who describes himself as "somewhat masculine" and one who describes himself as "slightly masculine" is far less than the difference between the "completely masculine" men and everyone else (with similar distinctions, though weaker, among women). As such, most of the analyses in this book divide men (and women) into just two groups of roughly equal size based on their responses: "completely" in line with the gender identity traditionally associated with their sex, and everyone else.

The Masculine Role Norms Inventory

In addition to measuring how people describe their masculinity or femininity, several of the surveys used in this volume also make use of a scale to measure the acceptance of traditional masculine roles. Combined with the gender measures just discussed, this allows us to identify the men who are falling into the masculinity gap.

For this purpose, I use a short version of the Masculine Role Norms Inventory (the MRNI-VB: McDermott et al. 2019; Levant et al. 2007). The

MRNI is based on work from the late 1980s (Thompson & Pleck 1986) and early 1990s (Levant et al. 1992) that tried to go beyond the suppositions of psychologists to see what, exactly, constituted norms of masculine behavior. Previous work had argued that masculinity consisted of a combination of personal achievement coupled with an avoidance of feminine activities and roles (Hartley 1959; Komarovsky [1976] 2004), while others argued that suppression of emotions was a necessary element (Pleck & Sawyer 1974); Brannon (1976; Brannon & Juni 1984) added aggression to the mix. To sort out this debate, Thompson and Pleck created a questionnaire that included all of the proposed elements of masculinity, added in a couple of questions looking at attitudes toward women,[15] and used factor analysis (a statistical technique that analyses correlations between items) to see which of these elements actually seemed to be measuring the same things. They found that of the questions boiled down to three areas: status (measured by agreement with statements like "success in his work has to be a man's central goal in this life"), toughness ("when a man is feeling a little pain, he should try not to let it show very much"), and anti-femininity ("it is a bit embarrassing for a man to have a job that is usually filled by a woman").

Over the following decades, researchers tweaked the twenty or so items identified by Thompson and Pleck, adding and subtracting dimensions based on results from different samples of men (mostly college students; see Levant et al. 2007). This process of addition and winnowing eventually led to multiple versions of the scale, with widely varying lengths and content, including a "very brief" version containing just five items (McDermott et al. 2019) that does a reasonable job of getting at all the elements of masculinity found in the larger versions of the scale.

The scale used in this book asks respondents to agree or disagree (with options for strong or weak agreement and disagreement[16]) with five statements about how men should behave.[17] The statements include things like "boys should prefer to play with trucks rather than dolls," and "men should not be too quick to tell others that they care about them." Higher scores—more agreement with these statements—indicates greater acceptance of traditional masculinity norms. While there are other, more detailed scales that can be used to measure views of traditional masculinity, the MRNI is well validated and, more importantly, short enough to be included on general purpose political surveys. As might be expected, scores on these kinds of scales are related to sexuality. Heterosexual, gay, and bisexual men seem to understand the items on similar scales in the same way, but gay and bisexual men tend to score lower, especially on dimensions

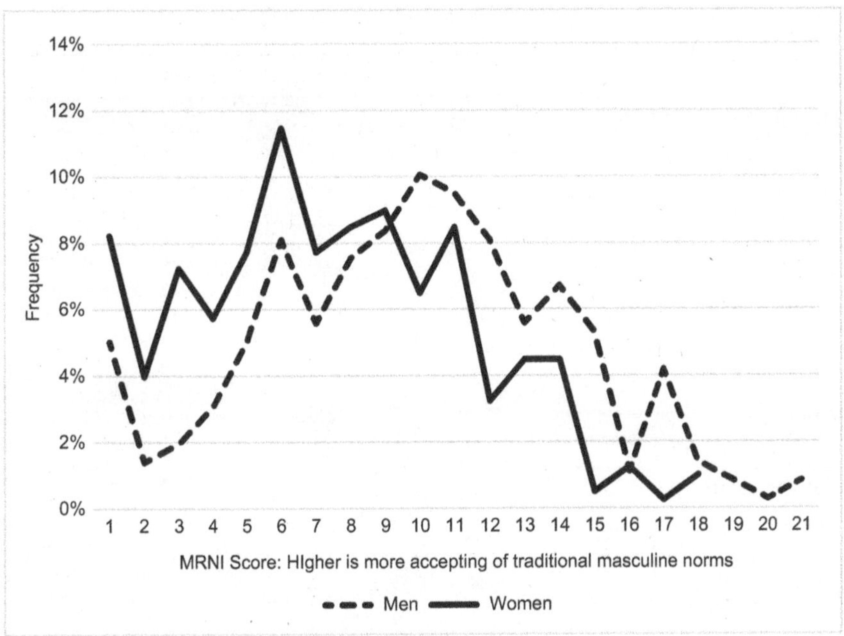

Figure 1.3 MRNI scores, by sex, August 2024 national poll.

related to masculine self-presentation and dominance over women (Anghel, Mahalik, & Harris 2023), but overall, men, regardless of their sexuality, are subject to many of the same social pressures relating to masculinity and seem to respond to those pressures in similar ways.

The MRNI is especially useful because there is significant variance in how Americans respond to it. It might be assumed that the overt nature of the scale—anyone taking it knows that they're being asked what they think about masculinity—would mean that people would give what they see as socially desirable responses, but views of what is socially desirable when it comes to masculinity vary widely.

Overall, US registered voters averaged 7.5 out of 20 on the MRNI scale; as Figure 1.3 shows, men averaged 8.8 and women significantly lower at 6.4. As might be expected, there was also a substantial gap between Democrats (5.7 average) and Republicans (9.4), as well as by education, as seen in Table 1.1.

Surprisingly, views of masculine role norms don't differ significantly by age, and this overall stability holds up even when we divide respondents by sex. Men aged thirty and under have a mean score of 9.1, no different from the mean of 9.2 among men aged thirty-one to forty-four. Nor are there any significant differences in the mean scores of women by age. It might be thought that older

Table 1.1 Mean and Median MRNI Scores (Out of 20) by Demographic Group

	Mean	Median
Overall	7.5	7
"Completely masculine" men	9.9	10
Other men	7.6	7
"Completely feminine" women	7.2	7
Other women	5.5	5
Democrats	5.7	5
Republicans	9.4	10
Men	8.8	9
Women	6.4	6
No 4 yr college degree	8.0	8
4 yr college degree	6.8	7
Age 18–30	7.9	8
31–44	7.7	7
45–64	6.8	7
65+	8.0	8
Whites	7.3	7
Blacks	7.6	8
Hispanic/Latino/as	7.5	7

people—or at least older men—express more traditional views of men's roles, but that just does not seem to be the case.

Some of the biggest differences in views of men's roles come from the interaction of sex and gender. As shown in Figure 1.4, men who say that they're "completely masculine" (remember, that's about half of men in the United States) have a mean score of 9.9 on the MRNI; among other men, the mean score is just 7.6. Women who assert a traditional "completely feminine" gender identity have a mean score of 7.2, well higher than the mean score of 5.5 among other women.

It shouldn't be a surprise that gender traditionalism in one area—asserting a gender identity "completely" in line with the gender traditionally associated with the individual's sex—lines up with gender traditionalism in another area (valuing traditional tropes of masculine behavior). But the correlation is far from perfect, and the gap between the two measures winds up telling us a lot. Remember that the proportion of men who say that they're "completely masculine" is much higher—almost double!—among the oldest cohort of men than in the youngest cohort. But if MRNI scores *don't* vary much by age, that means that there's a

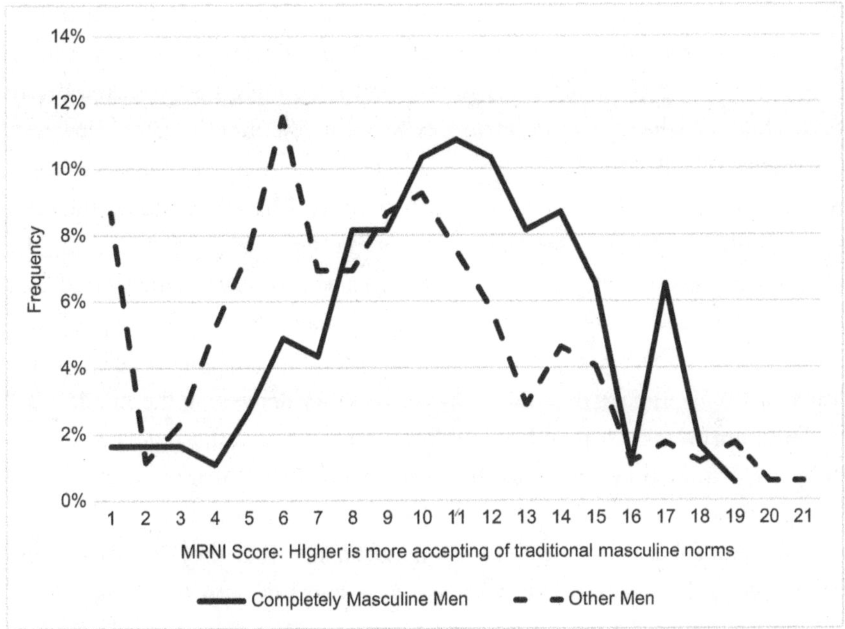

Figure 1.4 MRNI scores for US men, by asserted masculinity-femininity.

lot of young men who say that they value traditional masculinity, but, by their own assessment, aren't living up to it (that is, say that they're not "completely masculine"). These are the men who are falling into the masculinity gap. This represents a gap between how men—especially young men—*think* men should be and act, and how they see themselves. It is expected that men who value traditional masculinity (a high score on the MRNI) but don't see themselves as meeting that standard (placing themselves as something other than "completely masculine" on the masculinity-femininity scale) should be the most prone to look for things—like buying cryptocurrencies—that promise to help them achieve the masculinity that they value.

Looking at this interaction between beliefs surrounding masculinity and how men perceive their own gender identities helps to fill in some gaps in the existing research on men and gender role norms. For instance, Kaya et al. (2019) made use of a longitudinal (looking at the same people at multiple points over time) design to look at the relationship between acceptance of various dimensions of masculinity norms (not using the MRNI, but a related scale, the Conformity to Masculine Norms Inventory) among young men and their happiness over time. It might be expected that acceptance of traditional masculine norms, pushing men toward the impossible standards of hegemonic masculinity, would lead them to be less happy, but the findings were rather more complicated than that. On the whole, men who endorsed elements of traditional masculinity like being powerful or being what's euphemistically called being a "playboy" were negatively associated with happiness in measures taken a few months later. However, acceptance of other masculine norms, like the importance of being a winner, was positively associated with overall happiness. The key to understanding this seeming discrepancy seems to come from a separate measure used by the researchers, looking at gender role conflict: men who experience more conflicted feelings about masculinity are much less happy than men who don't experience such conflict. What's going on here is that acceptance of masculinity norms leads men to be unhappy—unless they feel like they're meeting the standard set by those norms. When men feel like they're not meeting these norms, they're unhappy, or sometimes even violent, as in Amato's (2012) work on prisoners in New England.

The manosphere provides young men who feel that they're falling short of the demands of masculinity with a smorgasbord of ways that they can try to perform them. Bujalka, Rich, and Bender (2022) note that one leading masculinity YouTube creator, Richard Cooper,[18] sells his own books titled *The Unplugged Alpha: The No BullSh*t Guide to Winning with Women & Life, Enough Is Enough: The DIY Debt Settlement Guide Your Creditors Don't Want You to Know about*, and a whole series of books about what he calls *Dark Psychology* (including *The Beginner's Guide to Learn Covert Emotional Manipulation, Covert Manipulation*, and *Dark Psychology and Manipulation*). It should surprise no one to find out that he is also all in on Bitcoin, letting his 200K followers on X/Twitter know that the upward trend in the price of Bitcoin "will continue for several decades."

While the set of ideas being sold here may seem scattershot—dating, psychology, and money—they're all linked by the idea that the mastery of esoteric or hidden knowledge can help men get access to the benefits of hegemonic masculinity that are otherwise out of reach. Those benefits—sexual access to attractive women, sufficient income to support a family—are, in his telling (and that of other masculinity influencers) impossible to achieve through conventional means, reflecting the extent to which hegemonic masculinity is impossible for young men to achieve. But these influencers hold that it is possible to get there via an alternative route. In the redpill forums, there are few types more despised than "Chads," attractive, athletic, wealthy men who get (supposedly effortless) sexual access to women. In the imagination of the posters, these men have met the standards of hegemonic masculinity, and achieved the rewards thereof, but they're despised because they didn't have to work for it: they were born into it, and may even be "NPCs," a term from videogames denoting someone who completely lacks an inner life. It would be reasonable to assume that men who are not meeting the standards of hegemonic masculinity would aspire to be like them. That's what traditional hierarchical models of masculinity would presume: that they would want to go to the gym, get a good haircut, get a good education and job, and make enough money to be a Chad themselves. But that's never really presented as a possibility. Rather, the Chads and anyone else who seems (to these outside observers) to have met the standards of hegemonic masculinity is seen as almost a different species.

Red Pill content sets up a binary, with society—and all of the institutions of it—on one side, and the audience, with access to esoteric and technical knowledge on the other (Bujalka, Rich, & Bender 2022). In this narrative, among the lies that the blue pill world has told men is that they can be financially successful by going to school, studying, getting a good job, and working hard at it. The system under capitalism is rigged, and they'll never get ahead by working within the system—they'll always be a Beta, plugging away for a more dominant male (or, worse, a woman) and never getting the financial freedom that they deserve.

Becoming like them is impossible: but it is possible to get to the same outcomes through the use of knowledge and mastery: that is, technical masculinities. Seduction strategies can lead to sexual access to women; wealth that will inevitably result from cryptocurrency investments. The respect that these men think that they deserve will come along with a day of reckoning—the collapse of government-backed currencies, or the "mother of all short squeezes" awaited by investors in meme stocks discussed in Chapter 4.

What about Women?

Throughout this chapter, I've been talking about masculinity and gender expectations among men, but women and nonbinary people have and assert masculine gender identities as well. Indeed, women in all of the samples discussed in this chapter are more likely to assert a masculine gender identity than men are to assert a feminine one. Less is known about the asserted masculinity and femininity of nonbinary people, as there just aren't enough of them in general population samples to allow us to draw concrete conclusions. It's not surprising that women are more likely to assert a masculine gender identity than men are to assert a feminine one: we live in a society that tends to value masculinity, so there may be benefits for women to exhibit masculine traits in some contexts. Scholars looking at political candidates, for instance, have found that female candidates can benefit from demonstrations of masculine traits (Bauer & Santia 2022, 2023). Similarly, scholars working in this area—like Monika McDermott (2016)—have shown that masculinity has a demonstrable effect on the sociopolitical behaviors of both men and women.

However, while masculinity, conceptualized as a personality trait or traits, is present across sex categories, men have a particularly fraught relationship with it. Because masculinity is valued in our society, and men are expected to demonstrate it, a failure to do so—even if that failure is only one that's perceived by the individual—can have substantial psychological ramifications. If a woman doesn't meet the unrealistic demands of dominant forms of masculinity, it's not necessarily a big deal. If a man doesn't, he's likely to have to find ways to cope with that failure.

The effects of masculinity on the behaviors of women and nonbinary people and the ways that they may perform such masculinities is an important topic; just not one that this book is going to delve into. There has been excellent work on the topic, like Mimi Schippers's (2007) work on how women borrow performances of hegemonic masculinity like promiscuity, sexual desire for women, and physical aggression as "pariah femininities" that, because of their similarities to men's behaviors, function as a rebellion against them.

Part of that is the need for any research agenda to focus on one area; part is my personal conviction that it's important to spotlight men's behavior, because men have long been taken as the baseline category, leading researchers to look at how other groups deviate from men's behaviors and ignoring the many ways in which men's behavior is puzzling. In the case of cryptocurrency, this means articles asking why women don't buy crypto, when I believe that the more interesting question is the one that foregrounds men's behavior. There's also a pragmatic issue: I'm a middle-aged het cis white guy, and while I feel perfectly comfortable talking about men acting weird and irrational, the last thing our society needs is someone like me trying to explain women.

The Monocausation Trap

While this book is making an argument about why men buy cryptocurrencies, any such argument is going to be incomplete. Human beings are weird and do things for all sorts of reasons; they're especially weird when it comes to gender. I'm arguing that men use cryptocurrency, memes stocks, and related assets as a way of performing a gender identity centered on technical masculinities, but there are lots of other ways that men can perform that gender identity. There are also lots of other reasons why men might buy cryptocurrencies or NFTs or meme stocks that have nothing to do with a performance of masculinity. Maybe they thought it was funny, maybe they thought it was a good investment, maybe they did it as a sign of support for a particular movement, or online personality, or political candidate. Maybe they saw an ad during the Super Bowl or bought an NFT or a meme stock because it gave them discounts for something that they wanted to do anyway.

I argue that the performance of technical masculinities provides a better explanation for the behaviors and attitudes discussed in this book than other approaches to masculinities (even the compensatory masculinities model that I've used in much of my other work). But I'm also sure that there are men using cryptocurrencies as part of a performance of compensatory masculinity. While women in these spaces are vastly outnumbered by men, there are plenty of women who have bought the sorts of assets I'm talking about, and while some of them may be driven by a performance of masculinity, many of them are surely being driven by other considerations (likely the same ones driving men). In some cases, men might even be using them as part of a performance of hybrid masculinities.

In social science generally, the specter of monocausation looms. Nothing in human behavior ever has just one cause, and the purchase of cryptocurrency is no exception. But the argument being made here isn't reliant on there not being causes other than technical masculinities: it's enough that it is *a* cause. Understanding the link between crypto and technical masculinities gives us a way into the worldview of the men performing these masculinities, which is important not just because they've been understudied, but because they have the potential to become the dominant performance of masculinities in our society.

Are all crypto and meme stock purchases linked to technical masculinities? Of course not, and while the statistics can show that the performance of technical masculinities accounts for some portion of the purchases, there's no way to directly compare that to other causes or even to just the random vagaries of human behavior. Let a thousand explanations bloom: it's enough to show that this one accounts for much of what we're seeing.

The Plan of the Book

The goal of this book is to explore exactly how attempts to perform technical masculinities are leading men to buy cryptocurrencies, and why cryptocurrencies and related assets, like meme stocks and NFTs, are so useful for these performances.

I start off by establishing why performances of masculinity are so important for men, and young men in particular, defining what technical masculinities are and how they fit into the overall conception of men's gender roles. Rather than just being an alternative way of asserting traditionally masculine roles, I argue that that technical masculinities are an attempt to supplant existing dominant performances of masculinity. Dominant forms of masculinity are continually shifting and come under pressure from economic and societal changes. Increasing economic inequality, and the (slowly) ebbing economic and social dominance of men, sets the stage for a shift in dominant forms of masculinity in the United States, in the same way that it has in many other countries. This means that people buying cryptocurrency isn't just a fad, or some niche interest, but is part of an attempt to make a wholesale change in the dominant forms of masculinity within our society, making it critical that we understand how they work.

With the stakes established, I proceed to dive into the history and underlying narratives of cryptocurrencies, which show why they work so well for young men flailing about for a way to demonstrate masculine gender identities. I make use of survey data and experiments to make an empirical case for the link between crypto purchases and attempts to assert a masculine gender identity.

The discussion of cryptocurrencies is followed up with a discussion of meme stocks, centered on the GameStop short squeeze that rocked Wall Street. The same factors that lead young men to use cryptocurrency to try and establish a certain kind of masculine gender identity can also lead them to other behaviors that are equally bad from a financial perspective but pay enormous dividends to their masculinity. Again, making use of survey data, I show that meme stocks purchases have been absurdly popular among young men and that those purchases are tied to the same masculinity gap that drives cryptocurrency purchases. However, these relationships are weaker for meme stocks than they are for crypto purchases, and there are good theoretical reasons why this might be the case.

The narratives underlying cryptocurrency and meme stocks wind up being very important to both their appeal and for the case that we're seeing something very different from traditional investment behaviors. In both cases, the narratives driving these investments are apocalyptic, profiting not from business as usual but from the collapse of existing power structures and a redistribution to plucky underdogs.

Of course, there have been other explanations for why men might buy into these kinds of assets, and Chapter 2 works to show that these other explanations don't fully explain what's being observed. Research in economics and finance has long noticed the seemingly irrational behaviors of investors like those that are buying crypto, and it's important to show that it's performances of masculinity, and not other factors, that are driving these behaviors. The traditional way to explain why people buy assets like this is through some kind of appeal to risk-taking or financial knowledge, so it's important to show that such explanations just don't work here. As this chapter shows, men are more likely than women to accept risk, or to express interest in certain kinds of financial activities, but these proclivities, too, are linked with men's beliefs that they're falling short of the demands of masculinity.

With survey and experimental data having been used to establish the link between masculinity and these financial assets, I then make use of content analysis data to look at how the people buying these assets understand them and the dynamics of the online communities that they're embedded in. The content of these discussions is often upsetting, but it's important to understand how the people caught up in these performances of masculinity talk and think about them and how they relate to each other and to the imagined power structures that they're rebelling against.

Once I've shown how the purchases of these financial assets are used to perform technical masculinities, and how these technical masculinities are attempting to supplant existing dominant performances of masculinity, I zoom out to see what the implications of this are. Crypto purchases may be the clearest marker of these performances, but they're not the only one, and the attempt to demonstrate technical masculinities shapes the behaviors of young men in many other ways. In this chapter, I show how the same factors are shaping men's behavior in other arenas that may be more consequential for our society, looking at how they're shaping other behaviors, like gambling, voting, and belief in conspiracy theories.

I conclude by examining what these trends mean for the relationship between young men and masculinity and what, if anything, can be done to ameliorate the problems that arise from these performances. As distasteful as the rhetoric surrounding technical masculinities might be, I think that these young men are best understood as victims, people who feel that they are falling short of an impossible standard and are taken advantage of by hucksters and pyramid schemes selling them a way out. And even if we don't have much sympathy for them, these performances of masculinity have real consequences for the world that we all have to live in: anything we can do to help these young men helps the rest of us, too.

While there are a large number of regression analyses, statistical diagnostics, and details of sampling and analysis underlying the findings that I discuss in these chapters, I don't want to force readers to slog through tables of coefficients to understand the arguments being made. As such, the details of sampling and analyses, the regression tables and the like have all been placed in a Methodological Appendix for interested readers, organized by chapter, in the order in which the analyses are presented in the main text. My goal is to present the results of the analyses, often including expected values derived from the regressions, in the main text, while keeping the details of how I arrived at those figures out of the way of the argument being made.

This is a story about finance, and there's a long tradition of books trying to figure out why people buy nonsensical assets: I have little doubt that Bitcoin will, someday, be mentioned in the same breath as the Tulip Mania of the seventeenth century or the South Sea Bubble of the eighteenth. But the fact that cryptocurrencies and similar assets are so attractive to some people despite *clearly* being a bad idea for most of the people who buy them reveals a lot about how performances of masculinity are changing and what that means for society. Traditionally, the technical masculinities being performed by buying cryptocurrencies have fallen into the category of marginalized masculinities: performances limited to a particular group that is shut out, for whatever reason, from ever meeting the dominant standard of masculinity within a society. If that were still the case, perhaps we could ignore these performances as being something very online young men do: but these performances are too common to be so dismissed, and this version of masculinity, with all of the deep misogyny that has become embedded in it, may be on its way to becoming the dominant performance of masculinity in the United States.

"Have fun staying poor." Technical Masculinities and the Gender Hierarchy

To understand why young men are buying up cryptocurrency, NFTs, meme stocks, and similar assets, it's necessary to understand how men construct and perform their masculinities. The plural on "masculinities" is important because there isn't just one way to be masculine, but many forms of masculinity, jostling for position within a contested hierarchy. When men buy these assets, they are often doing so as part of a performance of what I'm calling technical masculinities, a form of masculinity based around knowledge and mastery of technical or esoteric topics that are perceived to be masculine in nature. That gendered motivation drives these investments and is a big reason why any actual return on these investments is almost irrelevant to why men buy them. The payoff isn't monetary: it's in allowing these men to perform this version of masculinity.

It would be tempting to think of these technical masculinities as something that shows up on some corners of the internet among men sitting in their parents' basements, and not really worthy of our interests, except perhaps as anthropologists doing field work among a strange tribe. But such a dismissive view is belied by how many men buy cryptocurrency, meme stocks, and the like. As noted in Chapter 1, crypto ownership is not a marginal behavior; more than 40 percent of men under thirty say that they own (or have owned) cryptocurrencies. It's one in six registered voters in US elections. As will be discussed in Chapter 3, cryptocurrencies are also increasingly linked to larger financial markets. It's also not some marginal expression of masculinity, content to stay in the shadows of the dominant, hegemonic forms of masculinity within our society. Instead, it's challenging those existing dominant performances, making the case that these technical masculinities should be on top of the gender hierarchy. It's important to understand the version of masculinity that drives cryptocurrency purchases because it's showing us the future of masculinity in the United States, and that future isn't pretty.

Already, I've been throwing around terms like "hegemonic masculinity," and while people have an image of what that looks like, it's important to understand what gender scholars mean by the term. Rather than refer to one type of masculinity, hegemonic masculinity refers to whatever form of masculinity is in the top position in the hierarchy of masculinities, dominant over other masculinities, and justifying that position over both other men and over women.[1] The exact behaviors and traits that make up a performance of masculinity change over time, but the hierarchical nature of masculinity, its elusive and tenuous nature, do not (DiMuccio & Knowles 2025).

Early work on hegemonic masculinity arose largely from studies of high schools (as in Connell 1982; Kessler et al. 1985), a setting in which the jostling among groups of boys over what is, and what is not, considered masculine is perhaps more evident than in other settings. Messerschmidt (2018, 27) traces the initial idea of hierarchies within men to the experiences of gay men at the hands of heterosexual men, but looking at high schools (and later workplaces, in Connell 1982, 1995) made the gradations of masculinities more obvious.

Of course, women, men, and people of all sexual expressions can and do assert masculine traits, or put forward masculine gender identities, but masculinity is especially fraught for men, and a perceived failure to demonstrate masculinity is much more consequential for them. Sex and sexuality-based inequalities are justified by masculinities, so to question whether a man sufficiently demonstrates these traits is to question whether he deserves his position in society.

The idealized form of masculinity within a society, the one that best makes the case for why men—or at least the men who embody that form of masculinity—should be dominant over women as well as men who don't conform to that style of masculinity, is referred to be Connell as "hegemonic" masculinity. However, the gradations of masculinities mean that it's more complicated than just a distinction between men who perform hegemonic masculinities and everyone else. In addition to hegemonic masculinities, Connell describes four specific categories of masculinities (Messerschmidt 2018):

1. Complicit masculinities: those that are not hegemonic, but benefit from them, and work to prop up hegemonic masculinities in order to maintain such benefits. Such masculinities accept their lower place in the hierarchy, often express admiration for the hegemonic masculinities, and don't seek

to challenge them: think of water boys or equipment managers on a high school sports team.

2. Subordinated masculinities: those masculinities against which hegemonic masculinities are defined, and therefore necessarily lower in the hierarchy, like those of gay or trans men. Because hegemonic masculinity is set up in opposition to these forms of masculinity, they don't present a threat to hegemonic forms.

3. Marginalized masculinities: those performed by men that are of lower social status for reasons like race, ethnicity, class, or disability. Hegemonic forms of masculinity may borrow practices from these forms, but they'll always be held down by societal inequalities.

4. Protest masculinities: hyper-masculine forms that are performed by individuals who find themselves in social positions that lack economic or social power. Men performing these masculinities do not necessarily accept that hegemonic masculinities are actually superior and may seek to replace them in the hierarchy.

Of these, protest masculinities present the greatest potential danger to extant hegemonic masculinities. Complicit masculinities have no interest in dethroning the currently hegemonic forms of masculinity, as they're benefiting from them. Subordinated and marginalized masculinities are lower in the hierarchy than hegemonic masculinities and are defined almost entirely in opposition to them. Moreover, hegemonic forms of masculinity borrow freely from them, as in Demetriou's (2001) discussion of how heterosexual men have borrowed grooming behaviors from gay men (think the TV show "Queer Eye"). Protest masculinities are held by individuals who don't see any particular reason why they should be subordinated and claim to represent behaviors that are just as masculine as those of the hegemonic forms and make just as strong a case for male dominance.

It's tempting to think of hegemonic masculinities as being universal, or even transhistorical, and while those men performing such masculinities may claim that there are deep cultural (Ancient Rome) or biological (genes and hormones) roots to their behavior, this is belied by the regular turnover in what constitutes hegemonic masculinity within a cultural context. Messerschmidt (2018) cautions against the pop sociology understanding of hegemonic masculinity as being indistinguishable from a rigid machismo. Hegemonic masculinity isn't a type of man but a set of behaviors men use to position themselves relative to other men (Wetherell & Edley 1999). This means that hegemonic masculinities must remain flexible in order to maintain their position and that they may be unable to do so, especially in the wake of large-scale social and economic change.

Since hegemonic masculinities within any society or region are those forms of masculinity that best justify male dominance, societies that have seen substantial shifts in social or economic power structures have necessarily seen shifts in the masculinities that can be considered hegemonic. Morrell (1998, 2002), for instance, demonstrates the shift in hegemonic masculinities in post-Apartheid South Africa; Ozbay and Soybakis (2020) show how it changed in the wake of dramatic shifts in political power in Türkiye; Ferguson (2001) shows how it changed in Ireland in the wake of an economic boom; Dasgupta (2005) looks at the decline of the once hegemonic "salaryman" masculinity in Japan after the bubble economy of the 1980s burst. In all of these cases, the new hegemonic masculinity started off as protest or marginalized masculinities, until changes in society meant that the existing hegemonic masculinities no longer justified male dominance, or the men who exhibited them were not on top socially. As such, the masculinities performed by previously lower status groups (as in South Africa or Türkiye), or those who had been economically marginalized (as in the Japanese and Irish examples) became dominant.

The fact that such shifts in the economic and social structure of other societies have led to shifts in their gender hierarchy makes it clear that the same could happen in the United States. The transition from an industrialized economy to a postindustrial information economy has shaken up the nature of work and the skills required for men to be successful: it would almost be more surprising if the gender hierarchy remained stable. Hanson, Pascoe, and Light (2023), for instance, make an explicit link between reduced economic opportunity among working-class white men and gender revanchism, in which men seek to reclaim some mythical past (as in Carlson 2015). Changes in economic and social structure necessitate changes in gendered relations, so for men who don't want the gender hierarchy to change, attempts to revert to some previous economic and social ordering seem necessary.

Scholars have already identified signs of just this kind of transition and the gendered consequences thereof. University College Dublin professor Eugenia Siapara (2019), for instance, makes the argument that seeming boom in online misogyny seen in the manosphere is linked with these kinds of shifts in the overall structure of the economy. Just as scholars have linked the witch hunts of the early modern era to the transition to industrial capitalism and the resulting uncertainty about gender and sex roles, Siapara argues that the rise of online misogyny is linked with the transition to a knowledge and information-based economy. In this telling, understanding that the economy will be increasingly driven by computers and the internet, men online try to force women out of the spaces that would allow them to succeed in the emerging economy, excluding them from the new means of production (39), in much the same way that men might use gate-keeping strategies to exclude women from what they see as masculinized interests in pop culture.

In this book, I'm arguing that the technical, knowledge-based masculinities largely promulgated online, and which drive investments in cryptocurrency and similar assets, are functioning as a protest masculinity and seeking to unseat existing hegemonic masculinities at the top of the hierarchy of masculinities in the United States. I'm not the first person to make the argument that what have sometimes been called "nerd masculinities" are pushing out existing hegemonic masculinities in order to take over the gender hierarchy—the trend has been evident for some time, as in Mendick et al. (2023)—but I am the first to link these performances of masculinity with cryptocurrency, meme stocks, and show *why* the change is happening now.

What Are They Rebelling Against?

If we're talking about protest masculinities, it's important to know what, exactly, the men embracing them are protesting *against*. Throughout this book, I'll be referencing currently dominant performances of masculinity, and while there is expected to be significant regional variation, as well as change over time in what constitutes the dominant performance, there are some baselines that we can apply.

There are two ways to look at this. The first is to look at what men see as the outcome of meeting the standards of dominant forms of masculinity; the second is to look at the behaviors that, right now, seem best suited to get men to those outcomes.

The outcomes side is relatively uncontested in the United States (and with some variation, in western Europe and Australia) today: men who have met the standards of masculinity have a wife and children, are the breadwinner in the household, own property in a safe area, and protect their family. This set of behaviors and roles can be summarized as the three Ps: procreate, provide, protect.[2] It should go without too much comment that this ideal is nearly or completely impossible for most men to realize, but that's not the point. Rather than being a description of men, it's an idealized version, one that men are expected to measure themselves against (and fall short). They're economically productive, providing financially for a family, as well as providing them with a safe place to live and protecting them from the dangers of the world. Just as important as men being well suited for these roles, hegemonic masculinity assumes that women and nonheterosexual men are ill-suited for them: they're insufficiently rational or strong or able to protect or can't conceive children in a traditional manner.

While race, class, and sexuality aren't explicitly part of this definition of hegemonic masculinity, all are clearly implicated (Hirsch & Kachtan 2018). Poor men who don't earn enough money to support their families or keep them in a safe neighborhood are treated as failures by society, their families, and themselves (as in Randles 2020). Discrimination and reduced opportunities for educational and economic advancement mean that Black and brown men are also likely to be on the outside of this conception of masculinity (Wesley 2015).

The man who is able to get to these outcomes isn't just any man, but a white upper-middle-class man, and in societies with limited or contracting class mobility, even the possibility of reaching this ideal is out of reach for many. Men outside of that intersection of race and class are told to content themselves with the subordinated masculinities endemic to their communities and interests. Masculinity is made up of carrots and sticks: if men fail to meet the standard, they can expect to be ridiculed and marginalized. But if they do meet the standards, they can expect to be rewarded with these outcomes. The problem comes when men who feel like doing all the things that they're supposed to do aren't going to get them these rewards.

So, how are men supposed to get to these outcomes in a world where income inequality is growing, and they seem out of reach? Remember that dominant masculinities—which may or may not be hegemonic, as discussed in the next section—are defined as those performances of masculinity which best justify the position of men on top of the gender hierarchy, making a case for the correctness of men's disproportionate social, economic, and political power. Given the rise of global trade in the wake of the collapse of the Soviet Union, and the new age of globalization that has (so far) weathered the storms of the 2008–9 financial collapse and the Covid-19 epidemic, the baseline dominant performance of masculinity today in the industrialized world is built around being able to thrive in a globalized world (Connell 2005): this is the set of behaviors that's supposed to get men to the outcomes discussed earlier. The spread of culture and media has meant that local gender hierarchies are being challenged by global ones, which might lead to progress in gender equity in some cases but mean disruption in any case. In the global economy, gendered institutions like transnational corporations, international media, and global markets are the dominant actors, and the fact that these institutions are gendered necessarily imposes a degree of gender ordering wherever they appear (Acker 2004; Connell 2005).

As such, the dominant performance of masculinity—not the most common, as it must necessarily be out of reach for most men, but the ideal toward which traditional performances strives—is a kind of culturally sophisticated, transnational business masculinity (Connell 1998), with some local variation (for instance, greater emphasis on hedonism in North America; Connell 2005). This is not to say that these performances don't include behaviors like playing or appreciating sports—Connell (2010) quotes one finance worker in Australia talking the necessity of being conversant with sporting events, even if he doesn't really care about it, as evidenced by the proliferation of corporate boxes at sporting events (Connell 2005)—or being married and heterosexual or disciplining bodies through exercise. But those behaviors, while part of the performance of dominant masculinity, are subordinated to being able to prosper in the globalized economy.

To do so, these men have to be able to function easily in big cities around the globe, exhibiting a degree of cosmopolitanism that's reserved globally for the wealthy (though the middle class everywhere aspires to it and tries to copy it). They're also likely to be knowledge workers, generally tied to finance or other parts of the quaternary sector (like insurance or real estate), meaning that they're embedded in the international economy, rather than tied to local economies. As such, they're expected to have discerning social tastes and the physical markers that go along with it: expensive watches and cars, knowledge of fine food and wines, and tailored suits. This is only possible, of course, because their connections to cross-national capital flows ensure that they will be well paid. Well-taken care of children in a safe neighborhood and a big house are part of the deal, as is a partner who may work, but probably doesn't have to.

Even men who meet many of these standards might fall short if they are too tied to the local economy. Connell (2010) looks at a man who runs a successful business in Australia—but is therefore vulnerable to foreign competition in a way that men working in cross-national firms are not. The cross-national part is vital, not just because of what it means in terms of access to global capital markets, but because of how it is linked to global norms and mobility. The businessmen Connell talks about are not tied strongly to any one firm (Connell 1998) but tend to move between them to further their careers—an option simply not open to owners of firms in a single country and remain tied to that place. The money is nice, these men would tell us, but the real benefit is the freedom that money buys. Contrast that freedom with the nightmare scenario portrayed in ads for cryptocurrencies, where men are beaten down by their who boss—who may be a woman!—emasculated and never able to get ahead.

Despite being highly technologized, work looking at these transnational business masculinities has made the disconnect between them and "geek" masculinities explicit (Connell 2016). Technology and computers may be integral to the way in which these men perform their economic and social functions, but they are tools that enable the performance of masculinities rather than being the performance themselves. These men are expected to be ruthless, competitive, and able to win in a (metaphorically) kill-or-be-killed environment (Acker 2004).

This performance of masculinity also includes some degree of sex and sexuality-based egalitarianism. The businessmen that Connell (2010) talks to express support for ensuring that women are included in upper-tier management, even if there aren't many (or any) in those positions now. The emphasis seems to be on symbolic support for this kind of inclusion, even if that support doesn't translate into any concrete action (at least right now). Similarly, these performances of masculinity likely include some degree of tolerance for gay men, though, again, any statements of support are likely to be more theoretical than practical. Homophobia is looked down upon not to alter a gendered hierarchy, but because intolerance would be seen as provincial.

Elias and Beasley (2009) argue that the fact that these transnational businessmen hold enormous economic power does not mean that their performance of masculinity is necessarily legitimating and criticize this approach for drawing too heavily on class-based conceptions of power. As they put it, not many men are aspiring to be accountants (Beasley 2008). More generally, they argue that the varying degrees with which global markets and their underlying ethos have penetrated different parts of the globe means that we don't know the extent to which there really is a single global hegemonic masculinity. Beasley (2008) argues that it's misguided to think of globalization as a unitary force. Just as there are many masculinities, there are many forms of globalization, with uneven effects and interactions with local norms. This may well be the case, but it's also irrelevant to the argument being made here. For our purposes, it's enough that transnational business masculinities have become dominant performance here and now, providing a foil against which technical masculinities can rebel; if they're rebelling against other dominant forms locally, that's fine as well.

Is Sexism Inherent?

The nature of gender hierarchies, which place men above women, and straight men above gay men, and so on, certainly implies a degree of sexism. Women have masculine traits, as do men who aren't heterosexual and cis-gendered, but their performance of masculinity is always going to be marginalized.

In addition, some scholars have argued that it's not enough for men to display traits and behaviors that are perceived as masculine but that these masculine traits must be paired with the devaluation of complementary feminine traits (Schippers 2007). So, if men want to use the purportedly masculine trait of rationality as a way of asserting their gender identity, that's fine; but it only becomes part of a hegemonic masculinity if it's paired with the argument that women (or men performing other forms of masculinities) are *irrational*. Men being honest and forthright is an argument for the social and economic dominance of men only if women are said to be dishonest and scheming. Men's physical strength stops being a reason for male dominance if women aren't perceived as weak.

This sort of complementarity is clear in the discourse on online forums. Red-pilled men talk about the inherent deviousness of women and their supposedly genetic mandate to cheat on their spouses, as opposed to the honest men they take advantage of. Men who sell their crypto when the market slumps—rather than buying more—are acting emotionally, being governed by fear, rather than acting like real men.

While that existing dominant masculinities are just about universally sexist, there has been some pushback on the idea that dominant masculinities are necessarily sexist. This line of work comes out of a distinction between hegemonic masculinities and dominant masculinities.

To begin with, there is concern about the way that the term "hegemonic" is being used in the context of hegemonic masculinities. Such work starts with the original use of the term in the work of Italian Marxist philosopher Antonio Gramsci, who popularized the use of "hegemony" (i.e., Demetriou 2001). Much of this criticism is outside of the realm of the discussion here, but one insight is important to note: hegemony, as Gramsci argued, and as Connell did when introducing the concept into the study of gender, isn't inherently violent. The goal of hegemony is to ensure that subordinated groups consent to their lower status, to get them to buy into the logic of the system that disadvantages them. In political science, the term is usually used in the context of international relations: a hegemonic power is a nation-state powerful enough that other nation-states don't try to challenge it. In the wake of the collapse of the Soviet Union, for instance, the United States was briefly considered a global hegemon. It didn't have to invade (or threaten to invade) other nation-states to get them to do what it wanted: it was in the best of interest of other, weaker (and all states were militarily and economically weaker) states to play along with it. Violence, then, represents a failure of hegemony: hegemons only have to fight when their dominance is being challenged.

The same holds true with regard to hegemonic masculinities. In a high school, the boys displaying dominant masculinities—say, the star players on the football team stereotypically—don't have to force others to treat them as being in charge: the other boys know to stay out of their way. We see a similar dynamic in the online message boards that make up the manosphere: the men who seem to be obsessed with alpha males aren't angry at them.[3] Rather, they seem to accept the dominance of these men as being natural and acceptable and are trying to join them at the top of the heap rather than challenge the system that's kept them down.

Of course, hegemons are sometimes challenged, especially when a rival sees a vulnerability, potentially leading to a disconnect between dominance and hegemony. A hegemonic masculinity is one that is both the dominant—that is, the most celebrated—performance of masculinity within a group and the one that best justifies male dominance over women and other forms of masculinity. But there's no necessary reason that dominant forms must also be hegemonic.

Some theorists—especially University of Chicago sociologist Yuchen Yang (2020)—have made the argument that these two elements of the definition of hegemonic masculinity are potentially inconsistent, that the version of masculinity that is the most exalted within a society, and the version that best justifies the dominance of heterosexual men over other groups, might well be different. Imagine a world in which gender inclusive masculinities are dominant: the most celebrated form of masculinity wouldn't be one that is tied to sex hierarchies. However, while this may be theoretically possible—and there is little evidence for it happening outside of some educational contexts—in our society, it certainly seems that the hegemonic form of masculinity is both legitimating of male privilege and celebrated. Yang refers to this view, that the two elements are linked, as defeatist, but it remains the view of leading scholars in the field, like Michael Messerschmidt (2013, 2018) and Michael Messner (Messerschmidt & Messner 2018). It may be pessimistic to think that dominant masculinities are, and are likely to continue to be, tied to male dominance, but that seems to be the world that we live in.

Still, Connell and her coauthors have arrived at a distinction between dominant and hegemonic masculinities (as in Connell & Messerschmidt 2005; Messerschmidt 2018, 2019). Dominant masculinities are those that are the most socially valued within a population, but they're only hegemonic if they justify the social dominance of men who display them and lead to the consent of those beneath them in the gendered hierarchy. A dominant form of masculinity that only maintains its position through violence or the threat of violence wouldn't be hegemonic, nor would one that eagerly adopted feminist stances.

Two Levels of Conflict

In social science research on masculinity, scholars often treat masculinity as being synonymous with hegemonic masculinity, measuring the extent to which men accept this as a valid ideal and the extent to which they believe that they meet that ideal. For instance, in a review of how the concept has been used in the journal *Psychology of Men and Masculinities*, Connell (along with coauthors Nikki Wedgwood & Julian Wood 2023) finds that hegemonic masculinity is generally defined in research as a set of attitudinal traits, completely ignoring the extent to which it exists with a hierarchy. This is a simplification. Connell's work envisions conflict on two different levels: on the first is within men, struggling for the ideals of hegemonic masculinity and finding ways to cope when they inevitably fall short. The second is between performances of masculinity.

Most of the research on men who find that they've fallen short of the ideals of hegemonic masculinity looks at how they cope with that perception, often by finding elements of masculinity that they believe they are able to meet and focusing their efforts there. In the past, I've referred to these behaviors, in which men compensate for shortcomings in one area of masculinity by doubling down on a different one, as compensatory masculinities (Cassino & Besen-Cassino 2021). So, for instance, it might be expected that when men in heterosexual couples come to earn less money than their wives, they would do more housework, but research has consistently shown the opposite (i.e., Kaplan & Offer 2022; Thébaud 2010), with men apparently asserting their masculinity by refusing to engage in tasks that they see as feminine in order to compensate for the threat to their gender identity that comes from their loss of relative income. All this work is looking at the first level of conflict, and as valuable as it is, it's important to bring in the second level of conflict as well.

For men who accept hegemonic masculinity as a desirable—and perhaps attainable—goal, this sort of doubling down on some elements of hegemonic masculinity makes sense. But the fact that there are other masculinities means that there is another option open to them as well: giving up on the currently dominant performance of masculinity and working toward a different, competing performance. Such a shift in focus can be understood on two levels. On one level, men are conceding that they will not be able to meet the (nigh impossible) demands of hegemonic masculinity and are opting into a different form that they think they have a better shot at achieving. On another level, they may be making a case for this alternative form of masculinity to supplant the existing notions of hegemonic masculinity, either in whole or in part.

This brings us into the second level of conflict, *between* performances of masculinity. This conflict has generally been ignored in scholarly research (Jefferson 2017) but potentially has even greater impact on societies. Because hegemonic masculinity is defined in terms of what traits justify men's social and economic dominance, it necessarily changes along with society. Upper body strength, for instance, is likely to be an important part of hegemonic masculinity in societies where economic production is based on manual labor and becomes less important in the transition to a knowledge-based economy. This creates an opening for versions of masculinity that were previously lower in the gender hierarchy to take over the dominant position.

Connell's seminal work on masculinities is very much focused on the ways that hegemonic forms of masculinity are used to dominate other forms, especially those performed by homosexual men. Hegemonic masculinity is there to make a case for why those men (and, of course, women) should be lower on the gender hierarchy than heterosexual (and, generally, white middle and upper class) men: here are the traits that justify men being in charge, men who don't have these traits shouldn't be in charge. But Connell's work also gives examples of how men establish alternative forms of masculinity that, within a social context, serve the same function. For instance, in her qualitative research looking at workplaces, Connell talks to workers who maintain aircraft and shows how they use their technical knowledge to differentiate themselves from the workers—mostly women—who do what they see as lesser work in the same spaces. They're defining their masculinity through knowledge, technical skill, and mastery of certain areas. Within their workplace, these traits justify a higher place on the hierarchy for the men who are able to demonstrate them, justifying their dominance over women.

In research on masculinities, the forms of masculinity other than the current local hegemonic form are mostly discussed in terms of marginalized masculinities. Marginalized masculinities are those forms of masculinity that are performed by groups of men who are excluded from the performance of dominant masculinities, generally on the basis of inherent traits like race, disability, or sexuality, but might also arise from interests or behaviors that are seen as incompatible with dominant performances. Coston and Kimmel (2012), for instance, look at the ways in which poor, gay, or disabled men try and construct masculine gender identities. Quam et al. (2020) look at how exposure to violence and poverty shape the construction of masculinity among young, mostly Black, men in poor neighborhoods. In such research, the focus is on how men who are shut out of the existing version of hegemonic masculinity construct their own alternative models, borrowing the elements of hegemonic masculinity that seem achievable and context-relevant, while ignoring those that aren't. In some cases, markers of these marginalized masculinities may be successful enough that they are incorporated into masculinity performances of other, more privileged groups (think of young white men adopting rap music in the 1990s), provided they work toward the overall project of making the case for why men should be socially and economically dominant.

All of this is also context dependent, with performances of masculinity changing along with social setting. Individuals think about the conclusions that the people around them will draw from their behaviors (West & Zimmerman 1987) and engage in reflexive self-monitoring of their own behaviors to ensure that they are congruent with the gender (or sex) identity that they're trying to perform in the situation (Archer 2007).

But dichotomizing hegemonic masculinities and marginalized masculinities tends to obscure the possibility that men might be engaging instead in protest masculinities. The theoretical argument being made here is that the construction of masculinity that goes along with buying cryptocurrency is best understood not as an attempt to join the ranks of existing hegemonic masculinities, but to replace them. The men performing these masculinities are responding to changes in social and economic structures by deciding that currently hegemonic forms of masculinity just aren't applicable anymore, that they don't lead to the rewards that they promise, that they don't justify the social dominance of heterosexual men over women and other groups. The system, in this view, is broken. It's a scam, and the men who should be in charge are the ones who see it for what it is.

Protest Masculinities

The idea of protest masculinities significantly predates Connell's conception of hegemonic masculinity. In the 1950s, Harvard sociologist Talcott Parsons wrote about "masculine protest" ([1954] 2010), arising from the (very Freudian) notion that the mostly working-class boys who lacked proper male role models would try to distance themselves from femininity by playing the role of the bad boy (see Burton & Whiting 1961; Whiting 1965).[4] They participated in petty crimes, rejected schoolteachers and other authority figures, and used violence and macho posturing to both perform their own version of masculinity and symbolically separate themselves from other members of the working class. An early example of this sort of dynamic comes from British social scientist Paul Willis. His 1977 book, *Learning to Labour*, shows how rebellion against authority figures in school—seen as a masculine activity—arose from a degree of class consciousness among poor boys and served to prepare them for their subordinated role in society as working and lower-class adults.

These protest masculinities have mostly been studied among underprivileged, often working-class men (Messerschmidt 2018, 50; Walker 2006), who are excluded from the dominant form of masculinity within their society, but not because of traits like race or sexuality. Men who cannot participate in dominant masculinities because of their race, ethnicity, or sexuality are pushed into marginalized masculinities: the intersectional nature of dominant and hegemonic masculinities means that they have no real chance of achieving them. Protest masculinities arise from men who feel like they *should* be able to achieve these dominant forms but are excluded from them, often because of socioeconomic status. These are the forms of masculinity that are the most likely to present challenges to dominant forms, as they seek to move up the gender hierarchy. Other performances of masculinity might seek to join the hegemonic forms at the top of the heap or be content with a middling position in the hierarchy; protest masculinities seek to displace them.

Within the schools that form the settings for early work in masculinities, protest masculinities take the form of boys and young men rejecting the authority of the school, and the importance of education, opting instead for confrontations with teachers and a lionization of working-class aspirations. They still seek out a relatively dominant position in the gender hierarchy, as evidenced by their expressed homophobia and sexism (Connell 2005), but see no reason to opt in to what they see as the fixed game of social advancement through the normal means of education, hard work, and good behavior. Their masculinity, then, is in the form of "you can't fire me, because I quit": knowing that they can't meet the demands of dominant forms of masculinity, they performatively reject what they see as false paths toward them.

In sociologist Gregory Wayne Walker's (2006) telling, Connell's initial description of protest masculinities is very much tied to a Marxist conception of social class. Working-class men stress masculine traits like strength and sexual fecundity in what seems like a compensatory performance: "I might not be rich, but I am a man" (and perhaps more of a real man than the men at the top of the heap). Such performances serve to distance themselves from other working-class people, especially racial minorities and women, putting them higher on a gendered social hierarchy than the people who work alongside them. From a Marxist perspective, this is important because it limits class solidarity, getting working-class people to fight among themselves, rather than see where their larger interests lie.

Walker, however, argues for two different kinds of protest masculinities. The first are what he calls "anomic" protest masculinities, which lead to gendered anxieties and self-destructive behavior, as well as the intra-class splintering already mentioned, as working-class men seek to highlight what they have in common with men higher up in the gender hierarchy. He contrasts these with "disciplined" protest masculinities, as demonstrated by skilled workers in a grain plant. These men actively distance themselves from dominant masculinities, joking about their lack of sexual access to women, joking about homosexual attraction, and expressing deep suspicion of new workers who come in claiming mastery of tools or machinery. Walker ties this performance of masculinity to a substantial loss of permanent jobs at the plant. Cut off from the previously existing work structure, and now in a position of economic precarity, these men created new, alternative performances of masculinity. In this workplace, men who claimed to be too masculine, knowing how to do things already, are seen as dangerous, liable to get someone killed. As such, the men performatively distance themselves from dominant masculinities to show that they can be trusted.

Some scholars, like Richard Gater of Cardiff University (2024), have made the case that modern protest masculinities have evolved to include traits that might previously have been seen as feminine, like willingness to engage in physical contact with other men, and even some that might be seen as questioning the gender hierarchy, like a rejection of homophobia. This is part and parcel of a rejection of dominant performances of masculinity, taking up behaviors that are almost antithetical to it.

Past conceptualizations of protest masculinities have looked at them as being tied to poor men, but it's important not to confuse a position within a gender hierarchy with a specific set of traits. Just as the form of dominant masculinities can change over time and across place, so too can the nature of protest masculinities. Rather than think of protest masculinities as being linked specifically to working-class rejection of education and middle-class aspirations, we can conceive of protest masculinities more generally, as any masculinity in which men reject aspiring to existing dominant forms of masculinity as a way of explaining why they're not able to meet them.

Moreover, just as the content of hegemonic masculinities changes in response to economic and social shifts, so too should the content of protest masculinities. Remember that the work on protest masculinities that found them largely among working-class men came from an era when economic inequality was much lower, when class mobility was at least seen as achievable. Men who nonetheless felt that they had no chance to move into the middle class embraced these protest masculinities. So, in an era of increasing inequality, with lower class mobility, it would be expected that men from middle-class backgrounds, shut out of any possibility of moving up, and facing the very real possibility of downward mobility, would embrace them as well.

The fact that the men doing this kind of rejection are not intersectionally excluded from dominant forms of masculinity opens up possibilities closed to men who are excluded from them because of race, ethnicity, sexuality, or other factors. Rather than accept their position as lower in the gender hierarchy, protest masculinities, unlike marginalized masculinities, can make the case that their performance of masculinities are superior to existing dominant forms. Within a school setting, if masculinity is linked with traits like being strong or independent, dominant forms of masculinity might involve (as they do in Connell's early work) athletics teams, but getting into fights and slagging off teachers are certainly recognizable performances of the same traits.

This more generalized conception of protest masculinities allows us to reinterpret existing work on men's displays of knowledge in specialized areas. These might previously have been seen as marginalized masculinities, but to the extent that (1) the individuals performing them are not inherently excluded from dominant forms of masculinity, (2) the individuals performing them reject the idea that they can attain hegemonic masculinity, and (3) they believe that their performances of masculinity are actually superior to those made by hegemonic forms, especially in terms of justifying male dominance, they're better understood as protest masculinities.

Based on the discussion so far of technical masculinities, this should all sound familiar.

If men performing a certain kind of masculinity wanted to supplant dominant forms of masculinity, what would they have to do? Dominant forms of masculinity are those that best make the case for why men should be socially and economically dominant over women (and, in Connell's telling, gay men), so a protest masculinity wanting to supplant a dominant masculinity would have to assert that it does a better job of justifying existing hierarchies. Take, for instance, the sort of masculinities that become prevalent in rural areas of the United States, in which white men argue that knowledge of hunting, building, or nature is not only a way of being masculine but is actually a *better* way of being masculine than the dominant, more urban, and suburbanized forms of masculinity. To make such a case, these men must argue that their masculinities make them better able to achieve the goals that dominant forms of masculinity purport to achieve. If dominant forms of masculinity in the United States are all about protection, procreation, and provision, men performing these sorts of rural masculinities must make the case that they do a better job at all of these. They might argue that they live in areas with less crime and disorder, and so do a better job of keeping their families safe; that they can afford to have more children and offer those children a happier, freer childhood; that their skills mean that while their incomes might not be as high, their ability to provide for their families is more secure.

Howson (2006) makes the case that these protest masculinities are easily compatible with behaviors that might otherwise be seen as feminine, like caring for children. The argument is here clear: wealthier men might be able to provide more for their children materially than working-class men, but these men can claim to be better parents, spending more time with them, and imparting more skills. While most of the work on protest masculinities looked at men in urban areas, these rural men are an equally strong example.

Challenging the Hierarchy

These types of protest masculinities have long existed as locally dominant and hegemonic masculinities, but the current crop of protest masculinities based around the online manosphere is different in two ways. First, they're different in who is doing the protesting. It made sense for men in poorer, rural areas to come to the conclusion that they were permanently on the outside of dominant, affluent, urban, and suburbanized forms of masculinity, because they *were* excluded. But increasing social and economic inequality means that lots of men who otherwise would have felt that they had a chance to move into the dominant forms of masculinity no longer do. They know that they won't be able to be a breadwinner, support a family, and move to a big house in a nice neighborhood, and with that possibility cut off to them, they look for alternatives, for protest masculinities. These are not men who are intersectionally marginalized: they're middle class, but now find themselves on the outside looking in.

Importantly, the internet means that these protest masculinities can now transcend marginalized geographic areas. In the past, these sorts of protest masculinities were localized and could challenge larger-scale dominant masculinities within an area and perhaps even supplant them as the locally dominant form of masculinity. Now, these forms spread through online forums and can reach men everywhere. For men looking to perform technical masculinities, investments in cryptocurrencies and similar assets are so popular because they provide both a way for men to perform the traits that these forms of masculinity demand and provide a (almost entirely theoretical) path for men to get the benefits that normally accrue to men who perform currently hegemonic masculinities.

None of this is to say that investments are the only way for men to exhibit these kinds of technical masculinities, but such demonstrations of technical masculinities have become popular among young men for a reason. Men can demonstrate technical masculinities with a mastery of videogames, craft beer, sports, or any other masculine-coded topic, but what's made cryptocurrency and related assets so popular is that they combine costly markers of knowledge and mastery with a heroic narrative and monetary gain. Demonstrating knowledge about sports is certainly a way to perform masculinity, but there's no sense that sports fans are some kind of trampled minority whose fandom will eventually lead them to be able to get the social status that they deserve. As discussed in Chapters 3 and 4, both cryptocurrency and meme stocks carry with them narratives about a day—always on the horizon, never quite here—on which the underdog true believers will be recognized as having been right the whole time.

No one doubts that, for instance, men use weight training as a sign of masculinity, and visible signs of weight training like the amount of weight being benched, or the size of muscles, are markers of masculinity. As such, men who want to see themselves (or be seen) as more masculine might well choose to lift weights in order to do so. Physical strength is a marker of masculinity, and lifting weights is a display of physical strength; therefore weightlifting, regardless of any other reason a man might pursue it, can be used as a way to perform a masculine gender identity. In these online forums, knowledge is being used the same way. Knowing more about a topic is perceived as being masculine, and in the same way that men might discuss how much they bench, or how many women they've slept with, as a way of asserting their masculinity to other men, they can demonstrate how much they know about certain topics.

Some of these examples verge into the phenomenon known as "mansplaining," in which men unnecessarily explain things to a woman who may be more knowledgeable about the topic than the explainer is, but mansplaining is just one instantiation of the impulse to demonstrate knowledge. After all, it isn't enough to simply know a lot about something: that knowledge must be demonstrated, and the fact that some men seem to prefer demonstrating that knowledge to women simply reinforces the idea that this knowledge is being used to create or maintain a gendered hierarchy.

Of course, if someone is trying to demonstrate their knowledge of an area, knowing things that everyone around them already knows is hardly going to suffice. In Nanney et al.'s (2020) work on craft beer, for instance, respondents mention that asking for a beer from a large, relatively well-known craft brewery is seen as a credibility-destroying faux pas. In order to display knowledge, drinkers should be asking for a "challenging" beer from a brewery that few people have heard of. Arcane or obscure knowledge is favored, as it provides greater opportunity to explain and therefore demonstrate expertise.

Most past research takes it as a given that the nerd masculinities that have been previously studied—mostly those that deal with narrow interests or fandoms, like fantasy card games or videogames, or science fiction—are better understood as either marginalized masculinities or as instantiations of existing dominant forms of masculinity. If that's the case, then the technical masculinities being discussed might be interesting, but they don't really tell us much about the overall state of masculinity and the gender hierarchy. But this is exactly why cryptocurrencies and meme stocks are so important to how we understand technical masculinities. So long as nerd masculinities were restricted to narrow areas of interest where men sought to prove their knowledge and use gatekeeping techniques (challenging perceived interlopers into a masculine space to prove their knowledge before being accepted into a group) to keep girls out, they could be understood as marginalized masculinities. After all, the men performing masculinities in this way were pretty much definitionally those who were excluded from performances of hegemonic forms of masculinity for one reason or another: athleticism, attractiveness, sexual fecundity, economic success, or any other trait that meant that they had to resign themselves to a marginalized masculinity.

But this changes when those nerd masculinities become linked with the outcomes that had previously been thought to adhere to dominant masculinities. If mastery of esoteric knowledge can lead to money, sexual access to women, all of the rewards of hegemonic masculinity, what had been a marginalized masculinity becomes a protest masculinity, and a performance of gender that isn't necessarily excluded from dominant status, that can make a plausible case that it is the best way to demonstrate why men should be on top of the gender hierarchy. When demonstrating esoteric knowledge in masculinized areas of expertise means winning Magic: The Gathering (a popular fantasy trading card game) tournaments, it's marginalized. When it means getting rich, it's something else entirely.

Nerd Masculinities

The idea that knowledge and demonstrated mastery of certain masculinized subjects—like Connell's aircraft engineers—can be seen as a performance of masculinity isn't new, but the idea that they can form the essence of a protest masculinity is much less accepted. Much of the work on what I'm calling technical masculinities talks about them instead as "nerd masculinities" (Cheng 1999; Kendall 1999, 2000). In this work, they're categorized as marginalized masculinities, little different from the masculinities performed by Black men or disabled men. This may seem like a stretch—bias against men who really like videogames isn't really anything like racial bias—but Cheng (1999) works to shore up the comparison by arguing that the men performing nerd masculinities are different not just interests from other men, but also physically different, linking them with Asian-American men as being excluded from dominant forms of masculinity because of their physical characteristics (especially size) or self-presentation.

Kendall (1999, 261) makes the argument that these kinds of masculinities were presented as marginal in the pop culture of the 1980s (think movies like *Revenge of the Nerds* or *Weird Science*), but has since been rehabilitated, with many of the traits of what she calls "masculine nerds" incorporated into some performances of hegemonic masculinities. In the 1990s, Connell (1995, 165), too, seemed to argue that these performances of masculinity were a difference in what elements of hegemonic masculinity were being emphasized, rather than a wholesale alternative. This may well have been true in the past, but today, technical masculinities represent a protest masculinity seeking to become dominant, rather than a marginalized performance of masculinity. Mendick et al. (2023) argue that this shift comes largely because of the merger of technical masculinities with capitalism, and especially entrepreneurship. On the internet, the perception is that technical prowess and knowledge in the form of coding is what makes people rich (whether this perception is true, or not, is really beyond the point) and gets them all of the benefits that are thought to accrue to men who achieve hegemonic performances of masculinity. Technical knowledge might be something that men demonstrate to bolster their claims to dominant forms of masculinity—but it can also be the basis for an entirely different performance of gender.

Kelly (2023) looks at various forms of anti-feminist masculinities found in the online manosphere and focuses on these nerd masculinities. In her work, nerd masculinities focus on the extent to which they deviate from traditionally accepted norms of masculinity (like athleticism) and therefore (in their telling) don't receive the benefits of male privilege. At the same time, men who perform this flavor of masculinity argue that they demonstrate superior masculine behaviors than other men. Kelly quotes one of these men as arguing that videogame players are powerful, implacable enemies, saying, "We're a group of people who will sit for hours, days, even weeks on end, performing some of the hardest, most mentally demanding tasks" (30). These masculine traits of mastery, endurance, and dedication will, in the narratives these men put forward, inevitably lead to their success (in this case, in the misogynistic online conflagration referred to as #GamerGate). They don't see their behaviors as being less masculine than those of other men—they're just as, if not more, masculine but simply aren't recognized as such, leading them to be underestimated.

Kelly contrasts these nerd masculinities with what she calls "alpha" masculinities, found on manosphere sites like pick-up artist forums, but the two groups have more in common than is immediately evident. The alpha masculinities are premised on the idea that the benefits of traditional hegemonic masculinity are achievable, but only through exploiting the system, achieving mastery of psychological trickery to seduce women, or money hacks to build wealth. In both cases, though, the identified problem is the same: the impossibility of meeting the perceived standards of hegemonic masculinity. As a result, both groups feel unfairly subordinated within masculine hierarchies, the nerd masculinities below other groups that they feel are more recognized, and the alpha masculinities below women, who, in their view, are actually socially dominant and control men. And just as the problems are the same, so too is the solution: the application of knowledge, dedication, and mastery, which will inevitably lead to the perceived benefits of hegemonic masculinity.

What these researchers are calling nerd masculinities is based on a combination of knowledge as being a masculine marker and the perception that they are excluded from dominant forms of masculinity for one reason or another. A lot of the work on these nerd masculinities and related concepts arises from how men find and defend marginalized social spaces that they see as masculinized.

For instance, Nanney et al. (2020) surveyed craft beer drinkers about their experiences in various sites, looking at how men and women were treated differently when they ordered local, unusual brews. They found that when women attempted to order beers that were considered to challenging for them (because of a strong or bitter taste, or a high alcohol content), the bartenders or even other patrons would frequently attempt to dissuade them, pushing them toward beers that were considered to be more appropriate for women (lighter, fruitier, with lower alcohol content, and so on). Men in these environments try to educate women and other less sophisticated drinkers, telling them about the beers and offering them entry-level drinks. Men—especially those who look stereotypically masculine—are assumed to already know about beer and are offered "manly" or "real" beers, while women are assumed to be ignorant and are offered "chick beers" and given advice until and unless they're able to prove their bona fides.

Knowledge about a masculine-coded area—in this case, beer—is used by men to establish dominance over women (and men who are perceived as less masculine) within the male-coded environment. But knowledge needs to be demonstrated, and these men are doing so by talking down to women, by publicly explaining things to other people, even when they're not asked to do so, and by embracing more obscure or challenging beers to prove that level of knowledge and taste (despite some of these challenging masculine beers tasting, as one respondent puts it, "like pinecones"). By showing that they know more than someone else about a masculine-coded subject, they're able to claim a higher position in a gendered hierarchy. The explicitly sexualized way this process is described—"showing off their beer dick"—is no accident.

University of Sussex social scientist Ceri Oeppen (2023) contrasts what they call "geek masculinities" with the ideal of hegemonic masculinities. Their ethnography—looking at competitive players of Magic: The Gathering—notes the extent to which the players perceive themselves as being necessarily outside of the bounds of traditional masculinity, while performing behaviors and personality traits that privilege the aspects of masculinity that they feel that they can achieve. In doing so, the players downplay or reject some elements of hegemonic masculinity, like mastery of sports or sexual access to women, while focusing on knowledge and mastery of a given masculine-coded topic (in this case, the card game).

The players are alienated from traditional standards of masculinity, but rather than aspiring to reach them, they hold that their version of masculinity, based on mastery and knowledge of this remarkably complex game,[5] is actually superior (something that often comes up in online discussions of videogames as well). As such, they suffer from a sense of dismay that they're not afforded the benefits—like respect and sexual access to women—that they perceive as going along with hegemonic masculinity.

Oeppen's work looks at how these players react to a top-down change in the way the game is sold, as it moves from a hobbyist community to having large-scale sanctioned international tournaments and from being focused on teenage boys to a more sex-inclusive marketing strategy. The increasing presence of women in the tournaments led to sexist backlash among players who felt that their space was being invaded, that changes to the art featured on the cards, designed to be more inclusive to people of color and women, were an attack on them. In the discussions of these changes—including in major right-wing media outlets in the United States—it was argued that women just aren't interested in being competitive players or don't have the skills or instincts necessary to win. The women who call such assertions into question by doing well in tournaments are dismissed or the subject of sexist attacks on their appearance or personality. After all, if this is a masculine area of expertise, a woman doing well in it has to lack femininity in some sense.

This response may seem off: if playing this competitive card game is a masculine behavior, shouldn't the players *want* women around as an audience? If they want to demonstrate that they're better at the game than women are—because of their greater knowledge and skill—shouldn't it be useful to have women around to beat in a match?

But the real issue is that making the game, and the environment in which it is played, more inclusive threatens the idea that the game is a masculine area of expertise. In a hypothetical world where women are just as likely as men to play the game competitively, knowledge and mastery of the game are devalued, as it's no longer masculine. Knowledge and mastery are important—the most celebrated players are those who find novel, unexpected combinations of cards that interact in ways that aren't immediately obvious—but that knowledge and mastery only matter if it is expressed within a masculinized topic.

Sociologist Michelle Wolkomir's (2012) work on gender performances in poker games gives us another example. There's no reason that men should be inherently better at poker—a game that has no physical component—than women are, except for men's beliefs that it is an inherently masculine game. Wolkomir finds that men's desire to use the game to demonstrate a masculine gender identity by playing aggressively and trying to assert dominance winds up hurting them, as they are loath to fold (which is seen as feminine) even when they should, and underestimate female players (who, in turn, take advantage of the perception that they're necessarily worse at the game).

This kind of gendered gatekeeping might seem like it has low stakes—so what if someone isn't accepted as a *real* craft beer aficionado?—but it can easily spark a larger conflagration. The most familiar example of this might be the #GamerGate movement, in which videogame players decided that a woman who had designed a critically acclaimed game didn't deserve the positive reviews her work had received. Soon, the game designer, the reviewers who had praised the game, the journalists covering the story, and even individuals who spoke up in support of the designer, the game, or even against the online pile-on, were targeted with harassment campaigns, swatting, and worse.

Similarly, the 2013 incident now referred to as "donglegate" came out of a woman being present in a nearly all-male programming conference. When she overheard men in the audience nearby her making sex jokes, she posted about it online, including a photograph of the men. One of the men, who was quickly identified, lost his job; in retaliation, online vigilantes launched DDoS attacks against her employer, and she was fired (Siapara 2019; Ronson 2015).

Like #GamerGate, the "donglegate" incident, covered in newspapers and magazines throughout the United States and Europe, had serious consequences for the women being harassed and shamed, but also served as a warning for other women looking to get into male-dominated spaces in tech. The message was clear: if women work in this space, they're only here provisionally, and if they make a fuss about bad behavior, or even seem to be too successful, they can expect push back.

For most of the researchers who have been studying these ideas, these men are demonstrating marginalized forms of masculinity, maintaining control over some small overlooked social space in which their performance of masculinity can be valued by an audience of their peers (almost entirely other men). Across these examples, men are demonstrating what I'm referring to as technical masculinity, a form of gender performance that relies on demonstrated knowledge and mastery of subject areas perceived as masculine. Beer, various pop culture fandoms, computers, videogames, and finance—all are perceived as masculine areas of expertise, and so men can assert a masculine gender identity by demonstrating their mastery of these areas. Not all of these interests—nor the men participating in them—can be so easily dismissed as nerdy or geeky, even if that's where most of the ethnographies looking at them have come from. The breadth of interests that follow these dynamics means that "nerd" and "geek" become reductive and inaccurate, leading me to refer to the performance of these knowledge-based masculinities by the broader term "technical masculinities."

While demonstrated knowledge of masculinized areas of expertise is not at odds with traditional components of hegemonic masculinity, it's not a big part of how men assert those identities. Indeed, hegemonic masculinity, as currently constituted, is tied closely to actions, so much so that many measures of masculinity (such as the Bem Sex Role Inventory; Bem 1974) simply use agentic or active personality traits as the measure of masculinity. The extant version of hegemonic masculinity is performed by demonstrating the extent to which the individual is directly meeting the demands of hegemonic masculinity: money, job prestige, sexual fecundity, physical fitness, toughness, and so on, while avoiding any display that might be seen as feminine, such as emotional vulnerability. Knowing a lot about a topic—even one that's seen as masculine—just isn't part of how hegemonic masculinities are performed, save when that knowledge is being used as part of a display of some other trait (for instance, knowing a lot about expensive watches is less about technical knowledge than it is about demonstrating that the individual has enough money to afford expensive watches, or knowledge of fitness regimes can be a signal of physical strength). But that's clearly not what's going on here: craft beers are more expensive than Bud Light, but drinkers don't need to be wealthy to afford them. Sports, TV shows, movies, and games are available to just about everyone, so knowledge about them isn't a signal of wealth or any other element of currently hegemonic masculinity. But that knowledge is still being used by men within masculinized areas of expertise to create and enforce a gendered hierarchy.

In many ways, the social experience of buying cryptocurrency is not much different than the experience of playing a complex card game or getting really into craft beer. The groups of people who are into these subcultures gather in almost entirely male spaces, in person or online, make costly demonstrations of how much they know about the subject, use gatekeeping strategies to keep some people out, and revel in the complexity of the subject. What makes cryptocurrency (and, to a lesser extent, meme stocks) different is the connection with money. No one thinks that they're going to get rich off craft beer or Magic: The Gathering cards, but with cryptocurrency, the same traits that might make them successful at a game could get them the status that they feel is warranted by their masculine traits.

Other scholars have made the argument that technical masculinities should be considered as protest masculinities, challenging existing gender hierarchies, rather than as hybrid or marginalized masculinities. Mendick et al. (2023) make the argument that what they refer to as "nerd masculinities" have already supplanted past performances of masculinity as being the hegemonic form, pointing to a shift in the heroes that are presented in popular media. Iron Man is a hero not because he's strong, but because of his technical skill, as evidenced by his frequent use of indecipherable technobabble; the more traditional action hero, Thor, is presented as a comedic figure. When tech entrepreneur Mark Zuckerberg is presented in the film "The Social Network," he's not using feigned nerdery to avoid being lumped in with the traditionally masculine Winkelvoss twins: his technical prowess is shown to be a dominant form of masculinity.

It may seem odd to have a performance of masculinity based around—or at least observed through—the way that gender is presented in the media, but Ging (2019b, 53) argues that this can be seen as a response to how post-second wave feminism has become understood. In the 1970s, feminism was largely concerned with achieving material and legal equality for women, but by the 1990s, the presentation of feminism was less centered on politics and economics. Feminism in the wider culture was presented by, and understood through, cultural icons like the Spice Girls, Lady Gaga, Carrie Bradshaw, and Hannah Horvath. It makes sense, then, that the backlash against it would also draw on cultural icons. Men's rights activists may have benefited from the shift from a discussion of material and political equality to a discussion of cultural issues, but they didn't have to make that shift themselves: post-feminism did it for them (Ging 2019b, 59).

The fact that upheavals in the economy and society are what lead to upheavals in the gender hierarchy means that money—and the perceived opportunity to earn lots of it—plays a key role in how these masculinities are viewed and experienced. Cryptocurrencies are important to this story because they form a link between marginalized nerd masculinities and financial success. I'm going to argue that the linking of what was seen as geek or nerd masculinities with money, and therefore with the outcomes normally associated with currently dominant forms of masculinity, means that they're now best understood not as a marginalized masculinity, content to be on the outside looking in, but as a protest masculinity, actively contesting their place in the hierarchy, and looking to become dominant. These performances, then, impact not just the men using them but all of us.

Race and Technical Masculinities

In general, the picture being painted here of technical masculinities has not been a rosy one. A performance of gender based on demonstrated knowledge of masculine-coded topics might not be inherently bad, but many of the things that people carrying out this performance "know" are simply not true (as in the beliefs about evolutionary psychology discussed in Chapter 1, or beliefs about the ways in which financial markets are fixed discussed in Chapters 3 and 4) and are often actively harmful. It might be fine to want to show off knowledge about financial markets, but it becomes a problem when it leads people to make bad investments (or even just make a lot of trades that don't gain or lose money but carry significant transaction costs, as discussed in Chapter 5). Men mansplaining the minutiae of sports as a performance of masculinity might be annoying to the people around them, but when it leads men to lose money betting on sports, it becomes actively harmful.

But there are some ways in which a shift to technical masculinities as a dominant form of men's gender performances might be societally preferable to existing hegemonic performances, and one of those areas is inclusiveness. Performances of masculinity that are tied to owning a home in a good neighborhood, for instance, or being the breadwinner in a single-earner household, necessarily present barriers for poor men and, because of the link between socioeconomic status and race, for Black and Hispanic men. This link is one of the reasons why men from these groups are generally shunted off into marginalized masculinities, from which dominant forms might borrow especially effective performances. But there's no intrinsic connection between socioeconomic status and the ability to demonstrate knowledge over masculine-coded topics.

The issue might be even more accurate for Asian American men. In the United States today, Asian American men are considered to be less masculine than men from other racial backgrounds, a bias that has been found across contexts (Lu & Wong 2013; Chong & Kim 2022). A stereotype that Asian American men are bookish and nerdy might make it difficult for them to perform existing dominant masculinities—but might make it easier for them to be accepted as performing technical masculinities.

Does this mean that a world in which technical masculinities are dominant is one in which dominant masculinities will be more racially inclusive? Survey data, even in surveys that target young men, don't generally have enough representatives of minority racial groups to allow for detailed analysis, and qualitative work on technical masculinities hasn't paid a great deal of attention to the racial composition of the men being studied. However, there is reason to believe that the version of technical masculinities currently contesting the gender hierarchy is, like existing dominant masculinities, largely concerned with white people.

Other Approaches

The idea that technical masculinities are best understood as a protest masculinity is new, so it makes sense to look at other ways that researchers in the field have or might conceptualize them and show why their approaches don't fully explain what's going on.

One of these, the inclusive masculinities model (Anderson 2010), holds that, today, there are really only two masculinities: orthodox masculinity and inclusive masculinity. Orthodox masculinity is defined through a set of familiar traits: aggression, agency, misogyny, and homophobia. Inclusive masculinity is also trait-based, and, critically, the men performing inclusive masculinities aren't anti-gay. Given that Connell's conception of hierarchical competing masculinities puts gay men's masculinities as the antithesis of dominant masculinities, this represents a real challenge to her model. It also gets at a perceived weakness of Connell's account: in a culture that is increasingly accepting of gay men and lesbians, Connell's argument that masculinity is largely defined in opposition to gay masculinities can seem dated.

For the purposes of this research in particular, inclusive masculinity theory doesn't work well, as the performances of technical masculinities here are not inclusive and make use of homophobic and sexist language.[6] There's no indication that the men performing technical masculinities are seeking common cause with men performing subordinated or marginalized masculinities. Perhaps more importantly, they're making the case that their form of masculinity justifies a higher place in the gender hierarchy. The whole point of inclusive masculinity is that the dominant form is defined by a certain set of traits: how, then, can we explain a replacement, or attempted replacement, of one form of dominant or hegemonic masculinity with another that has different traits? Whatever the contribution of inclusive masculinity theory to our overall understanding of how men experience and express their gender identities, it doesn't fit well with the research questions and findings explored here.

Another potential alternative arises from hybrid masculinities (i.e., Bridges & Pascoe 2014). The argument here is that men use nerdy, knowledge-based performances in order to distance themselves from what are seen as the negative aspects of hegemonic forms of masculinity, while actually reaping the benefits of them. While these sorts of hybridized performances certainly happen, they don't do a great job of explaining the technical masculinities being discussed, both because of the marginalized nature of many of the men performing these masculinities, and their general rejection of the traits of currently hegemonic forms, if not the outcomes.

Ging (2019a) is among the scholars who have argued that masculinities very much like the technical masculinities discussed here should be understood as hybrid masculinities, rather than protest masculinities. The distinction is important: if technical masculinities are protest masculinities, they represent an attempt to upset the existing hierarchy and take over as the dominant form of masculinity within a society. If they're a hybrid masculinity, they're simply a way for men who are reaping the benefits of existing dominant forms of masculinity to claim that they shouldn't be blamed for the inequalities resulting from that hierarchy. When men in the online manosphere complain about how they're disadvantaged relative to other men, and distance themselves from dominant forms of masculinity, it can certainly sound like hybrid masculinities: "Don't blame me for gender hierarchies; I'm being disadvantaged, too."

This means that we must be very careful when men claim that they're outside of hegemonic performances of masculinity. Maybe they're embracing a marginalized masculinity, or maybe they're just putting on a show of doing so. How can we tell the difference? The key is the audience for these performances. Performances of hybrid masculinities are targeted at people who are lower on the gender hierarchy (especially women), while performances for peer groups snap back to hegemonic forms. Bridges and Pascoe (2014) point to three strategies that men use in their performance of hybrid masculinities: strategic borrowing of behaviors and signals from marginalized groups, discursive distancing from hegemonic forms, and fortification of the boundaries between themselves and other groups. As an example, Bridges (2010) points to men participating in a "walk a mile in her shoes" march, protesting violence against women by wearing women's shoes (and often dressing more fully in drag). This certainly looks like a performance of allyship and breaking down barriers, but it's leavened by the men involved complaining about how their bodies just aren't designed to walk in these shoes and trying to ensure that they looked like it was uncomfortable (even if it wasn't). They make exaggerated feminine gestures, stereotyping gays and drag performers (and often conflating the two), drawing secure boundaries between this performance of femininity and their everyday lives.

Sure, technical masculinities call out what they see as the undeserved privilege of men higher on the gender hierarchy than they are: Chads who didn't have to work for anything, who haven't taken the red pill to see how the world really works. Like men performing hybrid masculinities, they might well point out the ways in which they fall short of the ideals of hegemonic masculinities, playing up their lack of success with women (for now), or their social awkwardness. Men performing hybrid masculinities might be doing this in order to appear more vulnerable, or less threatening, and achieve romantic success, but those men are doing so for an audience of women, while the men performing technical masculinities are doing so for an audience of other men. The essence of hybrid masculinities is a disconnect between outward-facing performances and peer-facing performances that allows men to distance themselves from dominant masculinities while reinforcing them. While technical masculinities share some features with these performances, the contexts and goals are very different. Men performing technical masculinities aren't saying that gender hierarchies are bad: they're saying that they should be on top.

A Compensatory Behavior?

It's important to remember that conflict between performances of masculinity on the gender hierarchy doesn't preclude conflicts within those performances, and another potential explanation for the behaviors observed comes from this level of conflict.

Much of the research on masculinities deals with gender strain or threatened masculinity: how men use certain behaviors to bolster their masculinity when they feel that it's being called into question. Work in this line has demonstrated, for instance, that threats to their masculinity make men more likely to buy a gun (Carlson 2015; Cassino & Besen-Cassino 2020), consume certain kinds of pornography (Cassino & Besen-Cassino 2021), or vote for a conservative political candidate (Carian & Sobotka 2018; Cassino 2018; Vescio & Schermerhorn 2021).

The logic here is straightforward: when men feel that they have failed to meet the expectations of a desired form of masculinity, they look for behaviors within that performance that they can achieve and focus on them. So, a man might lose income relative to his spouse and thus believe that he is no longer meeting the expectation of being a breadwinner: he can compensate for that perceived shortcoming by buying a gun or getting a concealed weapons permit. So, even if he's no longer meeting the role of breadwinner, he's doubling down on a role as his family's (or society's) protector.

This idea of compensatory masculinities is tied closely with a line of research on gender role discrepancy stress (Eisler & Skidmore 1987; Reidy et al. 2014). It is that men who perceive that they are falling short of the demands of the masculine identities that they aspire to will act in ways to try and relieve that stress by doing—and often overdoing—behaviors that they see as linked to that identity. In contrast with the work on compensatory masculinities, which generally look at long term behavioral effects of this kind of disconnect, much of the work in gender role discrepancy stress makes use of experimental manipulations (often, giving false feedback to men implying that they are acting in a feminine manner, or forcing them to do so, as in Weaver 2013) to temporarily induce such strain.

Such lines of research present a different way in which we might understand the relationship between cryptocurrency purchases and men's gender identities: maybe buying up these assets is just a compensatory masculinity. Knowledge and mastery of these areas is masculine, so men who are worried about being seen as less masculine might well use it to shore up a gender identity that's under threat in a different area. Such an explanation is bolstered by the existing link between finance and masculinity: knowing about investments and money is linked with dominant performances of masculinity, so it could be used as a compensatory activity. If cryptocurrency investments are dominantly seen as a way to make money, we could easily see cryptocurrency purchases as a compensatory masculinity: men decide that they're falling short in one area of the currently dominant form of masculinity, and decide to redefine their masculine gender identities by stressing income. Technical prowess—especially with regard to computers and finance—could also be seen as part of currently dominant forms of masculinity, so a focus on these areas could also be used as a compensatory masculinity. If this is all that's happening, we don't need to bring protest masculinities, and the second level of conflict between performances of masculinity jostling for dominance.

Such an explanation is parsimonious and may even motivate some men to buy crypto, but it also seems insufficient. While many of the findings in this book could be seen as examples of men using financial behaviors as a compensatory masculinity, other findings indicate that the version of technical masculinities underlying cryptocurrency and meme stock buying behaviors isn't a supplement to traditional masculinity, but a wholesale alternative to it. This is clear from the narratives underlying these kinds of investments, as discussed in Chapters 3 and 4, as well as how these men talk about these investments, as discussed in Chapter 6.

In their own minds, at least, the man who masters these markets isn't someone who's fallen short in some other area, but rather someone who's found a different way to be a man, one more suited for the modern world. These men aren't aspiring to an elusive form of masculinity but performing a different one entirely: rather than reinforcing their claim to a dominant form of masculinity, they're tossing it out, and solidifying a claim to a protest masculinity, instead. Were dominant forms of masculinity even a little more achievable, they might very well make a different choice, but since social and economic shifts have put those forms solidly out of reach, there's little cost to moving toward protest forms, especially if there's a built-in audience in web forums for them. The difference here is subtle, but within the context of hierarchical masculinity proposed by hegemonic masculinity theory, it is important. In terms of the implications for society of these behaviors, there's a world of difference between threatened men finding a novel way to perform dominant masculinitiesand men who are trying to overthrow those masculinities and replace them with a red pill mentality.

From a theoretical perspective, there's a big difference between a behavior designed to reinforce existing dominant performance of masculinity and a behavior designed to supplant those performances. But the behaviors might be observationally equivalent, and while I think the data—especially the data from the content analyses in Chapter 6—push against a compensatory masculinities explanation, some men are likely using cryptocurrency as a way to aspire to currently dominant performances of masculinity, rather than performances seeking to replace them. From a societal perspective, this explanation might even be preferable, as it doesn't point toward an attempt to overthrow existing masculine hierarchies in the way that the technical masculinities argument does. In much of my past work, I've made use of a compensatory masculinities framework to understand otherwise baffling behavior on the part of men, so I don't have anything against such explanation, and would have been happy to build this book around them (in early drafts, that's exactly what I did). But as much as I would have liked to continue on with such an explanation, I don't think it fits all of the data presented in later chapters. The rhetoric around technical masculinities seems much more focused on challenging the currently dominant hierarchy of masculinities than being incorporated into it, pointing to a different level of conflict.

Across different conceptions of the gender hierarchy, there is widespread agreement that it is bitterly contested. While there has been a great deal of work looking at one level of that conflict—how men try to establish or maintain their placement within the hierarchy—there has been rather less looking at the second level of conflict, between various performances of masculinity for a place in the hierarchy. Such a discussion is necessarily theoretical, but it's important to establishing the stakes.

Technical masculinities are more than just an evolved form of marginalized nerd masculinities. The addition of money and social status to some performances of technical masculinities means that the men performing these masculinities can make the case that their version of masculinities is superior to the currently dominant ones. They are, in effect, making a play to become a new dominant performance, as they claim to offer a better path toward the purported benefits of masculinity for men, as well as a better case for why men deserve their social, economic, and political dominance. As the figures on the adoption of cryptocurrency and meme stocks make clear, these performances of masculinity have become enormously popular, and the next chapters lay out the case for why this is and demonstrate the relationship between a need for alternative performances of masculinity and the uptake of these assets.

"Buy the dip!" Men and Cryptocurrencies

In August of 2023, a new user on Reddit's cryptocurrency forums posted a question he had about buying a presale token. If the expectation is that the price of a token will increase substantially once it's released to the public—which might be a dubious expectation, but has happened—then buying at a much lower price in the presale would be a way to make a lot of money. For instance, some of the insiders who bought Andrew Tate's DADDY coin before it went on sale to the general public were able to multiply their initial investment more than 2,000x. This isn't unusual: meme coins often give away free coins before launch to "key opinion leaders" to incentivize them to talk up the coin and get more people on board.

This novice investor had been offered an opportunity[1] to buy a new, unknown coin at a presale rate, but was told that first he would have to have at least $500 worth of a more established cryptocurrency (Ethereum) in his account first. Since he only had $100 worth of it in his account, the people offering the presale wouldn't let him buy any more. This seemed odd, so he turned to the forum to ask why.

To be clear, this was almost undoubtedly a scam. There was perhaps some kind of malicious code that would steal whatever was in his account once he added the new tokens, or fees associated with the new tokens that wouldn't allow him to transfer them unless he paid some exorbitant amount (which would be covered by the money in the account). Some of the posts told him that the account he had used to interact with the new tokens was probably compromised by bad code already, and he should probably abandon it.

The consensus was that the novice, who was just excited by the idea of getting in on a token early, had been scammed and was probably already out the $100 in that account. The response of the more experienced investors wasn't outrage at a scammer, or even surprise: rather, the novice was told to treat the lost money as "tuition" and that he should "spend more time educating himself." There were no expressions of sympathy; he wasn't seen as a victim, but rather as a fool. Had he done his homework, he wouldn't have lost his money, and the fact that he had only lost $100 (so far) meant that he had gotten a good deal on a lesson that could have cost him a lot more.

For anyone outside of the world of cryptocurrencies, this interaction seems nonsensical on multiple levels. Why would anyone just give away something as apparently valuable as early access to a financial asset? How can buying something lead to a "compromised wallet" that would allow scammers to steal all of someone's money? What the heck is a "wallet," anyway? And why aren't investors upset at scammers targeting others in their community?

Moreover, this was, in the realm of crypto, a very penny-ante scam attempt. Large scale rug pulls—which might not even be illegal—can cost buyers of meme coins hundreds of millions of dollars. The collapses of crypto exchanges built on dubious assumptions about rates of return have cost crypto owners billions. In recent years, there's been a split in the crypto community between relatively respectable assets like Bitcoin or Ethereum, and the scammy, seedy wild west of meme coins (often referred to as "shitcoins," in a play on "bitcoin"), but the factors that lead individuals to buy into them are very similar. The fact that buying them is complex (and rather more for the smaller meme coins), and that there is ample opportunity for scams, theft, or simple catastrophic losses, isn't a problem but is intrinsically linked to the appeal of cryptocurrencies of all stripes. A man can perform toughness by walking into a seedy bar and picking a fight; if a man wants to perform technical masculinities, he can show that he can thrive by his wits and fortitude when things are complex, and he could easily lose everything.[2]

In crypto, the complexity comes at multiple levels. Suppose you saw an ad during the Super Bowl and want to buy some crypto. There are some big exchanges that will take your money and give you some crypto, some with an app, but then you're stuck operating within that exchange, hostage to whatever transaction fees they charge, unable to buy any assets that they don't support. Oh, and sometimes those exchanges collapse or get hacked, and you lose all of your money.

So, if you're serious about this, you have to set up a wallet, an anonymized account that allows access to your holdings (as discussed later, you never actually own crypto, you just have access to a code that lets you transfer that code to others). You can have a virtual wallet on one of those exchanges mentioned before, but as anyone in crypto will tell you, "not your keys, not your coins," so it really should be a hardware wallet, meaning that you're going to be buying an actual device that plugs into your computer (and, if you lose it, you've lost your assets with no hope of recovery). Then there's the debate about open source versus closed source programming underlying it, and it becomes very clear that this is not like buying something on Amazon.

To quote from the subreddit BitcoinBeginners, ostensibly aimed at people who just decided to get into crypto and are asking how to make a wallet:

> Electrum is great too, unless you're using an airgapped device that uses QR codes to communicate. It can do it, but the UI is very clunky for that, sadly. But if you're not using QRs, Electrum is great.
>
> Nunchuk for mobile is great for multisig, though the setup is clunky.
>
> P.S. If you ever decide to run your own node, all of the apps I mentioned can be set up to work with it. Nice!

A technically proficient reader can probably understand most of what's going on here, even if it's not clear why you would need your device to be air-gapped (never connected to the internet).

And once you do get yourself set up, buying and selling is far from straightforward, as is cashing out your gains into actual dollars that you could spend somewhere (assuming you're not robbed or scammed out of everything you have). But the arcane, technical nature of these discussions isn't a failure of the system: it's part of the point. If just anyone could do it—and really do it, not just pussyfoot around in a walled-off exchange—then it wouldn't function as a performance of technical prowess.

Buying crypto and talking about it is, then, a powerful way to perform technical masculinities, because it links traits that are seen as masculine with outcomes that are typically associated with dominant forms of masculinity, especially financial success. Its value as a performance is enhanced by the narrative that underlies cryptocurrencies.

People who buy and hold crypto are not just performing a form of masculinity but see themselves as part of a larger underdog narrative, where they are the plucky rebels, rising up against a monolithic institutional structure, despised in the moment, but certain to be successful. In the end, when they're vindicated, and cryptocurrencies have replaced government backed fiat currencies, they'll not only be proven right but will reap the rewards of their faith and perseverance. Often, as they express it, in the form of flashy cars. The combination of complexity, money, community, and the heroic narrative makes cryptocurrencies very attractive as a means of performing technical masculinities but also makes buyers vulnerable to those who are trying to take advantage of them.

These narratives are key to the argument that I'm making about the function of cryptocurrency purchases as a performance of a protest masculinity. Buying a financial asset that you think is going to make money isn't a sign that we're dealing with a protest masculinity, but using your technical prowess to burn down the existing system, replacing it in an apocalyptic moment that overturns existing power structures is. That means that in order to understand why crypto functions the way it does as a performance, we have to understand where it comes from and the narratives underlying it.

Cryptocurrencies and Fiat Currencies

To understand why cryptocurrencies are so attractive to some people, it's not necessary to understand all of the technical aspects of how they work, but a basic understanding is useful. Regardless of how they're used today, cryptocurrencies are intended as a potential replacement for the dollars, Euros, yen, or whatever is being used to buy and sell goods and services, and so it makes sense to look at them first as a currency. This is also useful for understanding how crypto has evolved over time.

Researchers examining attitudes toward cryptocurrencies have created detailed lists of their important characteristics: what makes them crypto and what makes them different from other financial assets (see Abraham et al. 2019). These lists mix three important characteristics of crypto: the way that the assets are created, the way that they're managed, and the way that they interact with the real world.

Cryptocurrencies can be understood as the bastard child of fiat currencies and stocks. In the past, national currencies—the dollar, the pound, and so forth—were directly, and later nominally, backed by precious metals in what was known as the gold standard. So, for every dollar that the US government printed, there was a corresponding amount of gold somewhere in a vault controlled by the government. This limited how many dollars the government could print—if they wanted to print more dollars, they needed to get more gold from somewhere—but the trade-off was that it facilitated international trade. Since the currency of other countries was also backed by precious metals, figuring out the exchange rate between two currencies wasn't a problem, and sellers from other countries didn't have to worry about accepting dollars, as they could always be traded in for gold (at least on some theoretical level). Modern proponents of the gold standard mostly center their arguments in favor of it on inflation: if the government can only print a certain amount of money, there's limited opportunity for an increase in the money supply to increase prices and reduce the value of existing money.[3] It also makes long-term trade deficits impossible, as too much currency flowing out of a country will lead to a lack of backing precious metals, limiting the ability of the country to import, as they won't have any way to pay for those imports.

Of course, currency backed by precious metals had enormous drawbacks: in addition to limiting the ability of countries to respond to economic crises, they also facilitated speculative attacks on currency, in which cartels could buy up enormous amounts of currency, betting that the government didn't have sufficient reserves of foreign currency or precious metals to back them, and forcing a devaluation. Countries largely started ignoring the need to back all currency with precious metals during the Great Depression, retaining it in principle while refusing to allow any currency to actually be cashed out, and by the 1970s, even this fig leaf was gone. Instead of being backed by gold in a vault, currencies were backed by the government issuing them, having value to the extent that, and as long as, people believe that they have value. These are what are referred to as fiat currencies: currencies that are backed only by trust in the issuing government. In the crypto community—as among fringe economic groups that push for a return to the gold standard—US dollars are frequently referred to as "FRNs," for "Federal Reserve Notes," implying that the *real* dollar stopped existing when the US government stopped backing them with precious metals. There is therefore a trade in very old US currency, driven by the extremely dubious theory that it could somehow still be traded in for gold (the sort of folks floating these theories will also happily expound on why a US flag with a gold fringe is a sign that you're not dealing with the actual government).

The fact that fiat currencies aren't based on any real asset isn't a problem for most users of a currency in relatively stable countries: they don't have to think about why a dollar can be exchanged for a candy bar, they just know that it works. Things get trickier in countries where trust in the government is lower— there, sellers might demand payment in foreign currencies, leading to lots of real estate transactions being carried out in bags full of Euros or dollars—but so long as a more trusted currency is available, people work it out.

But for some people, these fiat currencies present a number of (often theoretical) problems. The first is inflation: since fiat currencies aren't backed by tangible assets, governments can print money whenever they want, and this sometimes results in out-of-control inflation that can wreck an economy. Even more moderate levels of inflation can erode the value of savings. There are also concerns about monitoring from the government and the financial sector. Banks and governments can easily see how much money someone has and can demand to find out where that money came from. Transactions go from one account identified with a particular person or corporation to another identified with a particular person or corporation: who paid whom can be traced. For a cynic, this might sound like it's mostly a problem for criminal organizations who want to hide the movement of money, but it could also be a real problem for any group that a government doesn't like. A human rights organization could find its assets frozen or its donors arrested. Most people wanting to hide money may want to do so for illicit purposes, but that doesn't mean that there aren't good reasons for wanting to do so as well, especially for people living under repressive regimes (this is the most frequently cited example of a positive, prosocial use of cryptocurrencies, even if it has remained largely theoretical).

Cryptocurrencies can, in theory, address these problems. Since crypto accounts aren't necessarily identified with an individual, outsiders can observe when value moves from one account to another, but don't necessarily know who was involved in the transaction, or what, if anything, was gotten in return. If I buy a pizza from Domino's with my debit card, there's a record both in my bank account and Domino's bank account showing that I bought a pizza: potentially blackmail material for an Italian-American living in New Jersey. But if I were to buy it using crypto, like programmer Laszlo Hanyecz did in 2010, buying two Papa John's pizzas for 10,000 Bitcoin (Yaffee-Bellamy 2024), an outsider could see that one wallet had moved crypto to another wallet but wouldn't know that it was me, or what potentially embarrassing product I'd bought.

When someone creates a new cryptocurrency, they can establish rules for how many tokens (commonly called "coins") the system will have, either capping it or increasing it in accordance with certain conditions. For instance, the rules governing Bitcoin specify that only 21 million Bitcoins can ever exist, with the rate at which new coins are made halving at regular intervals over time. We're not yet at that cap, and more coins come into existence as payment for servers that process Bitcoin transactions.[4] As I'll discuss later, processing cryptocurrency transactions can be enormously costly and inefficient, so this payment serves to incentivize users to help out the system. From the perspective of crypto as a form of currency, however, this is important because no minting of new coins in response to financial crises or political pressure means (in principle) that there shouldn't be any inflation.[5]

Concerns about privacy and secrecy are addressed by the use of what's called a blockchain. Rather than all transactions going through a bank or some other body, cryptocurrency transactions are posted on a publicly accessible ledger: *this* account moved this many coins to *that* account. The fact that this ledger is public might make it seem like it's less private, but since the accounts are not linked with the identity of any individual or corporation, it's difficult or impossible to tell who is moving the coins to whom (though patterns in the movement can help researchers figure it out). In that sense, crypto accounts are less like traditional bank accounts, which require an ID to open, and more like numbered Swiss accounts, accessible by anyone who has the code.

The problem with such a system is that dealing with all of the transactions requires a great deal of computing power, and since there's not one central body—like a bank—that's profiting from the transactions, it's not clear who is supposed to pay for it. Solving this problem led to one of the more interesting aspects of Bitcoin (and many other cryptocurrencies that followed): a bounty system. To incentivize processing the transactions, accounts that do so get a payment in Bitcoin. Initially, this was fifty coins, but the amount has been repeatedly cut in half over time as the total number of Bitcoins in circulation rises.[6] As the price of Bitcoin has risen, the value of this bounty has gone up astronomically (even as the number of coins awarded has gone down), leading to some of the problems discussed later, but also ensuring that there's no shortage of server farms competing to process the transactions.

So, in addition to being motivated by the perceived failures of fiat currencies, Bitcoin and other cryptocurrencies have a great deal in common with them. They're (in theory) a medium of exchange that can be used to buy and sell, with no actual asset backing them,[7] just trust in the issuing body. Proponents argue that cryptocurrencies are actually superior to government-issued currencies because they allow (in theory) for greater privacy and less inflation.

But this raises a problem: getting people to trust this new currency. It's easy to understand why people trust the fiat currencies backed by the US government or the European Union and are wary of holding on to the currencies of states with weaker economies or less stable governments, but why should they trust a fiat currency that isn't issued by a government at all? For cryptocurrencies, the answer comes from smart contracts. Buyers don't have to trust that the people running the cryptocurrency are going to do what they say that they're going to do: all decision-making is set up in the algorithm that governs the coin. For instance, no one had to decide that the bounty for updating Bitcoin's blockchain would be cut in half every so often, or that the total number of Bitcoins would be limited to 21 million. These decisions were made when the coin was set up and built into the code that governs it. There's no need to be concerned that someone is going to steal the investment or change the rules of the game to devalue it (by, for instance, suddenly minting a lot of new coins), as the coin can only do what's in the code. It's called a "smart contract" because it's self-enforcing: it's a computer program that automatically follows the rules that have been laid out.

For a government, this is probably a bad thing: it would mean absolutely no flexibility to deal with financial crises or apply Keynesian solutions to economic downturns (which is a big part of why governments abandoned the gold standard in the first place). But it's easy to see why it might be attractive to savers, who may simply want to put money aside and be confident that it's not going to lose its value (even if, again, this benefit remains entirely theoretical). As we'll see, the earliest versions of crypto arose from communities worried about holding on to value in the *very* long term of hundreds of years, for reasons that probably aren't on the radar for most people.

Importantly, this case for crypto only really makes sense in contrast with existing power structures. The assumption is that nation-states and banks will collapse under the weight of their own contradictions, only to be replaced by cryptocurrencies, which lack the inherent weaknesses of existing systems of exchange. This view is hard to square with the idea that crypto investors want to join the ranks of the current elite but makes sense from the perspective of a protest masculinity, where the goal is to tear down existing power structures and replace them with something different.

Cryptocurrencies and Stocks

While the goal of a cryptocurrency like Bitcoin is to replace government-issued fiat currencies as a mode of exchange, in practice, cryptocurrencies are used much more like speculative stocks. In their earliest incarnations, stocks were a way for corporations to raise capital to invest in an undertaking large enough that no single investor or group of investors could back it: large-scale trading missions from Europe to Asia, for instance. In those early days, stockholders received a proportion of the earnings of the venture they were backing, spreading both risk and reward among all the investors, in proportion to how much stock they held. A secondary market in the stocks quickly arose, as investors bought and sold existing stocks: the first of what we now call stock markets. In a theoretically efficient market, the price of any stock is based on a combination of the future earnings of the company (discounted by the possibility that those earnings will not be realized) and the current assets of the company. A company that has few assets now, but the potential for strong earnings in the future (like many of today's tech companies), might well be more valued than one that has lots of assets now but less room to grow. If people are systematically overestimating how well the company will do in the future or its current assets, the price will be too high, and investors would be wise to sell the stock before it drops (or even short the stock, lending stock with a promise to buy back later, essentially betting that the price will drop in the interim). If the price is too low, investors would be better served by buying up the stock and waiting for it to rise. The key here is that there is, in theory, a correct price for the stock, and the fluctuations in the price are, essentially, investors fighting over whether the current price is higher or lower than that correct price.

But there's another reason why someone might buy a stock. Suppose that they don't believe that a stock is underpriced but have reason to believe that others will think that it is. It might make sense, then, to buy even an overpriced stock on the expectation that the price will rise further, under what's called the "greater fool" theory. That is, the buyer may be a fool for buying an overpriced asset, but so long as they can find a greater fool than themselves, they'll still make money on the deal. In a theoretically efficient market, any such gains from speculation will be short-lived, as the price of the stock will rapidly come back down to the correct price, but we don't live in a theoretical efficient world, and these asset bubbles can go on for some time.

The price of a stock can be thought of as existing on a scale ranging from being based entirely on the correct price of a stock to entirely driven by speculation about the behavior of other investors. We don't know where exactly on this scale a stock is, but old school blue chip companies like General Electric or Johnson & Johnson are probably closer to the correct price side, while companies that get lots of media coverage, or that are highly reliant on theoretical future earnings, are probably closer to the speculation side (meme stocks, like GameStop, discussed in Chapter 4, are perhaps the best example).

Bitcoin and other cryptocurrencies are even farther over on this scale than the meme stocks are. The price of GameStop might be out of line with its expected profits, but at the end of the day, GameStop owns a bunch of stores filled with stock that is worth *something*.[8] The price of the stock might be an unreasonable multiplier of that value, but it is a multiple of it. In the case of cryptocurrencies, the only value held by the asset is the expectation that other people will think it's valuable. In other words, it's propped up entirely by the belief in a greater fool.

Of course, if someone were buying cryptocurrency to use it as a currency, this would all be irrelevant: I keep dollars in my (physical) wallet not because I think they're going to appreciate relative to the Euro, but because I'm going to buy things from vendors who accept those dollars. However, only a relatively small portion of people who own cryptocurrency actually use it as, well, a currency: somewhere around 10 to 15 percent of US crypto owners have bought something with it in the past year (Federal Reserve 2023). The rest seem to be using it as an investment vehicle, holding on to it because they think the price is going to go up, a far cry from its utopian origins as discussed shortly, and making it more like a meme stock than anything else.

Now for the Problems

It's commonly supposed that Bitcoin and other cryptocurrencies are at least as safe as the contracts that underlie them: if the user trusts the smart contract, they can trust the currency. However, this ignores the meta-rules of the smart contract: the mechanisms built into it by which the contract can be changed. Just as the US Constitution has an amendment process, most cryptocurrency smart contracts are subject to change at any time, if (generally) a majority of participants want it changed (Baldwin 2018). There may well be good reasons for making these kinds of changes: adapting to technological changes or issues that were unknown when the smart contract was initially coded. But this feature also opens up the possibility of scams (perhaps like the one discussed at the start of this chapter): if someone owns more than 50 percent of a coin, and the rules stipulate the a majority can change the rules, there's nothing to stop them from changing the smart contract to steal everything else that's in the wallet (or force the user to pay an exorbitant amount to sell that coin or any number of other ways of taking advantage of minority stakeholders).

The smart contracts that underlie cryptocurrencies are thought to be desirable because they're self-executing and transparent. The user doesn't have to wait and hope that the other party in the contract decides to go along with the terms of it (and sue them if they don't): the terms of the contract happen automatically. But that also gives rise to the danger that any terms of the contract that disadvantage a user happen automatically, without giving them a chance to question them.

Such contracts are transparent—users can see them before they agree to take part—but face a problem well known to anyone who's scrolled through an end user licensing agreement before being able to start an app or sign up for a service: few people have the patience or capacity to fully understand what's in the contract. In cryptocurrencies, the smart contract is open for any user to look at, but without being able to read or understand the code it's programmed in (or without fully trusting any summary of the code that might be presented, or that it isn't going to change), that's not going to help much. Crypto users are told to do their own homework and examine what's going on with a coin before investing in it: but that's about as likely as anyone else reading all the terms and conditions associated with a purchase before agreeing to it.

Sometimes, the exploitation of code in the smart contracts can allow users to do things that most users would be opposed to, and this can lead to further complications. In July 2016, for instance, users discovered a vulnerability in the code of a prominent crowd-funded investment fund called DAO that was run on the Ethereum blockchain. Using this vulnerability, they were able to take control of more than a quarter of all of DAO's assets.

Now, this sounds like theft, but the group that took control of those assets was working entirely within the code that governed DAO, and if they were using it in a way that wasn't intended—well, it's a smart contract, and everyone involved apparently should have done their homework better. What's worse is that since all of the transactions are public and on the blockchain, it was very clear where the money had gone: there just wasn't a clear way to get it back to DAO.

In response, Ethereum held a vote, and instituted what's called a hard fork, reversing all of the transactions that had taken the assets from DAO. This meant, essentially, that there were now two different Ethereum blockchains: one that had the DAO transactions, and one that didn't. Both continue to this day (the one that didn't roll back the DAO transactions is now called "Ethereum Classic"). Instead of just giving everyone back the assets they were supposed to have in the first place, the only fix on the inviolate Blockchain is to create the equivalent of a parallel universe where they were able to fix it.

The smart contracts, combined with a lack of regulation, also mean that there is ample opportunity for less sophisticated scams, like rug pulls: essentially a classic pump and dump scam. For instance, in 2021, a memecoin inspired by the then-popular Netflix TV show Squid Game was listed on several sites (BBC 2021). Since these memecoins have no intrinsic value, they rise and fall based on whether memecoin investors are interested in them, and since the TV show was a hit, the coin—which didn't actually have anything to do with the show other than the name ("Squid") and a logo inspired by the program—quickly rose in price. According to the creators of the coin—on a website riddled with spelling mistakes—the coins would be used as in-game currency in an online game inspired by the show, which perhaps explained why investors who bought the coins wouldn't be able to sell them immediately (as specified in the smart contract). The price of the coin rose from one cent to nearly $3,000: at which point the creators of the coin, who still owned most of it, sold everything they had, pocketing about $3 million while the price dropped back down to where it had started. Similarly, one of the biggest stories about crypto in 2024 involved the social media influencer Haliey[9] Welch, colloquially known as "the hawk tuah girl"[10] for a viral video moment. Like many other influencers, she launched a meme coin; within a few minutes, it had a market capitalization of around $500 million (which in this context doesn't mean what that term generally means, but more on that later). The rapid rise encouraged buyers to jump in and get their share of what seemed like windfall profits, but within 20 minutes of the launch and rapid rise, the price cratered, dropping nearly 90 percent as buyers who had gotten in early (suspiciously early, in the views of some) sold their holdings. Buyers who had thought they were getting in early to ride the wave were instead wiped out. Of course, some people made enormous amounts of money from the rapid rise and fall (a group which may or may not include Welch, as the ownership of the wallets that benefited is unknown), leading to claims that this was a rug pull, in which insiders who get early access profited at the expense of everyone else. If this sort of maneuver were to happen on the stock market, people would likely go to jail, but in the world of memecoins, it's almost expected, and may not even be illegal.[11] This all happened on the same day that the Bitcoin hit $100,000, driven by the expectation of a favorable regulatory environment under the then-incoming new Presidential administration in the United States.

The nature of cryptocurrencies means that scams even less sophisticated than rug pulls can be successful. Holders of cryptocurrencies often make use of exchanges, in order to move their assets from one coin to another. This necessarily means giving those exchanges access to their crypto wallets: if the owner of the exchange decides to just take assets from them, or if an individual or consortium puts together enough assets to gain control of the exchange and unilaterally change the smart contracts governing it, those assets can be gone in a flash. This isn't much different from a smash and grab robbery, but it's facilitated by the nature of the asset, and as with rug pulls it's not always clear if it's even illegal.

Initially, when Bitcoin was the realm of hobbyists, Bitcoin mining was generally a money losing proposition: the coins users got for helping to update the blockchain were worth less than the electricity the PC was using to do the calculations. It was more akin to the wave of distributed computing projects like SETI at Home (in which individuals volunteered their idle computers to analyze radio signals from space) than any sort of business proposition. Today, however, Bitcoin mining is big business, with giant server farms using ridiculous amounts of electricity and water to reliably generate returns. This is bad for the environment—especially as developed states try to move toward green sources of electric power—but also undercuts the intended decentralized network (Baldwin 2018). One of the benefits of Bitcoin was supposed to be that no one would control too much of it, making it resistant to disruptions in the same way that the Internet was designed to allow for communication even in the wake of a nuclear war. But if a few big data centers are doing most of the processing, we're right back to a centralized network.

In addition to limiting the decentralized nature of Bitcoin and other cryptocurrencies, Bitcoin mining operations have also had an enormous environmental impact. They use enormous amounts of electricity to power the chips performing the complex calculations needed, and cooling them requires enormous amounts of water, though this impact has been made less visible by the even greater demands of large language model processing. Some cryptocurrencies have taken steps to reduce the environmental impact of processing transactions, but the biggest, Bitcoin has not, and as the value of Bitcoin (and therefore the value of the reward for Bitcoin mining) increases so too does the incentive to build more warehouses full of servers cranking out calculations and waste heat.

Where Does the Value Come From?

When users on the Reddit forums r/Cryptocurrency and r/SatoshiStreetBets decided (seemingly as a joke) to drive up the value of the Shiba Inu dog meme-based token Dogecoin (not to be confused with the other popular Shiba Inu dog meme-based token Shiba Inu), they were easily able to do so, with Dogecoin prices increasing 900x over the next three months.[12] A coin—not a real coin, but more the concept of a coin—with a picture of an admittedly cute dog, has as much value in financial markets as large, well-known companies that have inventory and real estate and sales and employees. How is that possible?

As already noted, the value of a cryptocurrency arises not from any valuation of its assets or profit potential, but rather on the greater fool theory: it's worth whatever the buyers think they'll be able to sell it to someone else for. This is one of the ways in which cryptocurrencies are actually pretty similar to fiat currencies: dollars have value in large part because of the belief that other people are going to accept them as currency. That means that while cryptocurrencies don't have assets or sales in the same way that companies do, their price is driven by fundamentals of the market; it's just that the market doesn't look anything like a stock market.

Since the prices of assets like cryptocurrencies and the related asset of Non-Fungible Tokens (NFTs) are driven entirely by expectations about what other people will pay for them, rather than being tied to any kind of underlying value (or, in the case of stocks, fundamentals of the company), actions like celebrity endorsements can dramatically increase their value (hence the practice of giving online influencers free coins, in the hope that they'll be incentivized to talk it up). When a celebrity buys, endorses, or mints their own coin or NFT collection, it drives coverage, which leads to more attention, and more people buying in, which leads to a higher price and, potentially, large returns for the celebrity and whoever else owned the asset beforehand (Garcia et al. 2014). This has been a common play, with Snoop Dogg talking up Bored Ape Yacht Club NFTs in 2022, or similar efforts from Jay-Z, Ye, and other musicians (Serada 2023). When mentions of a crypto asset on Reddit increase, the price of the asset soon follows (Phillips & Gorse 2018), not because the buyers necessarily think its value has increased, but because they believe that other people will value it more (what John Maynard Keynes called a beauty contest: Keynes 1936).

So, potential buyers looking to assess the "fundamentals" of a crypto asset look for indications of the degree of interest in the asset itself, with predictions of future value being driven by metrics like Google search data (Cheah & Fry 2015), or, early on, how often the Wikipedia page for "Bitcoin" was viewed. Tash et al. (2024) note that doing research on the likely price swings of cryptocurrencies generally involves looking at social media posts mentioning them. In stocks, price swings are a combination of fundamentals, real information, and vibes: with cryptocurrencies, it's all vibes. This means that it's reasonable to try and create artificial indications of the popularity of a coin: paying online influencers or botnets to talk about it, for instance. And while that may seem like cheating, or gaming the system, such concepts aren't really applicable in the way that they would be for a stock. In a stock, paying people to say nice things might distract potential investors from the underlying fundamentals of the asset. In crypto *there are no underlying fundamentals,* so it isn't "fake it until you make it," but rather, faking it *is* making it.

Serada (2023) puts cryptocurrencies, NFTs, and meme stocks in the same basket of "YOLO capitalism," investments driven not by trenchant financial analysis, or theories of the market, but rather by emotional responses. They're less related to investments than to slot machines, and one of the explanations for the rise in cryptocurrencies and NFTs during the pandemic (as well as meme stocks, as discussed in Chapter 4) is that they're basically just entertainment. People spend a lot of money on virtual assets within videogames, for instance, in order to show off to other players, and cryptocurrencies might be no different. They might go up in price for a while, but so did Beanie Babies and Dutch tulips, and cryptocurrencies have less intrinsic value than either of those. As such, normal theories of why the value of the asset might rise or fall aren't applicable.

We should note one thing about the apparently enormous market capitalizations of these meme coins: it's not at all clear how much of it is based on real money. Leveraged buys are common in crypto marketplaces, meaning that individuals can borrow against their existing holdings, often by huge multipliers. If, for instance, a marketplace allowed for 10x leveraging against existing holdings, someone who had $1000 worth of crypto that was viewed as relatively stable (Bitcoin or Ethereum, for example), many marketplaces would allow them to buy up to $10,000 worth of other crypto assets: in such a case, there would be $10,000 worth of market capitalization for these assets, but only $1,000 of real money backing them. Some platforms were allowing leveraged buys of more than 100x (McKenzie & Silverman 2023). Such extreme leveraging only works on the assumption that prices will only go up—so the new instruments will eventually be valuable enough to cover any losses—and that no one will ever try to convert the crypto assets back into cash (as there wouldn't be nearly enough cash in the system for that to work).

The market capitalization of cryptocurrencies can also be artificially driven up in ways that have little to do with any actual market value. If I were to mint 1,000 DanCoins and somehow persuade someone (perhaps my mother) to pay $10 for one of them, DanCoins would suddenly have a market capitalization of $10,000, despite only $10 ever having changed hands. I might even just buy the coin myself, from a different account (remember that they're anonymous), transferring $10 from one of my accounts to another, and somehow becoming $10,000 richer for having done so.

If the value of cryptocurrencies isn't really based on anything but expectations, and leveraged buys mean that there might be a lot less money in the system than it appears, Serada's dismissive view of cryptocurrencies as being something akin to slot machines or Beanie Babies seems to make sense. Perhaps they're worthy of attention, but we shouldn't take them too seriously.

Such a dismissive attitude toward cryptocurrencies was probably justified in the early days of their existence, but the amount of money at stake, and how it interacts with other financial markets, means that it isn't justified today. Early on,

Bitcoin and other cryptocurrencies were basically walled off from other financial markets: money that was in Bitcoin stayed there, money that was in stocks stayed there, and whatever happened in Bitcoin barely registered in the stock market, a dynamic driven largely by the extreme volatility of Bitcoin (Yermack [2013] 2024). Today, however, the markets are much more integrated. Yousaf, Pham, and Goodell (2023) find that when crypto assets go up in price, stocks go up as well; when they go down in price, demands for bonds and other safe assets increases. The volatility in crypto assets means that these sorts of transmissions driven by big movements happen much more frequently than they would with other assets, so even though the overall amount of money in crypto and related assets might be small, they have the capacity to be extraordinarily disruptive (Yousaf, Pham, & Goodell 2023). Recently, funds that deal in cryptocurrencies have been allowed to trade in regulated markets, potentially opening up (indirect) investments to investors who might otherwise be skeptical by giving them a patina of regulation (such a patina is potentially very dangerous, as it may lead investors to falsely believe that their investments are safer or more regulated than they are, as in the exchange collapse discussed in Chapter 8). So, even if the normal expectations about the valuation of assets don't apply to cryptocurrencies, even if their valuations are based on vibes, they are now widespread enough, and sufficiently incorporated into our financial sector, that they matter. In addition to how integrated they are into the financial system, about one in six US voters now says that they own, or have owned, cryptocurrencies or related assets like NFTs, and if they were playing in a walled-off market that didn't impact everyone else, maybe their numbers wouldn't matter, and the billions of dollars in valuation could be seen as something like the inflated price of rare Beanie Babies in the 1990s. But, however, the value of a crypto asset has been reached, the fact that it's integrated into the markets means that it now impacts all of us.

The Origins of Cryptocurrency

I've already made reference to part of the appeal of cryptocurrencies coming from an underlying narrative. People aren't buying into crypto just because they like that the numbers go up—though that's important—but because of the story of crypto, which turns owners from just the holders of a volatile financial asset to actors in a civilization-defining conflict.

To understand this narrative, it's necessary to go back to the roots of cryptocurrency. Most such accounts start with a white paper written by an individual or group going by the name of Satoshi Nakamoto, published in late 2008. That white paper described the structure of Bitcoin, and by January 2009, the first Bitcoins were mined. We don't know who Nakamoto is or was, but their early investments in Bitcoin may have made them very, very wealthy: Nakamoto is estimated to have somewhere around a million Bitcoins, putting them in the top twenty richest people in the world (Cuthbertson 2021).

The timing of the launch of Bitcoin is important, as the development of Bitcoin was made more urgent by the financial crisis occurring at the same time. The first block on Bitcoin's blockchain, the text a user would see if they were to scroll all the way up to the first transaction, reads:

The Times 03/Jan/2009 Chancellor on brink of second bailout for banks

In one sense, this is just a way of date stamping when the post happened, like a hostage holding up a newspaper. But it also means that the 2008–9 financial crisis is literally embedded in every Bitcoin transaction. The theoretical case for Bitcoin or other cryptocurrencies only makes sense if the buyer has decided that the existing system of central banks and fiat currencies is corrupt, doomed, or both, and amid taxpayer bailouts for banks that registered huge losses, that was an easy case to make.

However, the origins of cryptocurrency start well before Bitcoin, as skepticism about the value and future of fiat currencies, and the search for alternatives, arose decades earlier. Brunton (2020) links this strain of thought to the science fiction of the 1930s and stories like *The Moon Metal* (Serviss 1900), in which crises ended the existing currency regimes, but a new, better currency would replace it, solving many (or all!) of the problems facing society. The timing here is no coincidence, as this initial wave of concern about fiat currencies came just as currencies were separating themselves from the precious metals reserves that had previously backed them.

In the modern era, this connection is clearest in the writings of objectivists. Despite the degree to which their prophet Ayn Rand fetishized the US dollar, her modern followers believe that the US government and the dollar it backs have been fatally weakened, and a collapse is imminent (and has been for some time). After that collapse, US dollars and other fiat currencies will be worthless, with silver and gold coins rising to become the only real currency.

The push for cryptocurrencies—and against state-backed fiat currencies—also arises from hardcore libertarian economics, especially that which draws from Frederich Hayek. Hayek argued (non-controversially) that prices are essentially communications of supply and demand, and therefore (more controversially) anything that meddles with prices serves to weaken the information value of prices, inducing market inequalities. Since governments meddle with prices (by supporting some industries, or altering the money supply, for instance), they necessarily lead to inefficiencies, and therefore (very controversially) should be kept out of markets completely.

But, as Baldwin (2018) notes, the early days of cryptocurrencies made for strange bedfellows, bringing together fringe (but generally left-wing) utopian ideologies with these kinds of right-wing economics. By the 1990s, a second strain of concerns about fiat currencies led to very different fringe groups looking into alternative currencies. One of those was cryogenics enthusiasts, people who believed that their bodies (or sometimes just their heads) could be frozen before or just after their deaths, allowing them to be revived at some point in the future by means as yet unknown. Among the many problems faced by anyone taking these ideas seriously is money: how to pay to keep a body or head (which, today, costs a little less than half the price of full body preservation[13]) frozen until the technology exists to bring it back? And once our distant descendants do, where are they going to get the money to support themselves? If they keep their money in investments, there's always the possibility of a catastrophic financial collapse that could destroy them. Holding on to cash or government securities might seem safer, but if we're talking hundreds of years, how confident can anyone be that inflation won't devalue their frozen nest egg into oblivion, or even that the country whose currency they're counting on will still exist? What they need, then, is a currency that is (1) not tied to any particular country and (2) is immune to inflation.

Precious metals do a reasonable job of meeting these criteria, and there was a spate of attempts to use digital ownership of pieces of a precious metals reserve as currency: imagine that there's a pallet of gold sitting in a warehouse somewhere, and owners can trade portions of it with other users. Recording who owned how much of the gold in a transparent way is a problem solved by something like a blockchain, but such schemes faced the same problems governments did when they were backing currency with precious metals. The system only has so much gold, limiting the amount of currency it can reasonably create and therefore the size of the economy that can be supported, and there's no easy way of knowing whether the gold being traded is actually there. Later, some of the currencies backed by precious metals (like Pecunix and e-Gold) were briefly in vogue and appealed to many of the constituents of the nascent crypto communities, but faced logistical problems, and weren't able to reach wide acceptance (though they did become popular for money laundering and credit card fraud, among other financial crimes). The fact that they were backed with precious metals also made them perilously close to actual currencies, potentially attracting regulatory enforcement (as did the crimes people were using them for). Individuals interested in these sorts of alternative currencies realized (like governments had some time prior) that it didn't matter what was backing the currencies, so long as everyone agreed to accept them. For example, the DigiFrancs of the 1990s were backed by ten cases of (apparently lukewarm) Diet Coke stored in a vault in Washington, DC (Black Unicorn 1994). Eventually, cryptocurrencies, as we now know them, provided a more reasonable solution for individuals worried about being defrosted centuries hence as they had no ties to governments and no risk of inflation.

Cryogenics believers weren't the only strain of very online people, and generally left-wing groups in the 1990s were looking at alternative currencies. Some were interested for much the same reasons, like transhumanists who believed that they'd be able to upload their consciousness and live forever, or longevity hackers who thought that some combination of nutrition and behavior could extend their lives greatly.

Other early developers of alternative currencies were more worried about the increasing digitization of currencies and transactions, and the surveillance possibilities that went along with it. Cash, for the most part, is difficult to track; buying something via credit or debit card necessarily leaves a record of where the buyer was at what time, and what they purchased there. Founding figures of the crypto movement like David Chaum pushed for what he called "e-cash" that would combine the convenience of digital transactions with the anonymity of cash. While Chaum's approach is in some ways superior to the cryptocurrencies of today—it would not have been at all attractive to criminals, for instance (Brunton 2020)—it never caught on with enough people to become viable. The same fate—though for very different reasons—befell other attempts, like the "Cryptocredits" of the 1990s.

Serada (2023) argues that it was the rising distrust of financial markets— especially after the 2008 crash—that led these threads of cryptocurrency development to come together, and with widespread enough adoption to make them really viable for the first time (even if much of the initial use was, as with other cryptocurrencies, for illegal purchases). So while the roots of crypto come from right-wing economics and science fiction ideas about transhumanism, its widespread appeal has been much more about providing an alternative to government-run fiat currencies and existing financial systems and, in doing so, mounting a direct challenge to the hegemony of those systems. As noted in Chapter 2, and I can't believe this has come up twice, hegemony relies on consent, and so by withholding that consent, by offering an alternative, the early adopters of cryptocurrencies saw themselves as part of an effort to tear down that hegemony.

It seems unlikely, of course, that most people buying Bitcoin or Ethereum or memecoins have any idea that their purchases are linked with transhumanism and may not even think of them as being related to right-wing economics. Indeed, for a lot of them, the appeal of buying may be less about any ideology, and more about "price goes up." Remember, though, that cryptocurrency buyers are, almost universally, getting information about them from online sources, as is evidenced by the wild swings in the price of memecoins and similar assets driven by online chatter: the best predictor of price movements in cryptocurrencies is how much people are talking about it in web forums and on social media. While the survey of young men mentioned in Chapter 1 doesn't directly ask about where crypto owners got their information about cryptocurrencies, it does ask about information sources for those who report buying and selling individual stocks. Only about 60 percent of crypto owners also report buying and selling individual stocks, but a large majority of the crypto owners who buy stocks say that they get financial information about stocks from online forums (compared to only about a third of people who buy stocks, but don't own crypto), strongly indicating that crypto owners are generally engaged in online forums. The complexity of most crypto investing also seems to drive lots of potential buyers to the biggest forums for help and advice.

In these forums, speculation about the prices increasing, and picks for meme coins are presented alongside material about countries adopting crypto, about the mismanagement of the US Federal Reserve, about the coming hyperinflation. Potential buyers simply can't be engaged in the online discussion of cryptocurrencies without being exposed to the narratives that have been a part of crypto from the beginning. These ideas are also important because they help to build the heroic narrative that is part of the appeal of cryptocurrency. As discussed in Chapter 6, which dives into how crypto owners talk in these forums in greater depth, community support is a big part of the online crypto community. The idea that posters are generally supportive of each other, offering sympathy (in addition to the frequent gendered performances and attacks) belies the idea that this is a bunch of people just looking to make money. They really do seem to see it as a community, working toward the end goal of cryptocurrencies replacing fiat currencies, underdogs in a fight against an implacable institutional enemy.

The Allure of Volatility

If the goal of cryptocurrencies like Bitcoin or Ethereum is to replace existing fiat currencies, they're failing miserably. Any asset can become a currency under the right circumstances—think cigarettes in prison camps—but any currency must meet some minimal requirements, and the most basic of these is holding on to value over time. Prisoners might be able to use cigarettes as a currency, but eggs, which go bad, probably aren't going to work. Bitcoin has some of the requirements for being a currency, but relatively few owners actually use it as such, and for good reason. Think of Laszlo Hanyecz, famously buying two Papa John's pizzas in 2010 for what would now be about $1 billion worth of Bitcoin. If a crypto owner think the price is going to go up—especially if they think the price is going to go up a great deal—they'd be foolish to use it for anything (and should probably just pour any extra money they have into buying more).

While users may be prone to moving from one crypto asset to another, generally by using widely accepted coins like Ethereum as an intermediary, they're generally using crypto holdings as an investment, rather than using them as a currency. And while the value of Bitcoin has, on the whole, gone up over time, it's also displayed an enormous degree of volatility. Other, smaller coins have even greater volatility: a big upside if they explode in value, paired with a reasonable chance of going to zero. Though, as users note, the most that can be lost is 100 percent of what's put in, but the investment can potentially make a lot more.

As detailed in Chapter 5, risk isn't necessarily a bad thing for male investors, as they can use risk preferences as a means of performing masculinity, and the extreme levels of risk seen in many crypto assets add to their allure. Suppose that I buy and hold a stock that's relatively safe, increasing in value modestly, or giving a small dividend, like many utility company stocks historically did. I'm making money, but the stock doesn't give me any opportunity to display masculine characteristics like risk-taking, knowledge, or fortitude. But an asset that suddenly climbs in price gives men the chance to show off how much they've made—a marker of masculine success—as well as how smart they were to have bought the asset in the first place. When that stock suddenly dips, they have the opportunity to show off their endurance and rationality, by showing that they're not spooked by the drop, that they're going to hold on to what they have, rather than take their losses, and that since their original reasoning for buying the asset still holds, they're going to be rational, rather than emotional, and buy more.

Even if it takes some time to recover their losses, the fact that they're willing to wait shows their fortitude and toughness. In effect, they get a payoff in the form of a masculine display whether the price goes up or down—both of which are preferable on this dimension to a safe asset.

Who Owns Crypto?

Of course, no one can "own" a Bitcoin or other cryptocurrency—there's not a coin, real or virtual, to own. Rather, when someone buys Bitcoin, what they're buying is the right to assign that Bitcoin to other accounts on the blockchain, but to make things simpler, it's fine to talk about ownership of these assets.

I've used a series of surveys to measure who has actually owned cryptocurrency or related blockchain-based assets like NFTs. The numbers are pretty stable: about 16 percent of people in the Unites States say that they own (or have owned) crypto.[14] There are some areas in which people who say that they've owned crypto don't look much different from everyone else:[15] educational levels are about the same (14 percent among those with a four year college degree, 16 percent among those without), and there aren't big differences on race and ethnicity (13 percent among whites, 17 percent among Blacks). There are also some regional differences, with people in the Northeast of the country (17 percent) and in the West (23 percent) being more likely to say that they own crypto than people in the Midwest (11 percent) or the South (13 percent).

The big differences between crypto owners and everyone else are in terms of age, sex, and gender. The people who say that they've owned crypto tend to be younger than other respondents: 29 percent of Americans under thirty say that they've owned it, compared with 20 percent of those aged thirty-one to forty-four, 13 percent of forty-five- to sixty-four-year-olds, and less than 2 percent of those sixty-five and over. They're also disproportionately men: 22 percent of men, versus 9 percent of women. And the gap becomes even more stark when we look at the interaction of age and sex.

As seen in Table 3.1, the highest rates of owning crypto are among young men, with 42 percent of men aged eighteen to thirty saying that they have owned crypto or related assets, but even forty-five- to sixty-four-year-old men are about as likely to say that they have owned it as the youngest women.

Crypto owners are only somewhat different politically from other Americans. Republican women are much more likely to say that they've owned crypto than other women are, but partisan differences among men are minimal, whether we

Table 3.1 Percent Saying that They Own or Have Owned Crypto or Related by Age, August 2024

	18–30	31–44	45–64	65+
Men	42%	26%	19%	4%
Women	16%	16%	8%	1%

Table 3.2 Percent Saying that They Own or Have Owned Crypto or Related by Partisanship and Ideology, August 2024

	Democrat	Independent	Republican
Men	18%	19%	22%
Women	7%	8%	14%

	Liberal	Moderate	Conservative	Progressive	MAGA	Libertarian[17]
Men	17%	22%	20%	19%	18%	36%
Women	9%	9%	9%	8%	9%	5%

look at whether they're Republicans or Democrats, or which political labels they apply to themselves, as seen in Table 3.2.[16]

It's interesting that there isn't a big gap in reported crypto ownership by political views, with no big differences by either partisanship (Democrat vs Republican) or self-described political ideology, save for an elevated number of the small groups of self-described libertarians. Crypto owners are not more Republican, nor more conservative, though they are more likely to say that they would support Donald Trump over Kamala Harris in the 2024 US presidential election.[18] In many ways, the story about crypto owners would be simpler if it turned out that they were more conservative, or more Republican, but whatever is driving individuals—mostly men—to buy cryptocurrencies, it's uncorrelated with partisanship, but is driving them to support Trump (more on this in Chapter 7).

The key to what's driving crypto ownership becomes clear when we break down the results not just by age or sex, but by gender: the extent to which an individual says that they're masculine or feminine on the scales described in Chapter 1. Overall, there's a strong relationship between how men rate their own masculinity and their likelihood of owning cryptocurrency, but perhaps not in the way that would be expected. In the August 2024 survey, 16 percent of men who say that they're "completely masculine" also say that they own crypto,

Table 3.3 Percent Saying that They Own or Have Owned Crypto or Related, August 2024

	18–30	31–44	45–64	65+
"Completely masculine" men	30%	18%	19%	2%
Other men	49%	30%	20%	8%
"Completely feminine" women	13%	16%	4%	1%
Other women	17%	16%	13%	–

but that figure is 29 percent among men who say that they're anything other than "completely masculine." Cryptocurrency purchases are certainly *related* to masculinity, but that relationship isn't as straightforward as "men who express traditional gender identities are more likely to buy crypto."

Bringing in other factors that are likely to play a role in this relationship provides greater leverage in trying to figure out what's going on. The biggest interactions come from age, self-assessed masculinity, and the extent to which men say that they value traditional masculinity (whether they're traditionally masculine themselves or not).

Remember that a little more than half of men in the United States[19] say that they're "completely masculine." Those men tend to be older than men who give any other response on the masculinity-femininity scale, which could easily drive results (as older people are much less likely to say that they've bought cryptocurrencies), but even looking at self-placement within age groups, there's a substantial gap. Thirty percent of men thirty and under who describe themselves as "completely masculine" say that they've owned cryptocurrencies or related assets, compared with 49 percent of men in the same age group who place themselves anywhere else on the masculinity-femininity scale. This gap is smaller among thirty-one to forty-four year olds (as are the overall number of men saying that they own crypto) and is statistically insignificant among older Americans. The figures for women—which differentiate between those women who say that they're "completely feminine" (again, about half of US women) and other women—show no difference, which indicates that the gap among men is not driven by gender traditionalism, like differences on issues like abortion, but rather by some element of masculinity. Men who say that they're completely masculine are more likely to be Republican, more likely to support Trump in 2024, more likely to oppose abortion rights: they lean right on any number of political and social issues, but they're less likely to say that they own cryptocurrencies than other men.

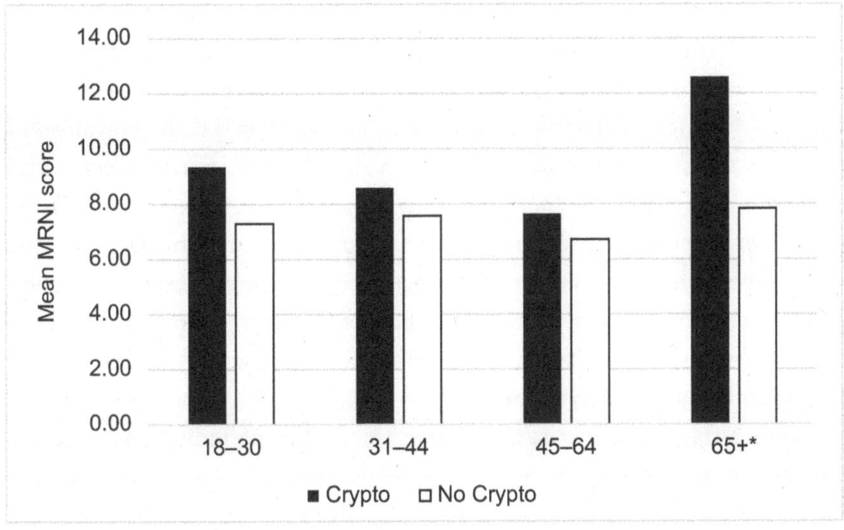

Figure 3.1 MRNI scores by crypto owner by age, August 2024 survey.

At first, this seems odd: if buying and holding cryptocurrency is tied to masculinity, shouldn't men who assert more traditionally masculine gender identity be more likely to own crypto? This finding is complicated by age. Remember that older men are much more likely to say that they're "completely masculine" (69 percent of men aged sixty-five and over, compared to 38 percent of men aged thirty and under), and that older people are much less likely to own crypto (or even know what it is) (see Figure 3.1).

Dividing by age group, sex, and crypto ownership means sample sizes too small to interpret with any confidence. But across all age groups, people who say that they own cryptocurrency or related assets have higher MRNI scores—valuing traditional masculinity more—than those who do not (with the difference being statistically significant for the youngest age groups, but not, largely because of smaller numbers of crypto owners, in the older groups). So the difference in MRNI scores isn't driven solely by differences in age or sex, but rather by some underlying difference correlated with crypto ownership.

All told, Americans who say that they've owned crypto also have higher scores on the MRNI scale than those who say that they haven't. Male crypto owners average 8.7 on the twenty-point MRNI scale embedded in the August 2024 US national survey, compared with 7.3 for men who say that they have never owned crypto or related assets. Combined with responses to the masculinity-femininity scales, this means that men who own crypto both value traditional masculinity more than other men do and are less likely to say that they're "completely masculine." If both of these relationships went the same way—crypto owning men being more likely to both value masculinity and assert a traditionally masculine gender identity, or the reverse—the story would be fairly simple. In that case, the story might be that cryptocurrencies and related assets appeal to traditionally masculine men who value masculine role norms. After all, the pitches for cryptocurrencies tend to revolve around the traditionally masculine roles that buyers will be able to fulfil once they get rich: fast cars, homes, and sexual access to attractive women. But the fact that cryptocurrency purchases are related to valuing traditional masculinity, and, at the same time, falling short of it, leads to a very different narrative.

While results from the national survey give us some indications as to the dynamics at play, there simply isn't a big enough sample size in the groups of interest (cryptocurrency owners, men, and especially young men) to carry out any sort of complex data analysis. For this, we turn to the previously mentioned survey of young men, carried out in December of 2022. This survey was just of people aged thirty and under, and because this survey was carried out online with a non-probability sample, the degree to which the respondents, overall, represent the wider population cannot be reliably established. As such, it's best to use results from this survey not to look at exactly what people in various groups think— because it might not correspond to values in the overall population—but rather to look at the relationships between different attitudes or traits of the respondents. It can't be known if these respondents look like the overall population, but there is no reason to believe that the relationships between masculinity, MRNI, and crypto ownership are any different for them than they are for anyone else.[20]

In this survey, men were asked to rate their own masculinity and femininity, and since this was an online survey, rather than a telephone survey, the question was given in the form of two sliders, both initially set to 50, that they could move all the way up to 100, or down to 0 on both masculinity and femininity. On average, the young men placed themselves at 80 (standard deviation of 25) on the masculinity scale and 30 (standard deviation of 32) on the femininity scale. Thirty-seven percent of the men placed themselves at 100 on the masculinity scale; most men placed themselves at 88 or above. Thirty percent placed themselves at 0 on the femininity scale, with most placing themselves at 18 or below (see Figure 3.2).

Interestingly, self-placement on the masculinity scale and scores on the MRNI scale (the same scale embedded in the August 2024 survey) are not strongly correlated (0.02), so there's plenty of variance to play with: men who have low MRNI scores and high masculinity scores, and vice versa.

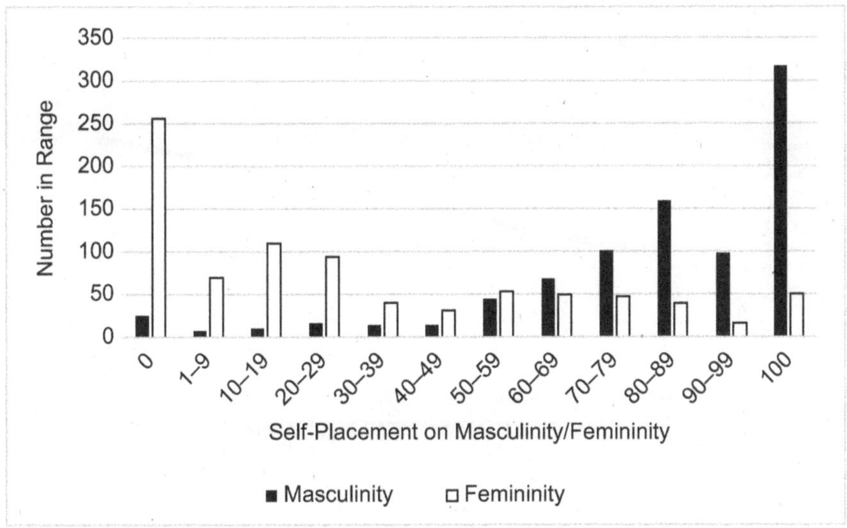

Figure 3.2 Self-placement on masculinity and femininity, December 2022 survey of young men.

To isolate the effect of this gap between MRNI scores and self-assessed masculinity, regression analysis is used (full results are in the Methodological Appendix). Controlling for race, ethnicity, age, and self-placement on the gender scales, the gap between MRNI scores and masculinity has a substantial effect on whether the individual reports owning cryptocurrency (since this is a sample of young men, 42 percent of them say that they own crypto, a figure very much in line with the responses of this group in the 2024 survey). Expected values are shown in Figure 3.3

At the lowest levels of the gap, when young men give themselves a high placement on masculinity but say that they don't value traditional masculinity (low MRNI), just 35 percent say that they own cryptocurrency. When the two are balanced—high, low, or moderate on both—52 percent say that they own such assets. When the gap is high—young men with high scores on the MRNI, indicating that they value traditional masculinity, but low scores on the masculinity self-placement—the predicted likelihood of owning cryptocurrency goes up even more, maxing out at 69 percent for men with the highest scores in the gap measure.

What this tells us is that cryptocurrency ownership is related to self-assessed masculinity—men who assert more traditional gender identities are more likely to say that they own crypto—and that it's related to views of traditional masculine norms, as those with higher MRNI scores are more likely to own it. However, the

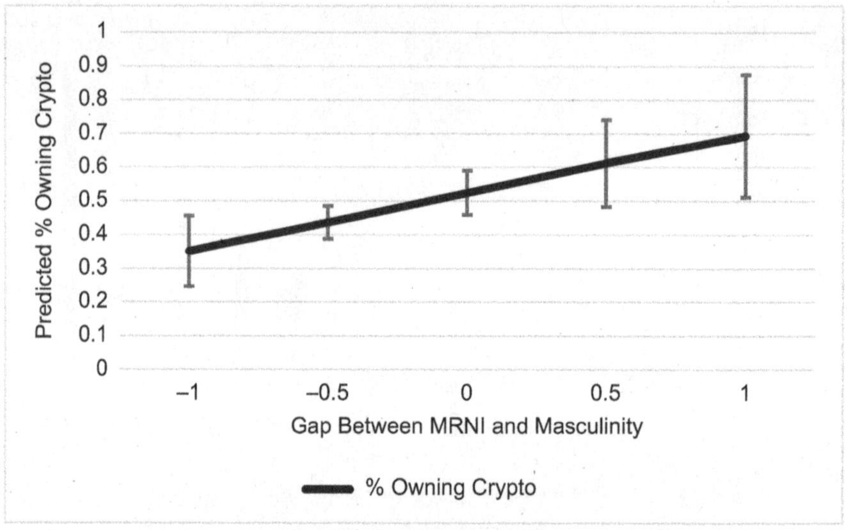

Figure 3.3 Predicted percentage of young men owning crypto, by gap between MRNI scores and self-assessed masculinity.

most powerful driver of crypto ownership isn't MRNI or masculinity, but rather the gap between them.

Going back to the August 2024 national survey shows just how big this gap is. Dividing MRNI scores at the median (eight, on the twenty-point scale) makes it easier to see how it interacts with men's expressed masculinity. Among the half of men who say that they're "completely masculine," MRNI scores have no effect on the likelihood of crypto ownership. But among the half of men who say they have a gender identity of anything other than "completely masculine," high MRNI scores are related to much higher rates of crypto ownership: 37 percent, versus 22 percent for non-"completely masculine" men with MRNI scores at or below the median. There's also no significant relationship between crypto ownership and MRNI scores among women, though any such analysis is complicated by the fact that there are literally no women in the sample who said that they were "completely feminine" and didn't have an MRNI score above the median.

As seen in Table 3.4, overall, 23 percent of men fall into this trap of valuing traditional masculinity but feeling that they've fallen short of its demands. Who are they? They're disproportionately young (38 percent of men aged thirty and under, 31 percent of men aged thirty-one to forty-four, and just 15 percent of men older than that), non-white (27 percent of non-white men, versus 21 percent of white men).

Table 3.4 Crypto Ownership, by Categorical MRNI Scores and Expressed Gender, August 2024 Survey

	Low MRNI	High MRNI
"Completely masculine" men	16%	17%
Other men	22%	37%
"Completely feminine" women	–	9%
Other women	14%	13%

An Issue of Causality

While all of these relationships between self-assessed masculinity, beliefs about masculine roles, and the gap between them tell a consistent story, they are all based on analyses of cross-sectional data. This is a serious limitation. Cross-sectional survey data like this is very good at establishing population validity—the extent to which the sample mirrors the characteristics of the population that it's drawn from—but they're not great at establishing internal validity: the extent to which change in one variable can be said to lead to, rather than be associated with, change in another variable. As such, no matter how carefully an analysis controls for the other variables that might be related to cryptocurrency ownership, there's always the chance that something has been missed. In this case, that means that there could be some other factor that's leading men to have certain attitudes about masculinity and to hold cryptocurrency.

Within a normal survey, there's really no way to fix this: researchers measure all of the variables that past research and theory indicate should be important, and hope for the best. To give strong evidence for causation, rather than just correlation, it's necessary to make use of other methodologies, like experiments, but there's no reason an experiment can't be embedded in a survey.

In an August 2023 national telephone poll, I did just that. Generally, questions about cryptocurrency ownership are placed toward the end of the survey, in the demographics section, as is the masculinity-femininity scale question. In this survey, I randomized the order in which these two questions were asked: half of the respondents were asked about their masculinity well before being asked about cryptocurrency ownership, and half were asked to rate their masculinity just afterward.

Men who say that they own cryptocurrency and are asked about it before being asked to rate themselves on the masculinity-femininity scale, are ten points more likely to say that they're "completely masculine," compared to men who say that they own cryptocurrency, and are only asked about it afterward. Among men who don't say that they own cryptocurrencies (and among women[21]) there's no difference between the two question orderings.

This indicates two things. First, that men who own cryptocurrency regard that ownership as being masculine: when the question order primes them to think about their ownership, they become more likely to categorize themselves as "completely masculine." Second, it tells us that this perceived link between crypto ownership and is limited to men who actually own crypto: men who don't own crypto don't think of themselves as *less* masculine because of that lack.

This result doesn't have the nuance of some of the cross-sectional analyses, which let us look at things like the gap between masculinity and MRNI scores, but it's valuable for building the case that, at least in the eyes of the men owning it, cryptocurrency is part of their masculine gender identities. Combined with the finding that crypto ownership is concentrated among men who value traditional masculinity, but feel that they're falling short of its demands, the data supports the idea that cryptocurrency ownership is seen by men as a way to get to traditional masculinity, rather than as a thing to be done once it has been achieved.

Importantly, this behavior is driven by trait-based threats to men's gender identities rather than state-based threats. State-based threats are common in experimental research on gender identities and rely on means like false feedback (telling men, correctly or not, that they're insufficiently masculine on some scale) to create a temporary gender-based threat in order to see how they react. In this case, the threat isn't coming from the researchers, but rather from the disconnect between the ideals and the identity of the individual man, and so the behaviors that it elicits can be much longer-lasting and require commitments of time and money. In state-based gender threat studies, men might be (for instance) more likely to say that they want to buy a big SUV after being threatened; this is the equivalent of them actually buying the SUV, rather than just talking about it.

Race, Ethnicity, and Crypto

One concern that arises from these kinds of analyses is the extent to which these analyses are just talking about white masculinities. While there are substantial numbers of Black, Hispanic, and Asian American respondents in these national surveys, the results don't show any signs of significant effects of race or ethnicity on these behaviors. This doesn't mean that people from other racial and ethnic groups are different from white men in their likelihood of owning crypto, but that after controlling for other differences correlated with race, there isn't a significant difference between racial groups left over.

There are two potential reasons for this. The first is that there really isn't a main effect of race or ethnicity on crypto behaviors; Black, Hispanic, and Asian American men are just following the same patterns as white men. The second is that there is an effect, but the surveys just don't have enough respondents from these groups for us to see it. To partially address this issue, I turn to a survey that does have enough Black and Hispanic respondents to allow us to identify an effect: a survey of 1,100 Newark residents (including 538 Black residents and 406 Hispanic/Latino/a residents) carried out in March 2024.

This survey didn't include the MRNI scale, but it does have the masculinity-femininity scale, as well as items about cryptocurrency ownership. In the survey, 17 percent of Newark residents, including 26 percent of men, say that they've owned cryptocurrency or related assets. Black men and Hispanic men are about equally likely to say that they've owned crypto, at about 24 percent of each. Among Black men, there is a small, but not significant, gap between men who identify as "completely masculine" and those that do not: 22 percent of "completely masculine" Black men say that they've owned crypto, compared with 25 percent of other Black men. Among Hispanic or Latino men, there's a larger gap, but in the opposite of the expected direction, with 28 percent of "completely masculine" men saying that they've owned crypto, compared with 16 percent of other men.

In surveys that include the MRNI scales but have smaller samples of Black and Hispanic or Latino men, these men are *more* likely than white men to fall into the masculinity gap, as they're both more likely to have high scores on the MRNI and less likely to say that they're "completely masculine." The fact that they don't seem to be more likely to buy cryptocurrencies than white men implies that there is something going on here.

While there isn't enough data to reach concrete conclusions, this is a place where theory can be helpful. The story being told about cryptocurrency and technical masculinities places it as a way of performing a protest masculinity, and protest masculinities are almost necessarily tied to race. The masculinities performed by racial minority groups are generally conceived of as marginalized masculinities, in which men are largely excluded from dominant forms of masculinity because of immutable characteristics, much in the same way that gay men are. Protest masculinities are built around the grievances of men who *aren't* excluded from dominant forms of masculinity by immutable characteristics: they could be in the dominant group but aren't and are alienated because of it. It would be surprising if large numbers of men from marginalized groups were participating in a protest masculinity, and might even be evidence that it's not a protest masculinity at all.

This shouldn't be taken to mean that Black and Hispanic or Latino men don't buy cryptocurrency: they do, especially among thirty-one to forty-four year olds (28 percent of men in Newark aged thirty and under say that they've bought crypto, along with 36 percent of men aged thirty-one to forty-four), but that the overall relationship between the masculinity gap and crypto purchasing behavior doesn't work in the same way, or doesn't have effects that are as strong, as they are for white men. More work, especially using qualitative methodologies, is needed to fully understand the role of race in these masculinity performances.

Why Crypto?

What is it that makes cryptocurrency so appealing to men in the masculinity gap? Research has explored lots of ways for men to express a masculine gender identity, from political behaviors to buying guns or joining a religious group. If nothing else, a lot of these compensatory behaviors are much less costly and time-consuming and might even be more easily recognizable as a symbol of masculinity than crypto ownership. This is where the argument about crypto ownership providing an alternative path to the rewards of dominant forms of masculinity comes in.

Generally, compensatory behaviors are used by men who feel that they're relatively close to the ideals of hegemonic masculinity. To compensate for a failure in one area, they double down on behavior in another area: so men who lose their jobs might be more likely to buy guns. A problem with the breadwinner role? No problem, so long as masculinity can be redefined around a role as a protector of the family or the community. But that's not what's going on here. The men in the masculinity gap aren't going out and buying a fast car: they're investing in speculative assets that they believe might eventually make them enough money that they'll be able to buy that car, and making that process, rather than the outcome, their expression of masculine gender identity. The best explanation for these behaviors is an embrace of technical masculinities as a substitute for traditional ways of demonstrating masculine gender identities. Rather than showing off success in achieving the pillars of hegemonic masculinity, these men are demonstrating their rationality, intelligence, and perseverance, sticking to the system with the understanding that doing so will inevitably lead to those pillars. Some men, of course, might be using crypto as part of a compensatory masculinity, but a generalized explanation based around technical masculinities seems to better fit what we know about crypto.

If nothing else, this is a fantastic sales job, and there are a couple of elements that make it possible. One is the way that cryptocurrencies are discussed and marketed online. No one is talking about cryptocurrencies as a reasonable, prudent investment that will reliably earn a slightly better return than a stock market index fund. Rather, cryptocurrency is marketed as something that can make buyers fantastically rich overnight and garner all the rewards that come along with meeting the standards of dominant forms of masculinity: fast cars, sexual access to attractive women, the ability to take care of a family, freedom from their low-paying, low-control, and soul-crushing jobs. In the forums, posters are encouraged to take even small amounts of money—$100 or less— and put it into the market so that they can start making gains.

From a distance, the unlikeliness of such an outcome is clear, making the behavior more akin to poor people's greater propensity for buying lottery tickets (Blalock, Just, & Simon 2007) than to stock market investments, but the emotional logic is clear. These men just don't see any way that they'll be able to meet the demands of masculinity from within the system: getting an education and working hard is never going to be enough, and even if the payoff of a cryptocurrency investment is only a remote possibility, at least it presents *some* possibility. The degree to which cryptocurrency is embedded in the online manosphere only makes this possibility more appealing: think about the extent to which red pill narratives argue that working hard to win over women makes a man not a winner, but a beta likely to be cuckolded. Crypto is the red pill applied to finance: you can invest in crypto and have a shot at being successful, or you can stick to conventional finance and be a cuck.

Those same online narratives also put forward the idea that cryptocurrency investing is a test of masculinity. According to the stories told about cryptocurrency in these forums, making money in crypto requires a cool head, rationality, and perseverance, even in the face of apparent losses. If the buyer loses money on an investment, it's only a failure if they give up. If they're cheated, well, that's tuition. So long as they persevere, stay rational, and hold on to the investment even as it craters, they're demonstrating the traits that they're being told comprise a masculine gender identity.

In this way, such investments give men a way to demonstrate masculine traits, to shore up a gender identity that's been threatened by a definition of masculinity that may be entirely unattainable. Such behaviors are only useful to the extent that they have an audience, meaning that the online message boards in which crypto investors share their tips, triumphs, and tribulations are a vital link in the process. More than just egging each other on and reinforcing the narratives around these investments, these message boards give investors the social element necessary for their performance of masculinity to have meaning.

While much of the discussion of cryptocurrency investment is centered around the possibility—or, as the investors would have it, the certainty—of getting very rich, they ignore the social and political underpinnings of the cryptocurrency project are also important. Cryptocurrency is a heady mixture of libertarianism, anarchism, distrust of power structures, and utopianism, and investors in cryptocurrencies see themselves as being part of this larger narrative in which they rebel against existing power structures and eventually win a brighter future. On the Reddit board r/CryptoCurrency on a given day (in this case, September 3, 2024), there will certainly be active discussions of which coins are tanking ("Crypto Whales Offload $26 Million in Cardano After Chang Hard Fork," "HBAR Slips Below $0.05 as HBAR Foundation CEO Steps Down") or spiking ("Whale buys 2,000 Bitcoin in 4 days"), or why people shouldn't panic in response to the latest volatilities in price ("Most of the people you see panicking are those who are new to crypto"). But there will also be stories about the spread and legitimation of cryptocurrency around the world: the day in question has stories about governments in Ukraine, El Salvador, Vanuatu, and Qatar buying, holding, passing laws in support of, or experimenting with various cryptocurrencies (mostly Bitcoin). It's hard to imagine anyone thinking that the tiny island nation of Vanuatu, or the political and economic wreck that is El Salvador, are going to be buying or holding enough of any cryptocurrency to move the markets, so why would anyone care? Because these stories aren't about getting rich off crypto, they're stories about the inevitable progress toward the dominance of crypto over the worthless fiat currencies that they will replace.

The frequency with which these stories appear tells us that they're important to users of the forum, even if they're not helping anyone make money right now. They're important because they reinforce the narrative in which the people buying cryptocurrencies might be misunderstood, dismissed, or despised today, but they are actually plucky underdogs at the vanguard of a revolution. When their inevitable victory and validation come, they'll be rewarded—money is still important!—and have the satisfaction of knowing that they were right all along. The investors aren't doing this just for their own benefit: they're heroes, Davids slinging stones, knowing that right is on their side, fighting for a better, more just world (a just world being one in which they're rewarded). This is why it's so important to see the signs of the impending victory—even if they come from a crypto experiment in El Salvador—to give meaning to the struggle and the losses that they're going through.

That sense of unity of purpose also helps to explain one of the more puzzling aspects of discussions of cryptocurrencies online. For instance, posters who post negative information or suspicions about a coin or a crypto exchange—and there may be a lot of blinking red lights—are accused of giving into FUD: Fear, Uncertainty, and Doubt. In any reasonable financial market, negative information is just as valuable as positive information, telling investors to stay away from an asset, so why is negative information so demonized in crypto forums? Part of it might be bad actors wanting to divert attention away from their actions, but it makes sense if we think of the crypto community as a *community*. The goal of that community isn't getting individual members rich (though that's fine, too) but moving toward an important societal goal: the fall of corrupt central banks, the anarcho-libertarian future posited by early adopters, the great restructuring of the financial and social worlds that will punish the guilty and elevate the humble. It may seem like the deep roots of cryptocurrencies have been lost in discussions of meme coins and the like, but it's still here in the many stories about more widespread adoption.

"Hodl to the Moon!" Men, Meme Stocks, and the MOASS

In January 2021, the price of GameStop rose as high as $463 a share, from a low of about $2.50 a few months prior (Yousaf, Pham, & Goodell 2023). This wasn't driven by any change in the fortunes of GameStop, a chain of (mostly) mall-based stores selling videogames and related merchandise. For a long time, GameStop had a lucrative business in used games: they would sell games new, at a high MSRP, then offer to buy the games back from customers who had finished with them, for a much lower price (typically one-quarter of the initial sales price, in store credit rather than cash). They could then resell the almost new game to a new buyer for a little less than what a new copy would have cost, potentially selling the same game multiple times.

This was a good business model, but one that was subject to disruption. The companies making the videogames in the first place were not necessarily happy to have GameStop collect all these resale profits, so they started offering games as digital downloads[1] that couldn't be resold, often at steep discounts a few months after the initial release. Before long, manufacturers were selling gaming consoles that could *only* use games that had been bought from their online stores.[2] Combined with the general collapse of mall-based retailing during the Covid-19 pandemic, institutional investors were confident that GameStop was on its way out and were short-selling the stock, betting that it was going to fall.

Essentially, when someone shorts a stock, they are selling the stock to a different investor, with a promise to buy the stock back at a future date for whatever price is prevailing at that time. So, if the price of a share goes down from, say, $5 to $3, the shorter sold a share for $5, then bought it back for $3, they still have the stock and they've pocketed a gain of $2. GameStop was, at one point, 140 percent over-shorted (Chiu & Yahya 2022), meaning that many of the investors who had been on the receiving end of the short (agreeing to sell the stock back later), had turned around and shorted the stock that they were holding (and contractually had to sell back at some point).[3] So as long as the price kept going down, the short sellers would make money, but the over-shorting is potentially dangerous. Suppose someone had been on the receiving end of a short—agreeing to sell it back later—so they held the shares, then turned around and shorted them themselves. Now, someone else has the shares that they're obliged to sell back. If they can't meet their obligation to get the shares back to whoever they got the shares from in the first place, they're in trouble: but they can fix the problem by just buying shares on the open market and using those instead. Shares are fungible, so problem solved; unless there are no shares to be had. In that case, the price of the shares would *increase* in what's called a short squeeze.

This potential danger did not go entirely unnoticed. Keith Gill, aka RoaringKitty, a regular poster on the Reddit forum r/WallStreetBets, had long believed that GameStop was undervalued by the institutional investors who had been shorting it. WallStreetBets is not the only subreddit concerned with investing—there's also r/Investing, r/Stocks, r/PersonalFinance, and others—but it is the one most concerned with relatively speculative and volatile investments. Gill held about $50,000 worth of the stock (Verlaine & Banjeri 2021), and when the price started climbing a bit, his claims that a short squeeze was possible gained attention on the forum. The plan was simple: buy and hold GameStop shares, and don't sell them. If all of the shares of GameStop are tied up with people who won't sell them, then there won't be any shares left for the over-shorters to pick up in order to cover their contracts. They'll have to offer more for whatever shares are floating around, increasing the price, making other shorters desperate to get out of their short positions (which lose money when share prices rise), which increases the demand for shares, which increases the price, and the feedback loop goes on and on. This sort of loss is especially dangerous to investors: if they buy a stock, and it falls, the most they can lose is what they paid for the stock in the first place. If they short a stock, and it rises, the potential losses are unlimited, as are the potential gains for those who hold the stock (with prices potentially going "to the moon").

This was more than a hypothetical: such "infinity squeezes" had happened a couple of times in recent years. In 2015, for instance, Martin Shkreli (now best known for buying up a pharmaceutical company and instigating massive price hikes for AIDS drugs and a later securities fraud conviction, for which he served four years in federal prison) led a short squeeze on a floundering biotech company, briefly driving up the price from about 50 cents a share to as much as

$45 (Farrell 2015). The stock was, apparently, actually worth almost nothing and was delisted only a few weeks later.

As with Shkreli's short squeeze, the fact that GameStop's stock price might wind up completely out of line with any reasonable value of the company didn't matter: there was a lot of money that could be made for anyone who got into the squeeze early, buying the stock and running up the price. Before long, the frenzy to buy and hold GameStop shares had spread beyond Reddit and was all over social media; the price kept rising, into the hundreds of dollars. At this point, those who had held the stock could have sold it for enormous profits: but on the Reddit forums and on social media, users were egging each other on to hold, on the logic that more people holding the stock would just make the price go higher. They were encouraged to HODL (which is either an intentional misspelling of "hold," as per Tash et al. 2024 or an initialism for "hold on for dear life," or an intentional misspelling that was turned into a backronym), and despite the share price starting to drop as some investors took their profits, many at least claimed that they were holding, even as the price went back to just about where it had started. The full extent of the losses incurred by the institutional investors who were shorting the stock in the first place are not known but was certainly in the billions (Newman 2023). The investors who had gotten in and held on to support the community effort wouldn't have made any gains, while anyone who had managed to sell at the top—betraying the community effort— could have pocketed huge profits. Lots of small investors may have wanted to sell at the top and been unable to do so, as a commonly used app for buying and selling temporarily stopped processing orders for GameStop during the squeeze (more on that later), locking users into their positions.

This could easily be a story about a group of small investors seeing an opportunity and taking advantage of it, but even at the time, accounts noted another aspect: the narrative that the individuals holding GameStop were attaching to their actions. As Chiu and Yahya (2022) put it:

> It was no longer solely—or ever—about making money personally, but rather about banding together to send a message about how the power of the individual could destroy even institutions as seemingly unshakeable as Wall Street.

This wasn't driving up the price of an apparently worthless company as in some previous squeezes: this was about fighting back against institutional investors and hedge funds that the WallStreetBets crowd thought were unfairly driving GameStop out of business. Emotional attachments to GameStop, a store many had frequented for years, certainly helped. As the posters on r/WallStreetBets said at the time:

> This is a new paradigm, the year of the retail trader. The old guard will fight us tooth and nail to maintain the status quo. This is bigger than just me, this is us. And if it costs me my last $1000, it will be worth every penny.

> Today, after so long of shame, I am proud to be American. There are no parties, races, or anything to separate us from our common enemy: the greed of corporate America and the ignorance of the government. This is a defining moment in history for the government, as they are being forced to choose between their greed and the people. MAKE THEM CHOOSE THE PEOPLE. STOP THE ILLUSION AND LIES THAT WE ARE DIFFERENT. TAKE NOTE OF THE POLITICIANS VOTING AGAINST THE PEOPLE. Today, we come together as one to make the greedy people who influence our lives and wellbeing where it hurts the most.

These are not the gleeful postings of users who have made a lot of money off a clever bet and are proud of it. These are the postings of investors who see themselves as part of a movement: the Davids going up against institutional Goliaths. This is very much the same narrative that we see in crypto: the little guys teaming up against these nebulous institutions that they feel have ignored them and bringing them to bay.

Of course the "guys" part of "little guys" is a key part of it. The most commonly referenced memes on the forum at the time were from the movie "300," showing the Spartan warriors, paragons of masculinity, "holding" against a seemingly unstoppable force.[4] The fraternity of the group, the need to prove their masculinity by holding the stock no matter what, is seen throughout the forums. This isn't just anti-institutional language; it specifically appeals to brotherhood and masculinity as a means of taking down these institutions.

> We done did it boys. Taking off 🚀 feels nice right about now. Continue to hold and we will all be in the moon together 🌑. LFG! Good shit holding them nuts boys this is where we separate the boys from the men.

> Stand your ground. Dont be a pussy and run scared. Together Ape[5] strong!!

Of course, the institutions were fighting back, and in the eyes of these small investors, they did so by hindering the ability of the little guys to buy and sell the stock. The rush to buy GameStop and other meme stocks ran into a wall when one of the leading apps used by individual buyers, Robinhood, halted trading on them, citing regulatory requirements (Chiu & Yahya 2022). This was immediately viewed by many in the online world as a betrayal (Newman 2023): a company that the crowd had thought was on their side slowed the frenzy, limiting the potential gains of the individual investors and therefore abetting their institutional opponents. Even figures who were not generally aligned with the posters running the short squeeze, like US Representative Alexandria Ocasio-Cortez, posted on social media questioning Robinhood's actions. The CEO of Robinhood was called before Congress to testify: he claimed that the halt in trading on meme stocks was necessary because of collateral and liquidity issues, though not everyone bought this explanation (Newman 2023).

Bradley et al. (2024) demonstrate the extent to which the success of the GameStop short squeeze transformed r/WallStreetBets. Prior to the GameStop squeeze, the investment information given on r/WallStreetBets was fairly similar to that given on more staid, moderated websites, like SeekingAlpha (at least in the section of r/WallStreetBets actually devoted to investment advice[6]). Afterwards, though, r/WallStreetBets became heavily skewed toward more speculative short-term gain stocks and toward "new users who place too much emphasis on coordinated trading strategies" (1433). Put another way, the users of the forum had smelled blood and were now looking for the short squeeze or other speculative attack, even at the cost of getting higher expected returns on more traditional investments.

After the success of the GameStop short squeeze, this crowd started to look for other companies that might offer similar opportunities: attempts to make GameStop happen with Blackberry, Bed, Bath & Beyond, and AMC Theaters soon followed (Yousaf, Pham, & Goodell 2023). Such efforts were, for the most part, quixotic: if nothing else, there was now enough awareness of the possibility of a short squeeze that few institutional investors would be foolish enough to get caught up in one the way some had during the GameStop run-up. Bed, Bath & Beyond went bankrupt; Blackberry didn't really go anywhere. AMC Theaters—which has a lot in common with GameStop, in terms of mall locations, emotional attachments, a seemingly outdated business model, and being badly hurt by the pandemic—was a little more successful. The investors haven't made much money, but AMC has done their best to take advantage of the influx of capital, refinancing debt, and encouraging individual investors with perks like free popcorn and special screenings for individual shareholders (Ciu & Yahya 2022).

I should note that none of this seems to be illegal. Chiu and Yahya (2022) tell us that these wild price shifts left regulators at the Securities and Exchange Commission flummoxed: it was clear that this was not the way that markets were supposed to work, but it also wasn't clear that any rules had actually been broken

(Bradley et al. 2024; though the meme stock forums argued that the actual crime was the naked shorts they believe underlay the volatility). Pump and dump schemes—in which someone talks up an asset in order to artificially inflate the price, before selling their shares, taking their gains and leaving other investors at a loss—are illegal (well, in stocks, not necessarily in crypto, as discussed in Chapter 3), but there wasn't any false information circulating, and the people hyping GameStop stock (1) seemed to really believe what they were saying, and (2) weren't dumping their stock after it rose. As a result, the price of GameStop wound up above where it had been at the start of the process. Shorters were hurt, but, overall, the volatility added to GameStop's market cap (which does not happen in pump and dump schemes). The wave of GameStop buyers was essentially playing by Air Bud rules: it may not be the way the game is supposed to be played, but if there's no rule against a dog playing basketball, no one can do anything about it.

The fact that the short squeeze on GameStop was seen as a huge victory is also very telling. Remember, the price of GameStop didn't actually go up by very much after the initial spike: so the victory wasn't about saving. Rather, it is seen as a success because of the harm it was thought to have inflicted on the institutional investors who were shorting GameStop and lost billions. The r/WallStreetBets apes might not have made much money, but it's just as important to them that they were able to bloody the nose of their enemies.

Who Cares?

It would be easy to dismiss this as a viral online phenomenon, one that people who are not very online could ignore, save for how shockingly widespread these meme stock phenomena became. This isn't just about a small group of investors costing hedge funds billions: a 2021 Harris Poll found that 28 percent of Americans had bought at least one of twenty different viral stocks, with AMC, GameStop, and Blackberry being the most common. To be clear: that's not 28 percent of young people, or 28 percent of people who buy stocks, or 28 percent of people using social media, but *28 percent of everyone* in the United States. This is pretty much in line with figures from the August 2024 survey of voters nationwide that I carried out. In that survey, overall, buying and selling of individual stocks is a bit more popular than the cryptocurrency purchases are. Twenty percent of registered voters in the United States say that they've bought stocks, options or traded foreign currency on an online platform (versus 15 percent who say that they've bought cryptocurrency), with some of that difference with the Harris numbers likely coming from the difference between the sample of all Americans in Harris versus just voters in the August 2024 poll, and the rest coming from a decline in the behavior between 2021, at the peak of the phenomenon, and 2024.

In both surveys, this figure is driven almost entirely by young men: in the Harris poll, 52 percent of men under thirty-five said that they had bought shares (with the modal dollar value of the investments being between $100 and $250), compared to just 28 percent of women in the same age group. One-quarter of all the men under thirty-five in the same poll said that they had bought shares of GameStop in particular (compared to 8 percent of women, who also had a lower modal investment, in the $26–$50 range). Some of this is certainly linked with the increased online presence that went along with pandemic lockdowns, but this was clearly a widespread social phenomenon, with *most* young men in the United States putting at least a little money into the effort.

Analysts have noted the extent to which individual buying and selling of stocks through apps like Robinhood, as well as activity on message boards like r/WallStreetBets surged during the Covid-19 pandemic. Several explanations have been given for this: boredom, increased disposable income due emergency government aid, even a perceived levelling of the playing field as institutional investors may have had less access to information not available to individual investors, since they were operating online as well (Bradley et al. 2024). But this could also be a gender story: the pandemic, and the response to it, led to enormous uncertainty and was experienced by many men as a threat to their gender roles: earning money on the stock market could very well be one of the ways that they were attempting to compensate for this gendered threat.

Moreover, it seems that these buyers—again, more than a quarter of Americans!—were engaging with the online forums that we've been talking about, bringing them into not just r/WallStreetBets, but likely the manosphere in general. The Harris Poll linked this stock buying behavior with increased "research" on US financial systems: about three-quarters (72 percent) of people who bought meme stocks said that they "researched how US financial systems work" in the past month. Men were twice as likely to say that they had done so (49 percent) than women (25 percent). This "research"—like the "research" that people were doing about Covid-19 and immunology at the time—was almost certainly just reading posts on web forums.

The MOASS

Just as the narrative underlying cryptocurrency has a built-in day of reckoning when fiat currencies will collapse, and crypto users will be validated, the meme stock narrative has the apocalyptic (and imminent) MOASS: the Mother Of All Short Squeezes.

If the GameStop squeeze was John the Baptist, foretelling a greater coming, the MOASS will be Jesus. The idea—often, but not always, tied to AMC (mostly because it's heavily held in the community, continues to be heavily shorted, and hasn't gone bankrupt)—is basically the same as in the GameStop short squeeze. If the individual investors on the forums can get hold of all of the outstanding shares and refuse to sell them to cover (what they believe to be) the naked shorts made by institutional investors, the price will rise. If they keep on holding them, the price will "go parabolic," rising to infinity. At that point, the institutional investors who have been holding the shorts will be bankrupted and the stalwarts who have held the stocks will get their reward, as the billions of dollars lost by the big investors will go to them, making them all instant millionaires, ushering in a new era for the global economy.

This is, of course, ridiculous. As when GameStop initially rose dramatically, any sudden unexpected increase in the price of a stock is going to lead to a halt in trading, whether on the part of the platform carrying out the trades (like Robinhood) or the exchange hosting the stock. There's also little chance that anyone would be caught as flat-footed as some institutional investors were during the GameStop squeeze. But even if it could work, it's also an unsurmountable collective action problem. If the price of GameStop were to rise from its current level—around $30 a share at the start of 2025—to $50 or $100, some holders would certainly sell, to say nothing if it rose to $200 or $500. In such a case, the first person to sell would reap an enormous profit, and once the selling started, the price would quickly come tumbling down as the shorters would be able to cover their losses. Within the community, everyone might well be promising to "HODL to the moon," but that's exactly what I would say if I wanted everyone else to do that while I took my profits.

None of that has stopped adherents from anxiously awaiting the MOASS. Any given day, there are dozens of posts on popular social media sites looking at the price of GameStop or AMC or some other meme stock and declaring it to be a sign of the imminent MOASS. Other posts detail their plans for what they'll do with their earnings from the MOASS: during the 2024 US presidential election, there was a spate of posts bemoaning a proposed increase in the capital gains tax, which would hit these (hypothetical) new millionaires hard. The question isn't if MOASS will happen—it's an article of faith that it will—but when it will happen. Driessen, Jones, and Litherland (2024) liken the belief in the MOASS to Q-Anon, and as these posts make clear, the comparison is apt.

How common are such posts? One morning, while I was writing this chapter, I did a search for "MOASS" on Twitter/X, which turned up thousands of results, with hundreds from just that morning. As on most mornings (this was January 6, 2025), some were breathlessly posting the data that *proved* that the MOASS was imminent ("Breaking: $24,800,000 $GME TRADE JUST HIT LIT MARKET FROM CHICAGO EXCHANGE"; "These mfers really thought they'd get an easy oop gap fill to $275 HAHAHAHA shorts are going to be absolutely annihilated come January 17 this will be the REAL MOASS"). Others were anticipating the validation that would come from their newfound wealth ("Here's to all of us who tried to explain this crazy fucking thing to our family and friends but eventually stopped trying because you kind of just had to be here to understand."). One of the replies to that post read, in part,

> This is what I said to my wife, get used to it. When MOASS comes, every relative
> that we told them to buy GME and they just read the convenient news provided
> by the media about GME, and laughed at us for buying a company that's dying.
> "It's a gamble, why are you doing this"?

Still others were trying to breakdown cryptic statements by RoaringKitty to calculate the exact date, like a preacher predicting the second coming (a typically bizarre post in this genre: "In @TheRoaringKitty Aladdin post, he says, "I'll tell you all about it when I have *the time*" (magazine cover) And "next time I'm gonna use a nom de plume" (alter ego = @greg16676935420). Greg just told us his birthday is Jan 13 and what do you do on your birthday?"). On Reddit, the main discussion about the MOASS that day was concern about Lamborghinis being sold out when all of the posters became fabulously wealthy overnight. What's shocking is that I could do this exercise on just about any weekday and find the same sorts of posts. One might imagine that years of such breathless predictions and anticipation would have eventually worn thin, but apparently not.

The bottom line is that the MOASS is never going to happen: the GameStop short squeeze, while not quite a one-time phenomenon (there are other stocks that are heavily shorted and could be vulnerable to a short squeeze), is unlikely to happen in the same way, much less happen at a greater magnitude. There isn't a shadowy cabal of institutional investors trying to put AMC Theaters or other national chains out of business. The mostly young and online people who buy these meme stocks are likely to lose their money. So why are they buying and holding stock in companies that more informed investors are shorting?

As with crypto buying behaviors, the heroic narrative underlying the meme stock phenomenon and the GameStop short squeeze, as well as the online communities bolstering them, seems to be playing a major role. Scholars have noted the links between these meme stocks and cryptocurrencies: Chiu and Yahya (2022) put them in the same basket at meme coins and NFTs, drily noting that they have "values seemingly disassociated from typical underlying expectations for profit." As they note, it is assumed that rational investors buy stocks because they believe that the stock is undervalued, but the people buying GameStop or AMC seem to understand that these stocks are actually overvalued, and buy it anyway, even doing so enthusiastically. This only makes sense if their payoff for buying and owning the stock was something other than financial, not the sort of motive economics or finance research is well-poised to understand. The best they can offer is to say that "these stocks have acquired some sort of symbolism among meme stock investors" (92) without having any idea what that symbolic value is.

As with cryptocurrencies, the heroic narrative attached to meme stocks like AMC and GameStop is about the eventual triumph of an ignored or maligned community against powerful forces (in this case, hedge funds) and that triumph resulting in a reversal: when the MOASS happens, the investors will gain as much money as the hedge funds lose. Like crypto, the meme stock phenomenon rests on a deep distrust of existing economic institutions and seems to have been spurred on by an economic crisis (in this case, Covid-19 lockdowns, rather than the 2008–9 crisis).

And while the meme stock phenomenon doesn't have the sort of intellectual (or quasi-intellectual) backing that underlies crypto, it still gives an opportunity for people to demonstrate deep knowledge of an arcane topic, meaning that it provides an opportunity for men to demonstrate technical masculinities. Posts about the MOASS use complex price history graphs and screenshots of outstanding shares, all often covered with lines, annotations, and projections, to make the case that any time—maybe tomorrow!—the MOASS is coming. In one sense, the apparent analysis that's gone into such posts is meaningless, especially since they're trying to predict something that is never going to happen. In another, that detailed analysis *is* the meaning, independent of whether it predicts anything, because it demonstrates the technical proficiency that meme stock investors are trying to assert as a masculinity.

Meme Stocks versus Traditional Stocks

Generally, buying stocks would be considered a performance of currently dominant forms of masculinity, but meme stocks are different. The link between dominant forms of masculinity and investments is driven by three factors. First, the perception that stocks are the province of the wealthy, so owning stocks is a signal that someone has money. Given that being wealthy is a prerequisite for other performances of dominant forms of masculinity (having a house, providing financially for a family, being a breadwinner), having stocks—and talking about having stocks—is a reasonable way to signal this type of masculinity.

Second, finance and investment are considered masculinized areas of expertise (a relationship explored more in Chapter 5). In the same way that men looking to perform dominant forms of masculinity are supposed to know how to carry out home improvements, or understand baseball's infield fly rule, they're also supposed to know something about investment and finance. As such, women are less likely to buy stocks (Kaustia et al. 2023), invest less money in it when they do (Neelakantan & Chang 2010), and receive less early encouragement to start investing (Itzkowitz, Itzkowitz, & Schwartz, 2023). No surprise, then, that women are much less likely than men to work as stockbrokers or in the finance industry generally. More data on this, and how it interacts with the masculinity gap, is in Chapter 5.

Third, stock buying behavior is normally linked with currently dominant forms of masculinity because of the narrative underlying these purchases. Meme stocks are different not mechanically—someone buys a share of GameStop the same way that they would buy a share of a blue-chip stock like Apple or GM— but in the underlying narrative. When someone buys a share in a large company, they are literally buying into the existing system of economics and finance and putting their money on the idea that these large companies will continue to be large companies and continue to grow, reflected by perhaps modest, but reliable, gains in the stock price. But such a purchase is entirely at odds with the narrative underlying meme stocks like GameStop and AMC. The reason to buy these stocks is not because it's a good, solid company that's likely to deliver stable growth over time, but rather because of the perception that the entire system is rigged. If someone thinks that the companies that are big right now will continue to grow, and that the entire system will continue on as it has been for decades, it would be foolish to bet that the MOASS will lead to a collapse of institutional investment houses.

Put another way, the purchase of most stocks is an attempt to buy into, and profit from, the status quo, one that is incompatible with the red pill ethic that all of this is fake, fixed, and a scam. Small returns on big stocks are part of the scam—the only way to actually get ahead in the world is by making bets outside of the system, or even against the system.

Could someone buy up shares of GameStop, or some other meme stock, as part of a performance of dominant forms of masculinity? Perhaps. Maybe they think that there is a good fundamental business underlying the stock and that the short sellers mean that it has been undervalued. That logic might work when the stock was at $2 a share; it falls flat when the online support for the stock has it floating at $25 or more, as it is now. Either the MOASS is going to happen, and GME is undervalued, or the MOASS is nonsense, and it's substantially overvalued. Buying it for any reason other than the expectation that it's going to go vertical makes no sense. Could someone buy a meme stock like GME on the greater fool theory? That is, that they know the MOASS is never going to happen, but believe that enough other people are foolish enough to think that it might, and drive up the price on that expectation? Again, it doesn't make sense. Years of concerted effort and HODL on the part of online communities have only gotten the price this far—why would anyone think that it would go up even more? And even if they did, that is, again, a bet against the normal functioning of the stock market, that the actual value of a company has nothing to do with their market capitalization.

Truth Social as a Meme Stock

The past few years have given rise to what is perhaps the most prominent meme stock in the United States, DJT, representing the holding company behind the minor social networking app Truth Social and tied closely with Donald Trump. As with other meme stocks, the price of the stock seems to be completely untethered to the actual performance of the underlying company, which in recent quarters has reported multimillion-dollar losses on even smaller revenues. According to traditional metrics, this would be a penny stock at best, unlisted on major exchanges, but the link to a major political figure means that the market capitalization of DJT values it (as of late 2024) at about half the value of major brewery Molson-Coors, and about the same as athletic apparel company Puma, or contact lens company Bausch and Lomb, all of which are solid businesses that turn regular, if unspectacular, profits that are many times that of Truth Social.

It's not hard to see why people are buying this stock, regardless of the performance of the underlying company: it's a way for Trump supporters to put their money where their mouth is, to make a concrete and credible show of support for their preferred candidate in an election. It's also used as an indirect way to bet on the outcome of elections: political events that were thought to bode well for Trump's chances in the 2024 US Presidential election were linked with bumps in the price of the stock, under the apparent expectation that a Trump victory in the election would lead to a spike in the stock price.

In many ways, DJT has a lot in common with the other meme stocks that I've been talking about, like AMC or GameStop. Buyers are using it less as an investment tool than as a statement of identity (in this case, political identity). It's become attached to an underlying heroic narrative in which the faithful will be vindicated, despite what they see as the nebulous forces arrayed against them, when their preferred candidate is elected. That vindication will be accompanied by a spike in the price of the stock to unrealistic levels; perhaps not the infinite price associated with the MOASS but enough to make all the people who bought it very wealthy. Holders of the stock have faith that this spike in price will come, holding on to their shares even as prices drop, rather than giving in to fear, uncertainty, and doubt.

The difference between DJT and other meme stocks comes in which identity they're trying to perform and how effective the stock purchases are at bolstering that performance. Certainly, political support for Trump is tied to men's gender identities—there's a fuller discussion of this relationship in Chapter 7—but not in the same way that meme stock purchases are. Trump's strongest supporters are not men in the masculinity gap who may be trying to assert their gender through technical masculinities, but rather men who assert a traditionally masculine gender identity: those who call themselves "completely masculine" on the unidimensional scale. So, it's a different audience, one that's more likely to be concerned with traditional markers of masculine gender identity than the audience that's likely to be awaiting the MOASS.

DJT stock is also less likely to appeal to men looking to perform technical masculinities because the case for them is much less complex. Making the case for buying AMC or GameStop involves discussions of naked short sales and squeezes on institutional investors carrying out nefarious activities. The case for buying DJT is that someone thinks it's undervalued, they want to support Trump, and they think the price will rise. It serves as an identity marker, but doesn't lend itself to the detailed explanations, demonstrating a depth of knowledge and mastery of arcane concepts in a masculine-coded area that other meme purchases do.

Is DJT a meme stock? Sure, in that decisions to buy the stock are tied up less in any underlying value in the stock than in an attempt to perform an identity, but the types of identities being performed, and the men looking to do those performances, are likely to be very different.

Meme Stocks and the Masculinity Gap

Young men are much more likely than other groups to buy meme stocks than other Americans. In the 2024 national study, 47 percent of men aged thirty and under say that they've traded stocks on online platforms like Robinhood, compared to about 20 percent of older men. Young women are also more likely than older women to say that they've done so—25 percent of women aged eighteen to thirty, versus about 10 percent of other women—but the overall figures are much lower.

Of course, the fact that young men are buying stocks online doesn't mean that they're buying meme stocks, so we turn to the 2022 survey of young men for the more specific question. In that survey, 52 percent of men aged thirty and under say that they've bought individual stocks, not much different than the 47 percent found in the 2024 telephone sample (and the same as the 52 percent of men under thirty-five in the 2021 Harris poll). Even though the survey of young men is from an online sample, the fact that the topline numbers are very similar to telephone samples provides some confidence that it is a reasonable sample.

Of the group that says that they've bought individual stocks, a majority (61 percent) say that they've bought meme stocks, with AMC and GameStop used as examples in the question: that's 32 percent of all of the young men in the sample (a little lower than in the Harris numbers). To put it another way, *most* men aged thirty and under in the United States have bought individual stocks, and *most* of them have bought into at least some meme stocks.

Respondents in the survey of young men who said that they had bought individual stocks were also asked where they got their information about what to buy. About 35 percent said that they had spoken to a financial advisor, and 34 percent said that they looked at reports in the media, but 48 percent said that their information came from "online sources, like Reddit or Twitter." These men are "doing their own research" largely by going to social media and engaging with the online forums, exposing them to not just dubious investment advice but the narratives driving these investments and the often problematic elements of the manosphere linked to them.

As in the August 2024 national survey, respondents in the survey of young men were asked to complete the five item version of the MRNI (presented fully in the Methodological Appendix), and overall, results are pretty similar to the national sample, with a median score of eight, though there is more of a skew toward high numbers than in the other sample: 8 percent have the maximum score of fifteen, meaning that they "strongly agreed" with all of the items.[7]

As shown in Figure 4.1, young men who have an above median score on the MRNI are more likely to say that they have bought stocks on their own, but there's not enough of a difference to be statistically significant (48 percent for below median scores, 60 percent for above the median scores). However, there's a much larger (and significant) difference for men who say that they've bought meme stocks. Fifty-two percent of young men who say that they've bought individual stocks and have MRNI scores of eight or below say that they've bought meme stocks; but that figure is 83 percent among men with MRNI scores above the median. Among young men, valuing traditional masculinity more doesn't make them more likely to buy stocks overall, but it does make them more likely to buy meme stocks.

As would be expected, ownership of meme stocks is also related to young men's asserted masculinity: 55 percent of young men who say that they're "completely masculine" (only about 36 percent of the sample) and have bought individual stocks say that they have bought meme stocks; but that figure is 69 percent among men who identify any other way on the masculinity-femininity scale.

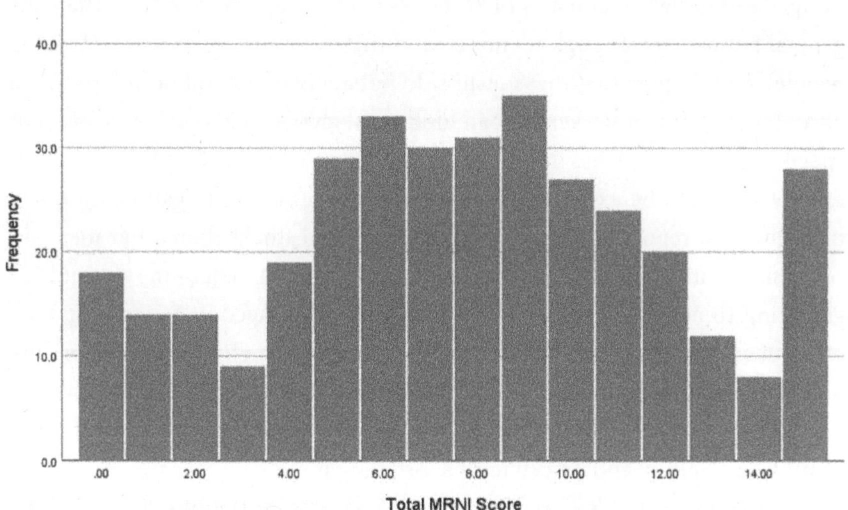

Figure 4.1 MRNI Scores, 2022 Survey of Young Men.

Table 4.1 Stock Purchases by Masculinity Gap, 2022 Survey of Young Men

	Men in masculinity gap	**Men not in gap**
Have bought individual stocks	54%	46%
Have bought meme stocks	50%	37%
Have not bought stocks	46%	54%

Put together, the data from the survey of young men suggests that there's a similar relationship between masculinity, valuing of masculine role norms, and meme stock buying behavior as there is for cryptocurrency purchases. It isn't men who say that they're traditionally masculine who are buying these stocks, but rather men who value traditional masculinity, but feel that they're falling short.

Overall, almost exactly half of respondents in the survey of young men say that they've bought individual stocks, and most of those who have bought individual stocks also say that they have bought meme stocks. However, while there isn't much of a difference between men in the masculinity gap and other men in likelihood of buying stocks overall, there's a significant and substantial gap in their likelihood of buying meme stocks, as shown in Table 4.1. Fifty percent of young men who are in the masculinity gap say that they've bought meme stocks, compared to 37 percent of young men who are not, a difference that remains when I control for other factors like age, race, and education.[8]

Of course, the fact that an online sample of young men is not a probability sample and certainly consists of respondents who are more online than the general population (though it's not clear if that's the case for samples of young people), could mean that these results do not apply to the public at large. As a partial replication, however, we can look at the prevalence of day trading (not specifically meme stocks) in the August 2024 national poll, and the results are exactly as would be expected, with men in the masculinity gap being much more likely to report buying and selling individual stocks than other men.

As shown in Table 4.2, this strong relationship—with men in the masculinity gap being 18 points more likely to say that they've engaged in day trading than other men—exists despite the fact that people in the high MRNI category are not much more likely to say that they've done so than others (23 percent versus 17 percent). It isn't MRNI scores driving this behavior, but the interaction of valuing masculinity and perceiving a shortfall in it.

Day trading activities are also not linked with assertions of traditional masculinity. On the whole, the half of men who identify as "completely

Table 4.2 Day Trading Activity by Masculinity Gap, August 2024 survey

	Men in masculinity gap	Men not in gap	Women
Have bought individual stocks	43%	25%	14%
Have not bought individual Stocks	56%	73%	84%
Don't know	1%	2%	2%

masculine" are *less* likely than other men to say that they've traded stocks online: only 20 percent have done so in the August 2024 survey, compared with 38 percent of other men (as with crypto, there is no significant difference based between "completely feminine women" and other women).

All told, the story about masculinity and meme stocks is more complicated than meme stocks (or day trading in general) appealing to men's gender identities: taking a chance on a stock might seem like a masculine-coded activity driven by knowledge and risk tolerance, but the men who say that they're masculine are less likely to take part in it. Rather, it's men who are falling short of what they perceive to be the demands of masculinity who are buying these meme stocks, and analyses of the narratives and discussions surrounding them help explain why that might be.

As with cryptocurrency purchases, the heroic narrative surrounding meme stock purchases seems likely to appeal to men trying to perform technical masculinities. The narrative, about a coalition of downtrodden disrespected men taking down hedge funds and other bad actors, both assumes that the participants in the narrative are currently not successful and promises that they will be in the future. It also, indirectly, gives these young men a target for their perceived lack of success: the financial system is rigged against them by these hedge funds, so any failure isn't individual, but the product of a corrupt system. Finally, it posits an apocalyptic reversal, where the high shall be made low, and the low made high, and the plucky underdogs will get all of the benefits of wealth and power currently denied to them. Also, the Lamborghinis.

Importantly, the arguments for why and how this will happen are all ridiculously technical, which might help to hide how flawed they are. As discussed in Chapter 5, the financial sphere is a masculinized area of interest, and the analysis of meme stocks presented in online messaging about them goes far beyond analysis of profits, losses, and growth projections. Rather, it looks at movement in the volume being traded and outstanding contracts and tries to extrapolate future movement toward the vertical in deep patterns of movement in the price. These analyses aren't really giving any new information—data, like people, will say anything if they're tortured enough—but getting the outcome correct isn't the point. The demonstration of technical masculinities comes not from actually making money from the MOASS but from the demonstration of the masculinized skills that go into the analysis in the first place.

What Makes Meme Stocks Different from Cryptocurrencies?

The analysis to this point has shown that meme stocks have a lot in common with cryptocurrencies, with both being linked to underlying heroic narratives and giving buyers the chance to demonstrate their knowledge of masculine-coded areas of expertise. And while there are lots of ways that men can demonstrate their knowledge of masculine-coded areas—craft beers, sports, fandom-based nerd masculinities—both cryptocurrencies and meme stocks are made more powerful as demonstrations of masculinity because they hold the promise of enormous wealth at some undefined future date.

However, there is reason to believe that cryptocurrencies might be a more powerful way to perform technical masculinities than the purchase of meme stocks. Part of this is because buying meme stocks is relatively easy. It's not a coincidence that the increase in the number of people buying meme stocks coincided with the availability of apps like Robinhood that made it cheap and easy to buy, sell, and cash out shares (most of the time). People started buying more stocks in part because it became easy and cheap to put twenty or fifty bucks into a stock without going to a broker. But that ease of use means that they're less appealing as a performance of technical masculinities. Buying cryptocurrency on crypto exchanges has gotten easier over the past few years, but trading crypto and cashing out on all but the biggest cryptocurrencies is still much, much more complicated than buying stocks on a trading app. The mere fact that someone knows how to navigate the world of meme coins and crypto exchanges is a sign that they know something about the masculinized areas of finance, investment, and technology. The fact that someone can buy a share of GME is a sign that they have $30 and an iPhone.

Meme stocks also have less volatility, on the whole, than cryptocurrencies do. They're relatively volatile by the standards of the stock market (over the course of 2024, GME had a low of about $14, and a high of about $50) but have far less day-to-day movement than even established cryptocurrencies like Bitcoin or Ethereum and far less than more speculative crypto assets like meme coins (the price of Bitcoin approximately tripled during that same period). These fluctuations in price give owners a way to demonstrate masculine traits like perseverance and rationality in a way that holding a stock that's pretty stable doesn't (though meme stock owners can fill in this gap with detailed nonsensical analysis).

The fact that cryptocurrencies are unregulated also gives an extra element of risk, especially when dealing with meme coins, but even on established crypto exchanges, which have been known to collapse unexpectedly. This adds an element of risk, of danger, to cryptocurrency investments that just aren't present in meme stocks, which are being sold via regulated, open stock exchanges with strict oversight. Regulation and consumer protections are generally a good thing for investors, but it means that meme stock buyers are deprived of one of the ways that crypto buyers have to perform technical masculinities.

One of the reasons to pay attention to meme stocks is that purchases of them are shockingly widespread, but this popularity also makes them less useful as a performance of masculinity. Any identity performance has to ride a line between being common enough that it's recognizable within a community as being linked to an identity, and rare enough that it actually serves as a marker of that identity. If an activity is too widespread, it's no longer distinctive enough to work as an effective identity performance, and the popularity of meme stock purchases may be putting it into this category, at least in some environments.

What Crypto and Meme Stocks Have in Common

The relationship between meme stock purchases—and day trading in general—and masculinity supports the larger story being told in this book about the use of finance to perform technical masculinities. As with cryptocurrencies, men are much more likely to buy these assets than women, but men who find themselves valuing masculinity, but falling short of it, are much more likely to do so than other men, even controlling for associated factors like age and education.

As with cryptocurrency, meme stocks make for a potentially powerful performance of technical masculinities. They combine complexity in a masculine area of expertise with an underlying heroic narrative and potentially leading to economic rewards. The fact that there seems to have been one instance—the GameStop squeeze—in which this heroic narrative seems to have paid off (at least in terms of hurting perceived enemies) only adds to the allure. Not only might buyers be able to get rich, in the same way that people who got into

Bitcoin early, or bought certain meme coins on their way up, but it's already happened once, and it might happen again.

These underlying narratives, setting up good guys and bad guys, leading inevitably (according to the story) to an apocalyptic day of reversal where the true believers will be rich and validated while the powers that be are laid low are vital to the appeal of meme stocks. Without that narrative, there's no difference between buying a meme stock and buying shares in anything else: investors buy it because they expect the price will go up. That sort of traditional stock purchasing behavior is, as discussed previously, a bet on the status quo and is therefore entirely at odds with the logic of buying stocks in anticipation of the MOASS. That narrative, that expectation, that logic is what separates normal investment behavior, which is more closely linked to currently dominant forms of masculinity, from meme stock purchases, which appear to be tied to protest masculinities.

While the data to this point supports the idea of a relationship between investing in these kinds of assets and technical masculinities, it's important to consider conventional explanations. There is, after all, a great deal of work looking at how men and women differ in their investment activities and supporting the argument that it's masculinity—and a particular performance of masculinity—driving these behaviors means showing that these conventional explanations don't fully work.

"It's all about winning." Masculinity and Finance

Having shown the relationship between men's gender identities and their embrace of cryptocurrency and meme stocks, I now need to deal with some of the more conventional explanations for the observed relationships. The fact that men are more likely than women to embrace risky investments, and that men are more interested in complex financial products—and finance in general—isn't new. However, as I'll show, men's risk preferences and interest in finance are not just driven by sex, but by a combination of sex and masculinity: for instance, men are more interested and knowledgeable about finance than women are, but men who say that they're meeting the demands of currently dominant forms of masculinity are *less* interested, knowledgeable, and risk-seeking than men who feel that they're falling short. It's important to show that finance is a masculinized area of expertise—it wouldn't make sense for it to be part of a performance of technical masculinity if it were not—but also that it's one sought out by men who feel that they need to prove their masculinity. Further, this is all in contrast with the sort of day-to-day concerns about household budgets, which aren't as useful as a demonstration of technical masculinity. As such, there aren't gendered differences in interest and engagement with them: the effects are not about money, so much as they are about being able to use money to perform gender.

Conventional Explanations

There has been an enormous amount of research in behavioral economics and finance looking at the differences in investment behavior between men and women. Generally, this line of work has found that men exhibit more risk-seeking behavior in their investments, while women are more conservative, and that men tend to be better at correctly answering questions about finance and investments than women are. While this research often refers to these differences as "gender gaps", the work rarely measures anything other than sex (see James & Agunsoye 2023; Parent, Kalenkoski, & Cardella 2018; Meier-Pesti & Penz 2008 for exceptions). This isn't just an oversight: sex differences might well account for many of the differences in how men and women deal with money. Risk-seeking among men (or risk-aversion among women) could be a gendered behavior, but it might also be sexed behavior: if, on average, men have more resources to fall back on, or simply earn more money, it would make sense for them to be less risk-averse just because of differences in the median financial situations of men and women. Similarly, if men are more likely than women to be encouraged to think about money and finances, or take classes that deal with them, it would be reasonable to expect a knowledge gap that has nothing to do with masculinity or femininity but is explained by differences in the socialization of men and women.

These elements combine to create a solid conventional explanation for the difference between men and women in cryptocurrency purchases. Putting aside the gendered aspects of their appeal, the two most basic characteristics of cryptocurrency (and meme stocks, to a lesser extent) investments are that they are risky and complicated. So, if men are more risk-seeking than women, and know more (or at least are more confident in their knowledge, correct or not) about finance, they should be more likely to invest in crypto than women are. No gender explanation needed, and to get women to buy more crypto, just educate them about it (perhaps by hiring a Kardashian to post on social media about it, as in Goldstein 2022).

The implication of these explanations is that masculinity shouldn't really matter in men's investment behaviors once we control for sex, and if there is a difference, it should be attributable to other differences between "completely masculine" men and other men, like income or education. As it turns out, this is not the case. On many indicators, there are sex differences—for example, men are more accepting of risk than women are—but these sex differences coexist with gender differences among men.

Moreover, the overall hypothesis requires not just a gender difference among men, but a particular kind of gender difference. Past work on, for instance, risk-taking and masculinity (Meier-Pesti & Penz 2008) has shown that identification with masculinity among Austrian undergraduates[1] was related to greater propensity for financial risk-taking in hypothetical scenarios. But if all we see is that traditional masculinity—operationalized here as men asserting a "completely masculine" gender identity—is related to risk-taking, or interest in finance, or perceived knowledge about investments and finance, that would actually be at odds with the larger story. Instead, the results should show that men become more likely to display the attitudes related to buying cryptocurrency when they're *not* completely masculine.

It might seem like this doesn't matter much: either way, masculinity is driving men's investment behaviors and the factors that would lead them to be interested in crypto (and, assumably, other complex, risky assets). But if a propensity for risk-taking and complexity is part of the overall package of currently dominant forms of masculinity—if the men taking risks and knowing about finance are the ones already at the top of the gender hierarchy—then they're not being driven by men looking to perform technical masculinities. The very broad strokes might be the same, with men's financial decisions being driven by gender performances, but the details matter.

Sex Differences in Investment Strategies

There is a long line of research describing the extent to which men exhibit much riskier behaviors related to money than women in areas like investment, but also anywhere that involves risk, like gambling.[2] This isn't always seen as a bad thing: Bajtelsmit and Bernasek (1996) make the argument that women are *overly* cautious when investing for retirement, which results in them having less money in their retirement accounts to pay for what is, on average, a longer retirement than men (though Watson & McNaughton 2007 show that any such differences are dwarfed by the effects of women's lower wages). The consensus, though, is that women's portfolios tend to outperform men's (Barber & Odean 2001), not because they're making better decisions about where to place their money so much as because they're making *fewer* decisions about where to place their money.

Given that most investors do not have any special information about the assets that they're buying or selling, selling one asset in order to buy another is essentially a random move, which might come out as a wash if there weren't transaction costs associated with buying and selling (Davison 2016). Since it almost always costs money to move assets, and the average gain from these moves is zero (a point empirically tested by Barber & Odean 2001), moving assets around almost always means losing money in the long term, meaning that men, on average, earn about 2.7 percent lower returns than women (Barber & Odean 2001), who are more likely to adopt the "buy and hold" strategy favored by most financial consultants.

Why would men be more active? Barber and Odean attribute the difference to overconfidence. That is, men, especially in areas that they perceive as being masculine (such as financial markets), tend to overestimate their own skill, leading them to make riskier bets. That is, they believe (incorrectly) that they can outperform the market and therefore make more trades in order to make that happen. Women also tend to believe that they can outperform the market, but by a much smaller margin.

In effect, this is like driving on a highway, with four lanes going in the same direction. Some lanes seem to be moving faster than others, so there's a temptation to move into those lanes. But since everyone else can also see that lane moving faster, they move into it as well, causing that lane to slow, relative to the others. A strategy that involves always switching to the fastest lane, rather than picking a lane and staying in it, might give the illusion of control, of mastery, but doesn't actually get a driver to their destination any faster and burns a lot of gas in the process (see Williams et al. 2014). Women, in this metaphor, are more likely to stay in one lane, getting to the destination at about the same time but without burning the extra fuel.

Of course, this tendency would likely be corrected by clear and unambiguous feedback: if people are told that their behavior is causing them to lose money, they would be prone to changing it. However, this is complicated by the fundamental attribution error: individuals tend to perceive their successes as being driven by their personal attributes, like expertise and skill, but downplay their failures as being due to forces outside of their control (bad luck, bad outside actors). As such, a trade that's successful will be remembered as the product of intelligence and skill and not counteracted by a bad trade that only went south because of bad luck.

In their content analysis of ads for day trading, cryptocurrency, and other dubious financial trading schemes on Instagram, Whybrow et al. (2024) liken the allure of these products to gambling. The gambling frame is illuminating, as there is ample research on why men are more prone to problematic gambling behavior than women (i.e., Walker et al. 2005): women are more likely to gamble in order to deal with emotional difficulties or to create opportunities for social interaction. Men are more likely to be driven by the illusion of skill: the belief that there is a system to the (basically random) wins and losses, and with sufficient practice and skill, they can become reliable winners. Winning at gambling, then, requires masculine traits, like a lack of emotion and willingness to take risks (Lopez-Gozalez et al. 2018). Whybrow et al. (2024) show that ads enticing young people to take up day-trading in crypto or other assets make the same claims, that there's a system, and if they have the rationality to trust it, they're guaranteed to make money. Of course, there isn't a "system" to day trading any more than there's a "system" that will guarantee making money off of slot machines, but the belief that there is one—though it's not one that just anyone can understand, appreciate or stick to—embodies both an appeal to technical masculinities (it's necessary to learn the system) and moves the blame for losses to the individual. Since there's a guaranteed system, any losses result from personal failures: "seems like a skill issue," being the common retort.

So, making more trades might sometimes pay off—which would be attributed to knowledge and mastery, perhaps in following an arcane system—but generally not, so the dominant result is losing the transaction costs of moving money around. This behavior raises the question of why men have such generally unfounded confidence in their financial acumen. One reason why men might be more likely to believe that they can outperform the market is that they tend to know more about personal finance than women and are rather more interested in learning about it (Chen & Volpe 2002), a finding that's been replicated across countries globally (Klapper & Lusardi 2020; Bucher-Koenen et al. 2017), with parent's embrace of stereotypes being a key factor (that is, parents are more likely to talk to boys about finance; Bottazzi & Lusardi 2021).[3] While there is a theoretical distinction between being interested in finance and knowing about finance, much of the work on the topic confounds them, making the assumption that people who are more interested in a topic will be more likely to learn about it. The analyses that follow will be looking at knowledge, rather than interest.

As Tinghög et al. (2021) point out, this gap in financial knowledge is especially puzzling in wealthy industrialized nations, in which women are now more likely than men to get a college education. They argue that some of this difference comes from the perception that finance is a masculine area of expertise, so men are much more likely to be confident—or overconfident—in their own assessments of how well they know it. While they show that the gap in financial literacy is not driven by how comfortable people feel with math-based tasks (the gap exists even in nonnumerical finance questions), stereotype threat does play a role: reminding women that finance is a masculine area makes them more anxious in in answering questions about it. Essentially, one of the reasons why women are less aggressive than men in investment decisions is that they understand that men are supposed to be better at it.

Setting aside for the moment how this difference might impact the ways in which men and women behave differently in finance, findings like this are important because they establish that both men and women understand that finance is a masculinized area of expertise. This may make women nervous about making finance decisions (which seems to actually lead them to greater risk aversion, and therefore greater returns overall under many circumstances), but it cuts both ways, potentially leading men to be *overconfident* in their investment decisions. After all, if this is a masculinized area, shouldn't men naturally know more about it, the same way that men are presumed to know more about craft beers? These findings also help to establish that investment is an area ripe for the display of technical masculinities.

This is suggestive, but more evidence is needed before concluding that finance is being used as a way for men to assert a masculine gender identity. To look at this, Mike Parent, Charles Kalenkoski, and Eric Cardella (2018), all from Texas Tech, made use of a traditional experimental set up for looking at whether behavior is part of a gender performance: scaring men and seeing if it changes.[4] In their case, male participants from an existing online panel were asked to fill out a psychological battery that included personality and masculinity questions and were then given false feedback about their results. They were randomly assigned to be shown a graphic indicating that they had scored at either the 27th percentile of masculinity or the 89th percentile. The idea is that men who were told that they were at the 27th percentile would perceive a threat to their masculinity and thus try and display masculine traits afterward to compensate.

In this case, the task given to the men afterward, and thus the medium in which the threatened men could make their performance of gender, was a hypothetical investment scenario. They had to divide up $10,000 between four different assets, ranging from low risk and low reward to high risk and high reward. In general, men who were in the threat condition invested more of their money in the riskier options. However, this effect was concentrated among men who were otherwise risk-averse (according to a general risk-taking questionnaire they had answered earlier).

Similarly, the same men were asked to allocate $10,000 between relatively simple (domestic) investments and relatively complicated (foreign) investments. Just as in the risk allocation task, men in the threat condition put more money into the relatively complicated investments, and the effect was concentrated among men who had lower baseline levels of financial literacy.

The takeaway from these tasks is that induced state-based gender identity threat led men to make riskier financial decisions and to prefer more complex investments. The clear implication is that men view these traits—financial knowledge and financial risk-taking—as being masculinized traits: otherwise, it wouldn't make any sense to exaggerate them in the face of a threat to their gender identities. But there's also the matter of the interaction effect, such that these responses were biggest among men who were otherwise low in these traits. Men who were otherwise risk-averse were the ones who sought out riskier investments; men who knew less about financial matters were the ones who took on more complicated investments. They weren't just blindly moving toward what they saw as more stereotypically masculine investment decisions but were strategically compensating for what they perceived to be their weaknesses.

Masculinity and Financial Literacy

So, men tend to know more about finance and investments or are at least more confident in their knowledge about finance, whether they know more or not. The question is whether this sex gap is related to gender identity among men, and if so, whether the relationship fits the story about technical masculinities that I've been telling.

To look at this, I make use of an online study carried out as part of the Understanding America Study in 2021.[5] In it, respondents were given a series of scenarios (essentially finance word problems) and asked what the people in the scenario should do. Three of them had objectively correct answers that anyone with a working knowledge of finance should have been able to figure out without too much trouble.[6] Here are two of the problems:

Jack and Jill are twins. At age 20, Jack started contributing $20 a month to a savings account. After 20 years, when he was age 40, he stopped adding to his savings but left the money in the account. Jill didn't start to save until she was 40. Then, she saved $20 a month until she retired 20 years later at age 60. Suppose both Jack and Jill earned a 6% return each year on their savings. When they both retired at age 60, who had more money?

Rita must choose between two job offers. She wants to select the job with a salary that will afford her the higher standard of living for the next few years. Job A offers a 3% raise every year, while Job B won't give her a raise for the next few years. If Rita chooses Job A, she will live in City A. If Rita chooses Job B, she will live in City B. Rita finds that the price of goods and services today are about the same in both areas. Prices are expected to rise, however, by 4% in City A every year, and stay the same in City B. Based on her concerns about standard of living, what should Rita do?

Table 5.1 Percent Choosing Correct Answer, by Sex and Scenario

	Jack and Jill	Rita City	Investment Club
Men	73.7%	65.3%	75.0%
Women	62.0%	56.2%	58.2%

Table 5.2 Percent Choosing Correct Answer, by Sex, Gender, and Scenario

	Jack and Jill	Rita City	Investment Club
Completely masculine men	73.5%	64.9%	74.0%
Other men	78.3%	70.3%	79.6%
Completely feminine women	61.9%	56.2%	61.1%
Other women	66.4%	59.1%	66.4%

Generally, respondents found these problems to be pretty easy: 67 percent got the Jack and Jill question right (Jack will have more money, since it has had more time to compound), and 60 percent correctly said that Rita should more to City B (since the raise in City A will be more than offset by inflation; 66 percent answered correctly in the third scenario, not presented above, about diversifying investments picked by an investment club). In line with past research on finance questions, men were more likely to answer correctly (and less likely to pick the "don't know" option) than women.[7]

As shown in Table 5.1, the sex gap in these questions is pretty big, and it would be reasonable to say that men know more about finance—or are more willing to venture a correct guess—than women are, very much in line with past results. But while men are more likely to answer correctly than women, men who say that they're "completely masculine" are *less* likely to get the correct answers than other men are. As shown in Table 5.2, men are about twelve points more likely to answer correctly than women, but men who say that they're *not* "completely masculine" are five points more likely than other men to answer correctly.[8]

Men in the "other men" category are also less likely than other respondents to pick the "don't know" option: on the Jack and Jill question, for example, 4.8 percent do, compared with 8.4 percent of "completely masculine" men and 10 percent among women (with no difference between "completely feminine" women and other women).

There is a sex gap in financial literacy, but it coexists with a substantial gender gap. In line with past research, men tend to know more about finance matters (or, at least, be more willing to guess on questions about them). This makes sense: finance is a gendered interest, men are more likely to be encouraged to learn about it, classes and professions that teach about it are highly gendered, historically women have had less money to invest, and so on. But what that past research misses is the effects of masculinity. Yes, men are more interested and knowledgeable about finance than women are, but there's a big gap among men as well, such that men who feel that they're falling short of the demands of currently dominant forms of masculinity—and thus might be attracted to technical masculinities—are more interested and knowledgeable than other men are. Given past findings linking masculinity and knowledge and interest in finance and investment, this is a high bar to clear, but the results are very much in line with the story about technical masculinities that I've been telling.

Now, the five-point gaps that we're seeing in these results are significant rather than huge, but they're telling. The fact that the relationship between masculinity and financial literacy is going in the expected direction at all means that there is something about falling short of the demands of traditional masculinity that is leading at least some men to use financial knowledge as a way to perform their gender. Conventional explanations, which link knowledge about finance and investment to dominant performance of masculinity, would suppose the opposite.

It's also likely that the results seen here are understating the true nature of the relationship. There could be a stronger case linking performances of knowledge about finance to technical masculinities if this data included the Masculine Role Norms Inventory. The lack of that data means that the results on "other men" are necessarily mixing not "completely masculine" men who value traditional masculinity (for whom strong effects would be expected) and those men who are falling short of traditional masculinity but don't value it (for whom no effects would be expected). However, this fact that there are effects even in such a mixed sample supports the case, as the bias from the missing data would tend to reduce, rather than increase, the size of the effects. The real effect among men in the masculinity gap is likely much bigger than what is being observed here.

Masculinity and Household Finance

The connection between finance and masculinity can be brought into greater focus by looking at other financial matters and showing that the connection is limited to performative behaviors, like stocks and investments, rather than day-to-day financial matters. This distinction is important because it gets at a potential explanation for the observed behaviors that has nothing to do with technical masculinities: maybe men are just more likely to deal with money issues than women are. Past research has shown that men are more likely to have taken classes or expressed interest in financial matters, so perhaps men are just more comfortable than women in dealing with money. If this were the case, and men who do not assert a "completely masculine" gender identity are more likely than other men to deal with day-to-day budget issues as well as investments, it would offer an alternative explanation for the results thus far. After all, the whole point of performing technical masculinities is the performance aspect of it: it has to be showy, it has to be big. Doing a household budget is very much the opposite: no one else is going to see it or care, and it therefore doesn't provide much of an opportunity to demonstrate the masculinized traits that I've been talking about.

None of this is to say that these quotidian money matters aren't important. Household budgeting, for instance, is money management just as much as investments are: they're just not showy. If there's some gendered behavior that's leading men to deal with money in general, it should show up in responses about household finance. But when respondents in the same survey as the financial literacy questions are asked how often they track household spending, there's no sex gap and no gender gap among men, as shown in Table 5.3.

Men and women are almost identical in their responses about how often they track household spending, and while "completely masculine" men are a little more likely to say that they "always" track it than other men, other men are higher in the next highest category, so the responses average out. The biggest gender gap actually seems to be among women who identify as something other than "completely feminine," who say that they're less likely to track household spending than "completely feminine" women. When regression analysis is used to control for other factors that might matter to tracking household spending, there are no significant effects of asserted gender: age and education are the only important predictors of whether someone tracks it or not.

Similarly, when asked whether they consider themselves to be good at dealing with day-to-day financial matters, as shown in Table 5.4, there is almost no gap between men and women: 46 percent of men and 43 percent of women "strongly agree" that they're good at it, with only 7 percent of men and women alike in the "disagree" categories.

But there is also no real gender gap among men: "completely masculine" men are a little higher than other men in the "strongly agree" category, but other men

Table 5.3 How Often Do You Track Household Spending? By Sex and Gender

	Men	Women	Completely masculine men	Other men	Completely feminine women	Other women
Always	38.9%	38.4%	41.9%	33.5%	40.5%	34.9%
Most of the time	40.3%	42.8%	37.6%	46.4%	42.9%	43.3%
Rarely	16.3%	14.3%	16.5%	16.1%	12.2%	18.2%
Never	3.3%	3.0%	3.2%	3.2%	3.5%	2.3%
Don't know	1.2%	1.5%	0.9%	0.8%	1.0%	1.3%

Table 5.4 Good at Dealing with Day-to-Day Financial Matters, by Sex and Gender

	Completely masculine men	Other men	Completely feminine women	Other women
Strongly disagree	2.7%	1.2%	2.5%	1.8%
Disagree	1.5%	0.8%	1.1%	2.8%
Somewhat disagree	3.1%	2.8%	2.0%	3.8%
Neither agree nor disagree	3.8%	6.8%	5.5%	4.3%
Somewhat agree	10.8%	12.1%	10.6%	13.5%
Agree	33.5%	36.1%	28.9%	29.8%
Strongly agree	44.7%	39.4%	48.8%	43.8%
Don't know	0.0%	0.8%	0.7%	0.5%

are higher in the next category down, meaning that there's no real aggregate difference between the groups (and any difference seems to go in the opposite direction of interest and knowledge about finance, anyway). The important finding here is that masculinity isn't driving men to say that they're better at the quotidian everyday work of money and budgeting. These sorts of money matters might be seen as more akin to the work of managing a household: cooking, for instance, is a feminine activity when it's getting dinner on the table every night on a schedule, when it might not be appreciated, but is a masculine activity when it's a special event (Neuman, Gottzén, & Fjellström 2017). Just so, the actual important money work like keeping a budget isn't masculinized, while investments and finance knowledge are. Men might be more likely to know about finance, and knowledge about investments is gendered, but it's traditionally feminine women who are the most likely to say that they're keeping the books at home.

Masculinity and Risk Tolerance

So far, the results in this chapter have shown that men are more likely to correctly answer questions about finance and investments than women are, but that "completely masculine" men are less likely than other men to do so. They've also shown that this knowledge about finance doesn't extend to more quotidian money matters like household budgeting, which seem to be more the domain of traditionally feminine women. But there's another aspect to crypto investments that hasn't yet been addressed: risk.

If the two major aspects of crypto that make it appealing to men trying to perform technical masculinities are complexity and risk, it should be the case that men who are falling short of the demands of traditional masculinity should be more likely to embrace risk than "completely masculine" men are. As with the questions about knowledge and finance, this is a high bar given past studies that have found a strong link between masculinity and risk tolerance. Even though results showing that completely masculine men are *less* risk tolerant than other men wouldn't necessarily be at odds with these results, the presumption has always been that risk-seeking behavior is associated with dominant forms of masculinity rather than the marginalized or protest masculinities.

Trying to get at exactly what drives the gap in financial risk tolerance between men and women, Lemaster & Strough (2014) look at a number of possible explanations: personality differences, gender traditionalism and even testosterone exposure.[9] Experimental studies have shown that, in general, men engage in riskier behaviors when they perceive a threat to their gender identities. In a lab study with undergraduate men as participants, Weaver, Vandello, and Bosson (2013) had the men test either a power drill or some hand lotion (the condition that was designed to elicit gender identity threat). After being primed, they were then asked to play a dice-based betting game: men who had just been testing the lotion (and were assumably facing a degree of state-based gender identity threat) were much more likely to take the maximum bet allowed on the throw of the dice. All of this makes the case for a link between masculinity and risk-taking, which could help to explain the appeal of crypto to men.

To look at the relationship between men's gender identities and risk preferences, I make use of an experiment run as part of USC's Understanding America Study (UAS) in late 2020 and early 2021. While the masculinity-femininity self-placement questions discussed previously were not included in that particular study, one of the strengths of the UAS is that it is a longitudinal study, so many respondents who completed the survey that included the gender items also completed the risk experiment, allowing the datasets to be combined.[10]

In the experiment, respondents were asked to choose between a guaranteed amount of money and a risky bet that could lead to a higher, or a lower, reward. For instance, they might be asked to choose between getting $3.55 and a coin toss where heads would get them $2.15 and tails would get them $4.95. The expected values of the two choices are the same: if the outcome get $2.15 half the time, and $4.95 half the time, it averages out to $3.55, so what the choice is really measuring is preference for risk. Each respondent played the game twenty times. To make sure that they were paying attention, one of their choices—randomly selected—was used to give them an actual payout. So, if they chose the risky side, and that bet was chosen as the one that counted, a respondent could have walked away from that bet with as much $4.95, or as little as $2.15.

While the safe option was set at $3.40 (moved up or down a little by a random factor, generally around 25 cents, as were the payoffs on the risky side), the expected value of the risky side increased slightly over time, from $3.40 in the first block of choices, to as much as $3.60 (though this increase was designed to be uneven: the biggest expected payoff of the risky bet came in games thirteen through sixteen out of twenty). This means that, in general, it makes sense to take the risky side of the bet more as the game goes on, but the potential losses (the gap between the high and low payouts on the risky side) get bigger. To make sure that they understood the game, respondents had to do a practice run first, correctly identifying what the payoffs of each choice would be, before starting the actual choices.

As might be expected, respondents chose the risky and the safe bets at almost the same rates: across the twenty trials, respondents chose the safe bet 51 percent and the risky bet 49 percent of the time. There also isn't much of a difference between men and women overall, and despite the perception from the economic literature that women are more likely to be risk averse than men, they were (slightly, but not significantly) more likely to take the risky bet: they did so 49.0 percent of the time, compared to 48.5 percent for men.

But while there aren't any real differences by the sex of the respondents, there are big differences between respondents based on their asserted masculinity and femininity. Overall, men who say that they're "completely masculine" are *less* likely to take the risky side of the bet than men who give any other response to the gender question (by 2.3 percentage points), while there's no similar difference among women (see Table 5.5).

The differences come into clearer focus when the responses are divided up based on the stakes at play. Remember that the expected value of the risky side of the bet—and the stakes—are higher in the second half of the game than in the first half, moving from as little as $3.40 in the first four rounds, to as much as $3.60 in rounds thirteen through sixteen. Just so, as the game moves from the first ten rounds to the second half, the gap between completely masculine men and other men expands from a nonsignificant 1.3 percentage points to a substantial 3.4 percentage points. To avoid concerns that this might be a learning effect, with respondents getting better at the game as they go, the results can also be divided between the highest risk and lowest expected value rounds, which results in an even larger gap of 3.6 points.

Table 5.5 Percent Risky Bets Taken, by Sex and Masculinity-Femininity

	Percent risky	First half	Second half	Lower expected value	Higher expected value
Completely masculine men	47.9%	48.1%	47.6%	48.3%	47.3%
Other men	50.2%	49.4%	51.0%	48.6%	50.9%
Completely feminine women	49.0%	48.6%	49.4%	48.9%	48.5%
Other women	49.1%	49.2%	48.9%	49.9%	47.3%

Of course, the "completely masculine" men are different from the men in the other category in lots of ways, so regression analysis (presented in the appendix) is used to control for all of the other potential differences between the groups that might be driving the results: age, education, race, income, employment status, and so on. Even controlling for all of these factors, the difference remains: overall, men who don't say that they're "completely masculine" are 3.2 percentage points more likely to take the risky bet, and 5.9 points more likely to take the risky bet in the higher expected value rounds (with no difference in the low expected value rounds, or among women).

This analysis indicates two things. First, that while risk tolerance is associated with masculinity, it's not that men who consider themselves more masculine take more risks. Second, that the men taking the risks are doing so in a relatively rational way. These results are consistent with a story in which men who feel that they're falling short of the demands of dominant forms of masculinity are looking for ways to perform their gender identity, and risk-taking is a reasonable way to do that. Men who feel that they're meeting the demands of masculinity aren't as likely to take these kinds of risks, because they have less to prove.

The fact that men who don't identify as "completely masculine" are more likely to take the risky bet when the payoff is greater also shows that this risk-taking seems to be calculated. When the expected value of the risky bet is higher, it makes more sense to take it, in that (over an infinite number of rounds) the player would make more money by doing so. While the difference in expected value between the higher and lower rounds is relatively small— dimes rather than dollars—the fact that we see such a marked difference makes it seem like the men outside of the "completely masculine" category are actually doing the math.

To some extent, these results seem to be at odds with past findings showing sex differences in risk tolerance, but the differences in results might be coming from the samples typically used in lab studies. Even as many disciplines within social science have become wary of student samples, economics and psychology still make widespread use of them. The logic isn't necessarily bad: the politics of undergraduate students might not look much like the politics of the broader population, so they'll likely respond differently to stimuli; therefore researchers can't generalize results from a student population to everyone else in a political science study. But so long as it is assumed that undergraduates' brains work the same way as everyone else's, results from psychological studies of undergraduates can be applied to the rest of the population, and if it is assumed that the ways in which undergraduates calculate risk and reward are like anyone else, they can use them for economics experiments. If researchers are worried about external validity, they might make use of an online convenience sample, through MTurk, Prolific, or a similar service that pays respondents a small amount of money to participate in a study. But either way, researchers are likely to be picking up a disproportionate number of young men, who are less likely than older men to identify as "completely masculine," and this bias in the sample could be driving the observed sex differences (as well as confusing the effects of masculinity on the results).

Of course, there are some limitations on this data. The biggest comes from the random variation in the payoffs on both sides of the choice, which introduces a substantial element of chance into the choices being made and is likely a big reason why the odds are all so close to 50 percent. The second is that while the difference between the lower and higher expected value rounds is interesting, the respondents are playing for low stakes, and it's reasonable to ask if we would observe the same differences if we were talking about large pots of money, rather than small amounts. The limited[11] research that has been carried out with large stakes, such as on the US game show "Deal or No Deal" (Post, Baltussen, & Thaler 2008), seems to indicate that the same biases that are seen in low-stakes experiments are also present in very high-stakes ones. The way people behave when dealing with low, but real, stakes seems very similar to how they deal with large stakes, so there's no reason to think that the risk tolerance effects seen here wouldn't also apply to real world investment decisions.

Men and Money

The key finding here is that the differences in financial knowledge and risk aversion between men and women are based not just on sex but also on gender. There are differences in the financial situation of the median man and the median woman, and such sex-based differences certainly matter to what sorts of investments people buy into: there's plenty of data on retirement investments showing that women invest more conservatively, even if it's unclear how much difference this makes to long-term outcomes. There are also differences in the amount of education on financial and investment matters that individuals have, and since these are considered masculine areas of expertise, men are both given access to, and seek out, more information about them. Some portion of the gap between men and women in financial knowledge may also simply be a result of men being more willing to guess—or less willing to say that they don't know—when given questions about financial matters, likely because they perceive it to be an area that they're supposed to know about.

But none of these differences between men and women account for the investment behaviors that are being observed among young men. If it were the case that older men, or wealthier men, or more educated men—or, most likely, men who are all three—were buying up lots of very speculative investment products like cryptocurrencies and meme stocks, it would make sense to tell a story about higher risk tolerance among people with greater financial resources. But the men who are most likely to invest in these risky assets are younger, poorer, and less likely to have a college degree than other men. In survey data, most of the people putting money into these assets aren't spending thousands or tens of thousands of dollars: they're buying a hundred dollars at a time, buying fractions of a coin or a meme stock, with money saved from a job they're desperate to be able to quit. It may be the case that men with more financial resources can afford to take more risks with their money, but that's just not the case with the men buying into crypto.

Greater financial knowledge, or at least a greater willingness to pretend to that knowledge, is related to masculinity, as is a greater willingness to seek out risky assets: "completely masculine" men are more likely to engage in these behaviors than women are, but the data here is consistent with a story that men who are falling short of dominant forms of masculinity are even more likely to do so. As past research has argued, these behaviors may well be linked to the same overconfidence that leads men to buy and sell stocks on their own, thinking (generally incorrectly) that they can beat the markets, and, in the long term, costing them returns because of the accumulating transaction costs. But it is also linked with performative financial behaviors: making risky or complex investments as a way of demonstrating knowledge and mastery of a masculine-coded area of expertise.

The results on household finance make clear that this is not a general orientation toward dealing with money. A desire to assert a masculine gender identity doesn't lead men to engage with quotidian money tasks, like budgeting. What's the difference? Part of it might be performative: running a household budget doesn't give men the opportunity to display knowledge and mastery in the same way that investments do. But it also doesn't give men as much of an opportunity to use their activities to display masculine traits like rationality, risk-taking, and fortitude. It doesn't work as a way of asserting a protest masculinity because it doesn't support the claim that these behaviors justify a place on top of the gender hierarchy.

As noted previously, the effect sizes seen in this chapter are rather smaller than those found in the other chapters, with gender corresponding to significant differences of less than ten percentage points between groups of men. While that's common enough in social science research, it's understandable here because of the lack of MRNI (or similar) data. The underlying hypothesis is that men who rate themselves as falling short of the demands of masculinity should be more likely to seek out risky or complex investments to display masculinities, but only to the extent that they value masculinity. Because we don't have a measure of the value men place on masculinity here, the groups being compared just aren't as clean-cut as they are in the other analyses. The other results make it seem likely that men in the masculinity gap—a subset of the men in the "other men" category—would be much more likely to performatively take risks and show off knowledge of financial markets, but the data here doesn't allow us to separate them out.

It's also important to note the extent to which young men are the targets of extensive marketing campaigns designed to convince them of the link between these sorts of investments and masculinity, even if they weren't already inclined toward it. In Whybrow's (2024) content analysis of financial services ads on Instagram, they find that the ads pushing investment systems or classes are not subtle in how they present sexual access to women as the reward for earning money through stocks, forex,[12] or cryptocurrencies. Attractive young women in revealing clothing talk about how they are "provided for" by their daytrading partners. The same ads make a point of the need to stick with the investments in the face of losses, showing masculine traits like courage (not being afraid of losses) and perseverance.

This creates what the researchers see as a feedback loop. The ads talk about the miserable lives of people—especially men—who have to work regular office jobs, who "live a life they don't really control," because of their lack of masculine attributes like risk-taking or intelligence. These regular workaday jobs are contrasted with "financial freedom" and the ability to get out from under bosses or other people who are oppressing the individual. Agency is masculine, and money buys agency. More importantly, working hard at that regular office job is never going to get these men the freedom and agency that they want: it's a scam. Sure, "they" say that men can get ahead by conventional means—but look at the life being led by the men who have instead invested in crypto or whatever else is being pushed: isn't that preferable?

The problem, of course, is that the individual seeing the ad doesn't know how to start or has tried and failed in the past. But the ads present a solution: a formula for trading cryptocurrencies, or stocks, or forex that makes the process riskless, so long as the individual being targeted has the masculine qualities to keep it up and a community that supports them in the endeavor (all for a very reasonable price). As long as they follow the formula and put aside their negative (unmasculine) emotional responses, they'll make money and get all of the benefits of having done so, like expensive cars, watches, and sexual access to beautiful women. And, of course, if they wind up losing money, not only is it their fault (remember, the formula *always* works), but there's another set of ads emphasizing how they can make back the money that they've lost with a system that actually works (unlike whatever system they were using before) and is really simple.

Of course, not everyone making risky and complex investments is doing so because of some scammy ad they saw on Instagram, but these ads provide an insight into the appeal of these investments and how they're linked to technical masculinities. When the ads posit that young men are never going to be able to get ahead by getting a good education and working hard, they're not wrong: increased inequality and lower levels of college completion mean that, for many young men, there isn't a path toward financial stability, much less prosperity. In the face of home prices massively outstripping inflation, the idea that men can save up to buy a house in a nice neighborhood is a cruel joke. The misogynistic, red-pilled logic of gender relations tells them that women will, at best, use them and cheat on them. The markers of dominant forms of masculinity are not aspirational: they're unattainable.

But, the ads promise, there is a way forward: by giving up on the traditional means of getting ahead, giving up on dominant forms of masculinity, and embracing technical masculinities. This means doubling down on rationality and fortitude, on knowledge of finance and investments, on a willingness to take risks, to pursue that alternative path forward. The men who can meet the demands of dominant forms of masculinity—or at least see a path toward those performances—don't have to stress their knowledge of markets or their risk-taking. Instead, they see a path forward that relies on traditionally masculine markers like hard work. Given that finance and investments are seen as masculine-coded areas of expertise means that these appeals may work on men in general, but as the findings in this chapter have shown, they're going to appeal more to men who feel like they're falling short. It's these men who need to show that they're knowledgeable about finance and investment, that they're risk-takers, that they're rational, and there's a reason why the ads stress the communities underlying their systems: they need to have somewhere that they can show off these traits.

Of course, to this point, the analysis is just positing how men see and talk about these assets. The last piece of evidence needed to support the connection between the masculinity gap and cryptocurrencies comes from taking a closer look at how users of these communities talk about these investments.

"Bro. You don't realize how ignorant this comment is." How Men Talk about Crypto

To this point, the analysis and claims have been based on a combination of survey data and survey experiments, but that work can't tell the whole story. The surveys can tell us about the extent to which men's gender performances are linked to crypto and meme stock buying behaviors, regression analyses can eliminate other explanations; the experimental results can help to establish causality. These techniques can tell us about what is happening and why it's happening, but they don't tell us much about *how* it's happening. Much of the story linking technical masculinities to cryptocurrencies is about what cryptocurrencies mean to these men, and how they interact with each other in discussions about it. To address that, it is necessary to make use of rigorous analysis of how participants in web forums actually talk about crypto.

Throughout the book, I've been mentioning how men talk about cryptocurrencies in these forums, and while some of that comes from years of dipping into them and seeing what's going on, or looking up what people are saying about the MOASS today, that's not rigorous enough to draw valid conclusions. To get such conclusions about how cryptocurrency is discussed in online forums, I make use of a large-scale content analysis of various web forums.

Full details about how this content analysis was carried out are found in the Methodological Appendix, but what's important to know is that it provides a valid technique for examining both the stated and implied ideas found in the posts made on the forums. To ensure that those ideas are really there, and not just a projection of the coder, multiple coders independently look at the same material, and the overall validity of their judgments is measured by the extent to which they look at the same texts and independently agree about what category it should be put into.

In this chapter, I'll go through the results of the content analysis. The coders systematically looked at several platforms, recording all of the responses to posts dealing with cryptocurrency that had substantive responses. The coders who carried out the content analysis made use of a range of online forums, including YouTube comments, Instagram, Twitter/X, various subreddits, and even some of the seedier side of the manosphere with 4Chan. In this, I'm following the example set in the online content analysis of masculinity presentations carried out by Kenneth Hanson, C. J. Pascoe, and Ryan Light (2023). While their work centers on a particular subreddit (r/unpopularopinons), they point to 4Chan and 8Chan as other forums attractive to men who want to express controversial ideas (or just troll) anonymously to avoid the threat of public censure. 4Chan, likely because of the unmoderated, free-for-all nature of the forum, had some sentiments that weren't seen in the discussion of crypto on the other platforms. These included nakedly racist and white supremacist statements and encouraging others to commit suicide (perhaps these posts, generally telling others that they should just kill themselves after suffering losses or making a bad decision, were in jest or trolling). In most respects, though, the patterns of posts across the forums were very similar.

Why This Matters

This analysis is critical to the argument being made in the book. While I think there's a compelling story about technical masculinities being told by the data to this point, many of the findings could also be explained through a compensatory masculinities approach. That is, men who feel that they're falling short of the standards of dominant forms of masculinity could try and make up the gap through the performance of traits that they associate with those dominant forms. In doing so, men often wind up doubling down on those performances, overdoing their gender.

So, how can it be shown that the behaviors we've been associating with technical masculinities aren't these men just doubling down? In many cases, there are examples of behaviors associated with men in the masculinity gap that aren't associated with men who say that they're meeting the demands of masculinity: crypto purchases in general fall into this category. It wouldn't make sense to double down on a behavior that isn't part of the portfolio of dominant masculinities. But the case can be furthered by focusing on the protest component of technical masculinities. Protest masculinities by definition reject the behaviors and institutions of dominant masculinities, making the case that their performance of masculinity is better suited to justifying male dominance. This necessarily means dismissing or denigrating the behaviors and institutions that constitute those performances. Throughout this book, I've been making the case that the narratives underlying crypto and meme stock purchases are incompatible with support for existing institutions and hierarchies. Both of these investments are, essentially, a bet that existing financial structures are going to collapse, taking the men currently at the top of the gender hierarchy down with them.

There's no necessary reason why support for crypto on these forums would have to include denigration of existing institutions: to the extent that financial firms are starting to trade in crypto (at least indirectly), references to them could very well be positive. However, entrenched negativity toward currently dominant institutions is a clear sign of a protest masculinity, rather than people trying to integrate themselves into existing hierarchies.

In addition, the technical masculinities argument would lead to the expectation of a lot of sparring on these forums, as men try to perform mastery over a male-coded area of expertise by demonstrating how much more they know than someone else (especially someone who is, themselves, trying to make a technical argument).

How the Coding Was Carried Out

While there is a complete description of the coding process found in the Methodological Appendix, it may be useful to sketch out how the coding was done. Three trained coders identified public web forums that hosted substantive discussions of cryptocurrency, including Twitter/X, Instagram, TikTok, Reddit, and 4Chan. Private servers on Telegram and Discord were considered, but the fact that individuals on these forums may not want their posts to be seen publicly makes their use in research ethically dubious.

The coders then went through multiple rounds of categorizing the posts that they found, then throwing out the posts[1] that led to those coding categories, refining them until they had reached a final list of nineteen categories (though only sixteen were found in the final coding set). They then went through the various forums on separate days, looking for posts about cryptocurrencies that generated substantive responses and discarding any posts that they suspected were from bots.

Each of the posts was then independently coded by two of the coders, with the process continuing until they hit a saturation point, at which the new posts didn't seem to offer anything that wasn't already present in the corpus, at 485 posts (not counting all of those that had been used to build the coding categories, and had been discarded). I then did an independent check, coding 150 of the posts. Because the coders had spent so much time developing the categories, it was not surprising that the analysis had a high degree of inter-rater reliability. Inter-rater reliability is important, as it serves as a measure of how well-defined the coding categories are: if different people independently look at the same post and categorize it the same way, that gives us some confidence that the coding is getting at something intrinsic to the post, rather than just reflecting the whims of the coder.

What's Being Said

The coders told me that they were surprised by some of the aspects of the communications they were witnessing on the various forums. While they were expecting toxicity, and found a great deal of it, in their reflections on the process they also spoke about how surprised they were by the degree of community support that they found. In addition to the posts questioning the intelligence of someone else on the forum, or mocking them for their mistakes, there were plenty of congratulatory and encouraging comments, telling people who had lost money to keep their heads up.

The coders also encountered a great deal of nigh indecipherable jargon. To some extent, this happens whenever individuals with a shared narrow interest talk to each other, but the use of technical jargon is also a potent way to display knowledge and mastery. Other work looking at the technical nature of crypto discussions has found substantial variance between different cryptocurrencies as to how technical the discussions about them are: Tash et al. (2024) find that online discussions of Ripple (a company attempting to displace the SWIFT system for interbank transfers), for instance, are largely about affiliation and power; discussions of Fantom (a blockchain network competing with Ethereum) are generally highly technical.

The most common sentiments across the platforms, far more common than any of the other coding categories, were statements demeaning the intelligence of other posters on the same forum (often the original poster, in responses to them), which made up 16 percent of all of the posts coded, followed by community support posts. These supportive posts, which accounted for 14 percent of the posts coded, were generally shorter and more direct than those in the other categories, congratulating other posters or encouraging them. Close behind these were statements that were dismissive of existing institutions like banks or stock markets, or of the financial world in general, constituting 10 percent of all of the statements coded.

In the second tier of comments—about half as common as those in the top tier—were unsupported assertions of knowledge (making a prediction or dismissing someone else's argument without any evidence), bragging about gains, and negative comments about crypto (especially losses).

Less common than these were comparisons of crypto to gambling or games of chance, discussions of government and politics, and, interestingly, supported assertions of knowledge. This last category, which tended to be rather longer and more detailed than other posts, and often included graphs, figures, and calculations, only made up about 5 percent of all of the posts coded but attracted far more responses and engagement than any of the other categories of posts.

Some of the posts were so bizarre that they resisted any easy coding—a particular post in which white nationalist icon Pepe the Frog was drawn as a sex worker for a meme coin comes to mind—but these were the exceptions. For the most part, the posts and the responses to them fell into quickly recognizable patterns. There's no reason to go through all of the coding categories here—full descriptions of each are found in the methodological appendix—but it is useful to focus on those categories which are very common and those that have the most say about what seems to be driving these behaviors.

Questioning or Demeaning Intelligence

The most common posts in discussions of crypto were ones mocking other posters—most commonly, in the same discussion thread—for their ignorance. Oftentimes, these are basically content-free insults ("Has no idea he's calling himself an idiot. Smooth brain."), but sometimes they were rather more substantive. An informative example comes from a Reddit post, responding to another user who had given details about his[2] Bitcoin investment strategy:

> Paper hands[3] McGee here has lots to learn if he's taking profits at 90, entering at 65 and holding for years. The truth is (bitcoin = log(dollars)) AND he's identified it in plain logic. Yet he exits to USD because he's unwilling to separate

from dollar hegemony? His reserve denomination is entrenched, deeply in a 20th century psyche. We are in the proto years of the bitcoin global reserve age.

Posts like this serve multiple functions.[4] It demeans the knowledge of the original poster, insulting him and claiming that his foolishness is causing him to miss out on potential gains (above the 38 percent profit that he's claiming to have made). Second, it demonstrates the knowledge and mastery of finance of the poster making the attack, including a (rather questionable) mathematical assertion about the price of Bitcoin being tied directly to inflation in the US Dollar. Third, it ties the whole discussion back into the underlying cryptocurrency narrative, positing that Bitcoin will become the new global reserve currency, and that the original poster fails to understand that "dollar hegemony"[5] is now over. In the attack, the failure of the original poster to fully realize his gains results from his failure to understand how cryptocurrency is *just about* to change the world. If someone doesn't buy into the larger narrative, they're dismissed as a fool, even if they did just make enormous profits on their crypto holdings.

Detailed responses to relatively technical posts explaining a profitable transaction often made reference to the larger narrative surrounding cryptocurrency.

> Bro. You don't realize how ignorant this comment is. We are currently slaves to the fiat system that prints trillions of dollars debasing and devaluing your currency which is essentially stealing the fruits of your labor. Bitcoin fixes that. No one can print more bitcoin like the fed reserve does with the dollar. Maybe it will start to make sense to you when Bitcoin is crossing 1 million. It's a deflationary asset. The best store of value known to mankind. Follow the white rabbit and God speed.

The implicit claim of these responses is that even if the original poster is demonstrating mastery by having made money, they're failing because they don't understand how cryptocurrency is going to change the world. Making money isn't enough to prove knowledge and mastery: posters also have to reject existing institutions and buy fully into the apocalyptic narrative (note the reversal of fortune implied by the claim that Bitcoin will hit a million dollars, while the Federal Reserve will drain all of the value from dollars).

Posts in this category more commonly relied on unsupported assertions of knowledge ("Learn about marketcap my friend, then you will understand why XRP values 7x more than chainlink"), but they serve the same purpose: to perform knowledge and mastery over finance in general, and crypto in particular. The high frequency of these posts—again, more common than any other type of post in the corpus across the platforms studied—fits in nicely with the argument that these men are working to perform technical masculinities. If someone is saying something I think is foolish, why engage with them? A post like the lengthy one quoted above isn't aimed at telling the original poster they're wrong—note that it's directed to "him," not to "you"—it's aimed at the other readers of the post on Reddit, explaining why the original poster is foolish. As we'll discuss later, posts like the one this is responding to, ones that get into the details of an investment strategy, attract the greatest amount of attention and responses on the forums studied. They generally contain supported assertions of knowledge—"here's what I did, and here's why I did it"—as well as elements of bragging—"and look how much money I made in the process." They're not asking for advice, or even really telling others what to do, so much as making a claim for mastery of the topic area. This seems to be taken as a challenge by other posters in the forum, who then pick apart the original post to explain why the original poster was foolish and how different actions would have been better. Basically, detailed posts provide an opportunity for responses that perform knowledge and mastery better than the original, revealing the whole point of the exercise.

Tellingly, posts in which the original poster talks about how they've *lost* money don't attract nearly this level of mockery. Few people, if any, chime in to say what they should have done better. Rather, those posts tend to attract community support, with responses chiming in to say that they've lost money too, commiserating, and encouraging them to stick with it. If someone isn't claiming knowledge and mastery in the first place, there's no premium in demonstrating superior knowledge.

These posts are some of the most direct evidence for the link between technical masculinities and cryptocurrency purchases. The individuals making these posts are doing their best to demonstrate knowledge and mastery, and the easiest way to do this is by denigrating the knowledge of someone else. If someone has lost money, or been scammed, it might be easy to dunk on them, but there's no point: who cares if you know more than someone who's admitted that they've failed?

Community Support

Nearly as common in the platforms studied were posts in which users commiserated over losses or encouraged each other to keep going. For instance, a response to a relatively technical video in which the individual talked about how distressed they were over losses didn't lead to explainers about what they should have done differently, but rather nontechnical statement of support ("i love this video, i saw myself in you lol made me feel less crappy about my loss:D").

Nearly as common were short, nontechnical supportive comments in response to the reported victories of other individuals, like finally owning a whole Bitcoin ("Congrats on becoming a whole coiner! 🎉🚀").

When someone posts that they're selling crypto assets, and frames it as profit taking, and *especially* when they claim that doing so is the smart thing to do, it attracts posts like the ones in the previous section. But there are also plenty of posts in which someone talks about selling crypto assets grudgingly, and rather than being attacked, responses tend to be supportive.

> Take some profits and enjoy your life. We are set on BTC mooning but what's the point of living to see numbers when for a small fraction of your wallet you could take a trip somewhere or buy your Mother something nice for example. Well done 🙌🏻

Since these posts aren't claiming mastery, responses can't demonstrate their superior knowledge by talking about what they've done wrong. This might seem odd. Sure, in the outside world, beating up on someone who's already down isn't a demonstration of knowledge; it's punching down in a way that's unseemly. But those rules of engagement don't generally seem to operate in the often toxic world of internet forums, so why here? These reactions underline the collective nature of the cryptocurrency (and meme stock) enterprises. If everyone is just out for themselves, trying to maximize their own profits, there's no reason to be supportive of others in the community: anyone's gain is necessarily someone else's loss. But the narrative of cryptocurrency highlights the community aspect of the asset: it isn't *just* a vehicle to get rich, it's part of a larger project that pits crypto (or meme stock) investors up against larger institutional forces.

Posts showing this kind of community support are differentiated in the coding from the related category of loyalty in crypto (which is rather less common, found in about 2 percent of the coded posts in the final corpus). Loyalty in crypto is about expressing solidarity with individuals not in the forums, especially figures in politics or business that are believed to be part of the movement, like Donald Trump, Elon Musk, and various crypto business founders. In the forums, references to these figures, and the need to support them, are used as a way to rally the other posters, often in the form of saying that these people are on our side, so we're sure to come out on top. These posts could also be lumped in with category of posts expressing masculine solidarity, often marked by the use of the word "bro," which constitutes another 2 percent of the coded posts.

Disdain for Existing Institutions

The third most common code in the content analysis is for statements expressing disdain or dismissal of existing financial institutions, most commonly banks, investment firms, and the US Federal Reserve. These statements constitute about 10 percent of all of the codes in the content analysis.

The most revealing statements in this category are responses to anti-crypto news stories or posts that attract the attention of these forums. The most common criticism levied at cryptocurrencies in these posts is that they're not based in anything, and therefore aren't worth anything. In response, posters in these forums generally attack the basis of the US dollar, pointing out that they're also not backed by anything (except the full faith and credit of the US Government, which also comes under attack).

> How do you think the Feds make money? Physical currency is backed by nothing these days. The american bank note is pretty much worthless these days. Hell, the government is even in debt for the ink and paper, it is printed on at this point.

Such posts often get relatively detailed, frequently referencing the end of the gold-backed dollar as a reason why the dollar can no longer be trusted as a currency. This reduces fiat currencies to the same status that crypto is accused of having—being backed by nothing—leading others to argue that since crypto and fiat currencies are essentially the same, the currency that runs better is preferable.

> I was Ne'ing at "rEaL aNd fIcTiOnAl MoNeY" Wtf is the real and wtf is the fictional? It's all just friggin' numbers on a screen with perceived value. Nothing more, nothing less. Some systems are just obviously better than others.

Some of the most furious activity in this vein comes in response to posts advocating for gold as an alternative to cryptocurrencies. From a theoretical perspective, this represents a more serious problem for proponents of crypto, as most of the arguments against fiat currencies don't apply to gold (which is also untraceable and isn't susceptible to inflation from central bank activity).

> Our dollar only has value bc we are a military superpower and we pulled thru for the world in WW Gold has absolutely experienced crashes. Also gold is continually being found and added to the supply. And good price is controlled

by powerful entities. Bitcoin is controlled by the people and for the people. It is an incorruptible ledger that can not be coaxed or manipulated without everyone on the blockchain being able to point out the error. And it self corrects. Bitcoin is the future. I agree hold gold but if you are storing your value in fiat expect to lose 10% year over year over year over year etc.

In addition to skepticism about and disdain for the system of fiat currency in general, posts in this category also demonstrate disdain toward banks, markets, and financial institutions in general, often using them as a straw man opposed to the underdogs backing crypto.

Hell no. The market is a black box. You have the institutions saying " dont do this we are the professionals" and a bunch of tards online saying "bullshit." The tards seem to be right.

Posts in this category point out all of the problems with existing financial systems as a reason why individuals should embrace an alternative and posit that cryptocurrency is the only one on offer. Banks are invariably referred to as being malicious actors (closing down accounts for suspicious activity, profiting off of late fees, cooperating with government investigations); institutional investors and stock markets don't come out much better.

This level of hostility toward existing institutions is important because it shows the extent to which crypto buyers see themselves as being in opposition to them. Even when banks are believed to be profiting from crypto on the sly—the belief that banks are investing in crypto without telling anyone is weirdly common— they're not part of the crypto community and are therefore the enemy, only in it for the gains, not for the big picture. This puts crypto buyers outside of the system of globalized finance that has been the basis for the transnational business masculinities that have become the dominant performance of masculinities in the past decades. This isn't about trying to use investment acumen to get a job at a big firm, or even to beat them at their own game. The goal is to completely tear down the system, which is invariably corrupt and oppressive, and replace it with something better.

If the goal of these discussions was just picking assets, and making a case for why crypto, as an asset class, or particular coins were going to outperform other assets, none of this would be necessary. Indeed, the fact that a big firm had chosen the same asset to invest in would be a good sign that the posters were on to something. If an individual were investing in platinum, for instance, and found out that one of the biggest investors was doing the same, they'd be trumpeting the fact. Instead, these institutional investors, with their legions of analysts, are presumed to be not just evil but missing out on the apocalyptic change that's coming any day now, the one that crypto (and meme stock) investors are wise to. Buying or selling crypto could be like any buying or selling any other asset; but the performance of buying and selling crypto is tied to this anti-institutional narrative. They're not trying to join the ranks of the elite who are currently at the top of the gender hierarchy: they're mocking them and claiming that their expertise, and therefore their performance of gender, is superior. The fact that Bitcoin has risen is seen as rock-solid proof of their superiority.

As such, the relative popularity of these posts makes a case for the link between cryptocurrencies and protest masculinities. These purchases aren't just about getting rich: they're about replacing the currently dominant power structures, about tearing it all down, about the fact that they, the plucky underdogs, have masculine qualities that make them more deserving of that wealth and prestige than the corrupt institutions that now hold them. Their strategies are defined exclusively in opposition to those of the existing power structures and posit a zero-sum game (reflecting the underlying logics of crypto) where they can win or the institutions can, but not both.

Assertions of Knowledge

In the coding, statements in which a poster tries to demonstrate their knowledge of finance or investments, generally by making an analysis or prediction, are divided into two categories. The most common, making up about 10 percent of the statements in the coding, are unsupported by any detailed analysis. These are largely assertions that something will (or will not) happen, but don't reveal the reasoning behind the assertion.

> Just a reminder. Santas bringing us a buck fiddy by Xmas.. By my 50th in April, $250k will be this 90k norm. These Coins have been paying like clockwork, atleast here in my timezone. Went down the Ol "Multiple Mortgage, CCs tapped out, Title loans against the Duc & Hudson" gamble during Dec '17s fiasco … and quickly got a taste of the most puckered up asshole of a dip the following month

Here, for instance, the poster is *colorfully* predicting a surge in the price of Bitcoin, without giving any reason why it would happen. This sort of post is, essentially, low-effort posturing: "I know more than you do."

Less common than these posts (5 percent of the codes) are supported assertions of knowledge, in which the post includes the reasoning behind the assertion. Some of these are almost incomprehensible to outsiders ("Depends on your finances . 1000$ in XAI213K is 4000 XAI213K if it goes to 50% of ath in 2024 thats a 600% gain. If it goes equal to ath . Its a 1200% gain."), while others are making clear arguments for or against strategies proposed by another post. This one, for instance, is making a case against selling Bitcoin at what seems to be a high point and buying it back on a dip (excerpt from a much longer post).

> Having a bitcoin is for the longrun. If you want to trade it. Take longs and shorts. Unless you are trading at least a million a month in volume the fees alone for buying and re selling will cut into your profits even if u do sell at let's say 99k and buy back in at 94k. And selling a few thousand and buying back in a few thousand lower will actually cost u w fees. U will have to sell entire bitcoin and re buy entire bitcoin thousands lower for it to be worth it if your fees aren't low from regular trading

These more detailed posts are what the much more common negative posts questioning or demeaning the intelligence of someone else on the forum are generally responding to. These posts tend to be longer and require a great deal more effort from the writer. They also seem to include more jargon, abbreviations, and technical terms than other posts. If the performance of buying and selling crypto is about asserting technical masculinities, posts like this are where that performance is clearest.

Of course, this raises the question as to why these kinds of posts aren't more common, and a lot of that has to do with the sampling process. The sorts of detailed, technical arguments as to why something is going to happen (or not happen) might not be too common on the forums that were coded, but they are the basis of popular YouTube videos (note that the coding looked at responses to YouTube videos, rather than the videos themselves), podcasts and the like. They were also much more common on private forums excluded from the content analyses because of research ethics concerns. These kinds of posts play a large role in the overall ecosystem of online discussions of cryptocurrency, and generate lots of responses, but are valuable and time-consuming enough that they just don't show up as often in the sampling process used here.

What's Not There

In addition to the types of statements that are present in the content analysis, there are some that might be expected to show up, but don't. Chief among these is references to crypto as gambling. As will be discussed in Chapter 7, the same factors that lead young men to embrace crypto also seem to lead to gambling behaviors, so it wouldn't be surprising if crypto investments were seen as being similar. However, there's just no indication of this in the data. There are references to gambling ("Why not just put it all on black, if you want to gamble?"), but these are almost all done in order to contrast cryptocurrencies with gambling or mock posts that seem to be taking an overly risky strategy. Posts referencing gambling, or non-systematic approaches to investing that are akin to gambling, make up 4 percent of the codes in the content analysis, and the few that are likening crypto to gambling make a contrast between meme coins and crypto that's seen as more established and stable (" 'crypto' is thousands of shitcoins made for insiders profits.Bitcoin is truly decentralized scarcity without an issuer Stay away from the shitcoin casino.").

The most common way in which gambling was referenced in any sort of positive way in the statements coded was in references to gambling systems: the idea that there is a random process at play, but that the process can be gamed by someone with a system and the skill to carry it out.

> It's an entirely different guess. Perhaps if you'd said that first of all that op had to become an expert in card counting so as to guess at the cycles of the cards then you might have been able to put together some kind of comparison. But you didn't. So playing random blackjack is very different to using multiple historical halving graphs to try and get a reasonable prediction of what will happen in the next year. Not the same thing.

References to this sort of systematic gambling were relatively rare—only about one percent of codes—but are telling. Investing in cryptocurrencies might be like a casino, they're saying, but more like a game of skill than one of chance. Some people may be blundering around and betting randomly, and they're going to lose money, but those of us with a system and the masculine traits needed to see it through are different.

Despite the frequency of scams in the crypto space, especially in meme coins, there is relatively little discussion of them in the posts coded in the content analysis. Posts mentioning having been scammed, or warning about a real or potential scam only constitute 5 percent of the statements. This doesn't seem to be because posters are reticent to talk about their losses—negative statements, in which posters talk about their losses, are more than twice as common!—but rather because it goes against the community ethos of the forums. Since this is a community moving together toward a larger goal, there's a presumption of good faith. It's outsiders, people who don't understand crypto, who spread fear, uncertainty, and doubt by claiming that things are scams. Of course, there are scams, and users should look out for them, but falling for a scam is likened to tuition: paying for the knowledge that will help avoid scams in the future.

This also fits in with the performative aspect of these posts. Posting about losses provides much the same opportunity as dips in the market: it's only when things are going poorly that posters can display masculine traits like rationality and perseverance, showing off their "diamond hands." As such, they're relatively willing to talk about losses. But falling for a scam is almost necessarily a failure of the knowledge and mastery that posters in these forums are trying to display. Scams are bad, but according to the narrative being promulgated in these forums, only fools fall for them.

In a space that's so concerned with performances of masculine traits, explicit statements that another poster is insufficiently masculine, or even openly misogynistic posts, might be expected. Neither comes up too often. Both of these types of attacks are much more common on 4Chan than on the other platforms in the content analysis, but none come up very often. Attacks on other posters—discussed earlier—are common, but those attacks are almost always based on the intelligence of the person posting, not other aspects of their presumed masculinity. When these attacks happen, they're pretty bad ("Do you watch while other guys bang your wife?"), but they simply don't happen very often.

This fits with the technical masculinities story. Posters on these forums don't have to perform their masculinity by contrasting physical or sexual traits: they do so through assertions of knowledge and mastery. As such, putting someone down by calling them gay or a woman isn't as effective as calling them stupid, which happens all the time.

Patterns of Responses

Aside from the coding of individual statements, the content analysis also allows for an analysis of common dynamics in posts about crypto. One of the most seen in the posts and replies across the forums is a supported assertion of knowledge, often detailed, in which an individual lays out their strategy or prediction, followed by a series of negative posts questioning their data or conclusions. On the other hand, posts in which an individual talks about losses or failures tend to lead to mostly positive, encouraging comments.

This dynamic would seem to explain the gap between posts making substantive, supported arguments and those making unsupported ones. Unsupported arguments—a post saying that someone's analysis is wrong or claiming that the price of a coin is going to rise (or, less frequently, fall)—don't attract much attention. There's simply not a lot there to reply to, making it a less valuable target for an assertion of knowledge. The sort of substantive, supported arguments that are seen less frequently attract a great deal of negative attention, with a smattering of positive community support messages thanking them for the analysis.

Unsurprisingly, the posts that attract the most negative attention are the ones that criticize the narrative of cryptocurrencies. If this were just about making money, then the only thing that would matter is whether the price of the assets were going to increase; claims that fiat currencies aren't really going to fall or that inflation in fiat currencies isn't really that bad wouldn't matter. But instead, there's enormous vitriol toward any post that questions the underlying narrative. These attract lengthy, highly negative responses asserting that fiat currencies are worthless, that the government can't be trusted, and that the original poster will be singing a different tune when Bitcoin hits \$1 million (as well as a small number of posts talking about the superiority of the gold standard). The narrative of cryptocurrencies is important to the posters in these forums, seemingly more important than the expected short- and medium-term changes in price. People certainly could buy into crypto solely because they think the price will increase without buying into the narrative, but there's no sign in the actual posts that anyone is doing that.

In essence, substantive arguments are being treated like an assertion of dominance, and when they're put out, other posters are liable to respond in kind, trying to demonstrate their own knowledge and mastery of the area. These responses generally aren't as technical or substantive as the post they're responding to, but they don't have to be: it's enough to point out a single flaw in the post and mock it based on that.

It also seems that posters are using criticism of existing institutions as a way of demonstrating knowledge. While supported assertions of knowledge tied to particular assets or strategies are relatively uncommon, posts that expound on the virtues of cryptocurrency in general or point out flaws in financial institutions are often very detailed and lengthy. These commonly arise in response to posts about news or political events that could impact crypto markets. This happens even when the news might be interpreted as being good for crypto prices: big investment firms getting involved in Bitcoin, for instance, don't attract praise, but disdain. Similarly, news about figures that are seen as allies—Donald Trump, Elon Musk, and such—results in some posts praising them, but more posts contrasting them with existing leaders and institutions.

It would be perfectly reasonable to respond to these sorts of news posts with a discussion of what the implications of the news are for the prices of assets, but that's just not what happens. Such posts—coded as supported assertions of knowledge—are relatively costly and difficult. They attract a lot of attention, but most of that attention is negative, as other posters look for ways to tear down the analysis. Posts expressing disdain for existing institutions, and contrasting them with crypto, serve a similar purpose, giving posters a way to show off how much they know about finance in a display of knowledge, but don't attract the same kind of negative attention. No surprise, then, that they're much more common, and users seem to take any opportunity to make such criticisms.

External Validity

Overall, the results of the content analysis fit in nicely with the technical masculinities story being told, but it's important to ask how much they're really telling us about the people buying and selling cryptocurrencies and meme stocks. Sure, this represents the ways in which people who post on internet forums talk about cryptocurrencies, but how do we know that these posts represent crypto buyers in general? Isn't it possible that individuals posting in these forums are using finance as a way to perform masculinity, but other users aren't?

In general, researchers can't discern much about the behavior of the overall population by looking at online activities. Not everyone has access to the internet; not everyone is online enough to post on Reddit or other forums. A survey that tried to measure attitudes of the general public by looking at posts on any social media site would be badly skewed. However, the population of interest here is crypto owners: being rather younger than the general population, they're much more likely to be online. And given the technical difficulties that arise in buying, selling, and trading cryptocurrencies with any degree of sophistication, they almost have to be very online. Finding out about the views of crypto owners by looking at online activities is less like trying to understand the general public, and more like trying to understand players of online games: it's already clear that the population of interest is engaged and online.

The surveys discussed in previous chapters also provide a strong indication that these users are at least somewhat representative of crypto investors in general. Remember the surveys discussed in previous chapters in which online sources like the sites coded were the most popular way for crypto owners and meme stock traders to learn about these assets. Even if these individuals aren't all posting in these forums, these forums are the communities that they're being socialized into, shaping the way that they understand the meaning of these assets.

Perhaps more importantly, the argument being made about crypto being a way for men to perform technical masculinities doesn't require that everyone buying cryptocurrency or meme stocks is doing it in order to perform technical masculinities, only that they *are* being used in that way. The issue of how common it is to use crypto purchases in this way is important to the question of whether or not technical masculinities will be successful in displacing transnational business masculinities as a dominant performance, but not to whether it represents a protest masculinity in the first place. Suppose that only 10 or 20 percent of crypto owners are using their investments as a way to perform technical masculinities as a challenge to whatever they see as the currently dominant performance of masculinity in their communities. Nothing in the data presented so far makes that seem at all likely, but it would still be enough to support the idea that these purchases are being used as part of a demonstration of a protest masculinity and that such performances are driving the otherwise surprising popularity of these assets.

Crypto as a Rejection

Aside from the ways that crypto is used as a way to demonstrate knowledge, the big takeaway from the content analysis is the extent to which it's seen as a rejection of existing financial structures and institutions. This shows up not only in the statements coded as disdain for institutions, but even in the more common statements diminishing the intelligence of other posters. The poster being dismissed is so dumb that they don't understand how bad the existing institutions are, that the dollar is worthless, that the Federal Reserve is debasing savings, and that banks are corrupt. This is all part of the narrative surrounding cryptocurrencies that has been referenced throughout this book, but it's important to realize that there's no reason that this has to be the case. People could certainly be buying up crypto or meme stocks on the greater fool theory, looking for the price to go up without buying into the underlying narrative, but they're not.

A world in which the discussion about crypto is centered on which coins are going to go up or down, and when, and how much, is a world in which buying and selling crypto is compatible with existing institutions. But the fact that the users themselves are linking support for crypto with deep suspicion and even disdain for these institutions and the people working in them is good evidence that acceptance of the underlying narrative—wild as it may be—is intrinsic to these purchases. The upside of this connection is that it creates a degree of fraternity and community that wouldn't otherwise be expected. Trades in financial markets inherently have winners and losers: if I buy an asset, it's either going to go up or down, and either I or the seller would have been better off not having done the trade. But the narrative underlying cryptocurrencies and meme stocks put the buyers of these assets in an antagonistic relationship with existing financial institutions, anticipating the apocalyptic reversals in which they'll be rich (Bitcoin at $1 Million, the MOASS), and the institutions (the Federal Reserve, the Banks, Hedge Funds) will crumble. Within these communities, this isn't a zero-sum game: there will be plenty of money (if perhaps not enough Maseratis) to go around.

From a theoretical perspective, this is important because it shows the extent to which buying crypto is a performance not just of knowledge and mastery but of rejection: rejection of the stock market, of the institutions of finance, of the people working in them, of the dinosaurs who don't know that they're about to be extinct. This is very much a rejection of cosmopolitan financial elites that top the social, economic, and gender hierarchies, as well as a statement that crypto and meme stock buyers are smarter than they are. The basis of a protest masculinity is the claim that the protest masculinity makes a better case for male dominance than existing dominant performances. Finance and investment are both masculine areas of expertise and provide the means by which men might be able to get rich enough to fulfil the increasingly unrealistic demands of masculinity. The performance of technical masculinities we're seeing in these forums claims that the crypto buyers not only know more than the men running the existing institutions, but also that they're going to wind up much richer, and more able to buy property and support and protect their families.

This link between technical masculinities and financial success is likely a big part of why cryptocurrencies and meme stock purchases make for such a powerful and popular performance of technical masculinities. But the logic of technical masculinities allows for all sorts of other performances that might not be tied to financial outcomes but might be even more compelling in certain communities. In the Chapter 7, I look at some of these other ways in which attempts to perform technical masculinities might lead men to otherwise bizarre, inexplicable, and sometimes harmful behaviors.

"Put it all on black." Other Performances of Technical Masculinities

In Chapter 1, I showed that the online forums related to cryptocurrency and meme stocks were tightly integrated with those covering many other topics. The implication of this relationship is that the purchase of these assets may be both politically and economically consequential, but they're only part of a larger constellation of activities driven by young men's attempts to perform technical masculinities.

Purchasing cryptocurrencies and meme stocks is a powerful way for men to perform technical masculinities, but they're still only one of the many ways in which men might choose to do so. Just as men performing currently hegemonic forms of masculinity might do so by earning lots of money, or through sexual fecundity or by buying a gun, men looking to perform technical masculinities have a lot of options open to them, many of them more socially consequential than the fandom-based nerd masculinities that have characterized much of the past research.

To give an idea of what these other performances of masculinity look like, in this chapter, I'll briefly describe some of the other behaviors that seem to be linked with young men falling into the masculinity gap. Any such listing is necessarily incomplete, but they can help to demonstrate how widespread the effects of these behaviors are.

Technical Masculinities and Gambling

In the content analysis of posts about cryptocurrency, one of the recurrent themes was the idea that the stock market, or meme coins, or some other asset, was like a casino, that buying into it was no better than gambling. Similarly, meme stocks were referred to repeatedly as being like slot machines—low-cost bets that are more amusing than anything, but might once in a while pay off big. It's no surprise, then, that the same factors that lead young men to invest in cryptocurrencies also lead them to be more likely to engage in various forms of gambling. Table 7.1 shows which gambling activities men partake in, by age.

It's only since 2018[1] that online gambling has become available in most of the United States. As of this writing, online sports betting is available in thirty states, with another eight allowing for in-person sports betting, and it has rapidly grown to be a multibillion-dollar industry that is closely tied with all the major sports leagues. Sports leagues are sponsored by sportsbooks; ads for gambling are omnipresent during games, and graphics during games now references odds.

Data for this comes from an August 2024 national survey that asked respondents about their gender, as well as their gambling activities, and a battery of questions designed to assess how much harm was associated with their gambling. About half of Americans say that they participate in some form of gambling or betting—lottery drawings are the most common—and for most people who do gamble, it doesn't lead to a gambling problem. However, some forms of gambling are much more likely to lead to problematic gambling behaviors, and it's those that seem to most attract young men.

The extent to which someone is harmed by their gambling behaviors is measured by the Problem Gambling Severity Index (PGSI). This battery asks respondents about how often various problems related to gambling come up in their lives. For instance, how often have they lost more money on gambling than they could afford, or had to borrow money to make up losses, or had friends or family tell them that their gambling was a problem? These items and others like them are combined into a single score, with a score of eight or above being considered a sign of problem gambling (or, as is the preferred terminology in the addiction literature, "gambling harm").[2]

By this measure, 2 to 3 percent of people in the United States are experiencing problem gambling, about the same percentage as have gambling problems in the UK. But for men under thirty, that rate is 10 percent, about four times as much. A lot of this difference is driven by the ways in which young men are gambling, as shown in Table 7.2. For instance, people who buy tickets for a lottery drawing are no more likely to exhibit problem gambling behaviors than anyone else, while about 5 percent of Americans who buy scratch-off tickets score eight or above on the PGSI. Playing slot machines in person is related to higher rates of high scores on the PGSI—about 9 percent of slots players are problem gamblers—but the games most likely to be linked with problem gambling are sports betting and online slot machines. Fully 17 percent of Americans who say that they bet

Table 7.1 Reported Types of Gambling Among Men, by Age, August 2024 Survey

Gambling activities reported

	All US	Men 18–30	Men 31–44	Men 45–64	Men 65+
Lottery tickets	43%	39%	48%	49%	44%
Scratch-offs	36%	46%	44%	32%	29%
Online sports betting	10%	26%	26%	10%	1%
In person sports betting	7%	16%	13%	5%	4%
Online casino games	7%	18%	14%	7%	3%
In-person casino games	17%	28%	22%	17%	11%
Online slot machines	7%	14%	12%	5%	1%
In-person slot machines	19%	23%	26%	16%	12%
Some other form	1%	0%	2%	1%	1%

Table 7.2 Rate of Problem Gambling by Gambling Type, August 2024 Survey

Rate of high PGSI scores

	Lottery	Scratch-off	Online sports	In-person sports
Less than 8 on PGSI	95%	95%	83%	87%
8 or above on PGSI	5%	5%	17%	13%

	Online casino	In-person casino	Online slots	In-person slots
Less than 8 on PGSI	86%	94%	83%	91%
8 or above on PGSI	14%	6%	17%	9%

on sports score at eight or above on the PGSI, twice the rate of those who play casino games in person, and 26 percent of men aged eighteen to thirty years old bet on sports (among Americans overall, the rate is just 10 percent). The only other type of gambling in which young men are similarly disproportionately likely to participate is online casino games.

The link between an attempt to assert technical masculinities and these forms of gambling is pretty clear. Sports, certainly, is a masculine-coded area of knowledge, so knowledge and mastery over it could be used as a demonstration of technical masculinities. There's also a distinction here between being good at sports—a trait more closely tied with currently dominant forms of masculinity—and knowing about sports. Men might be able to demonstrate traditional forms of masculinity by being good at basketball, but they can demonstrate technical masculinities by knowing a lot about it.

In the past, sports betting was largely limited to betting on the outcome of a game. But online sports gambling is much more immersive than that. Prop bets on games mean that there are multiple opportunities for betting on almost every play: the Super Bowl, for instance, generally has several hundred prop bets available for gamblers. A gambling website describes these bets explicitly in terms of demonstrating knowledge over relatively minor aspects of the game:

> Prop bets offer massive flexibility that you can take advantage of and rake in the profits. Say you have broken down every angle of the NBA showdown between the Rockets and Celtics. You might be unsure who is going to win or which side of the spread is showing value. But you're confident James Harden will struggle against the tough Celtics defense. You can eschew betting on the result of the game and focus on the value you've found. (Thompson 2024)

It's easy to see why these kinds of bets are both especially appealing to men trying to perform technical masculinities and problematic from a mental health perspective. For men trying to demonstrate knowledge of the masculine-coded area of sports, prop bets are appealing because they require much more granular knowledge about sports than simple bets on the outcome of a game. Any sports bet requires that the individual believes that they can outguess the wisdom of the crowds, but prop bets require that the individual know more about the nuances of a particular game, player, or match-up than the sports book does. If the goal is to demonstrate esoteric knowledge about sports, it's hard to imagine a better way to do so.

Like the purchase of cryptocurrency, this claim of greater knowledge about a masculine subject area is enhanced by the monetary element. Not only does being right mean that the bettor has demonstrated their mastery of sports, but they've coupled that knowledge with financial success, another aspect of masculinity. As with cryptocurrency and meme stocks, there's also the implication of a larger, nebulous force that the bettor is besting: in this case, the sportsbook, which sets the odds. Winning a bet necessarily means having won against a larger, supposedly more knowledgeable body, creating the David and Goliath scenario that should be familiar by now.

From a mental health perspective, the opportunity to place bets on hundreds of different aspects of a game, rather than just on the outcome, means that these sorts of bets would be expected to be much more addictive in nature. The difference is akin to the gap between buying tickets for a lottery drawing and buying lottery scratch-off tickets. The fact that the latter gives instant feedback—and potentially instant wins that can immediately be turned back into more tickets—makes it much more likely to lead to problem gambling behaviors. Just so, bets that can be made and paid off during a game are more likely to keep bettors glued to their phones throughout a match, making more bets, and potentially rolling winnings back into more bets.

Online sportsbooks also offer parlay bets, which are essentially chained prop bets, in which individuals can bet not just on one outcome, but on a chain of outcomes. So, someone could bet not just on the winner of a game, but on the winner and the MVP, and the number of field goals, and the bet would only pay out if all of the elements were to be guessed correctly. The appeal of such bets comes from the potentially enormous payouts associated with them, with bettors able to win hundreds of times their initial bet if they guess right on a long chain of low-probability events.[3] While such bets may be less common—even betting sites recommend against them for most gamblers[4]—they would be

                    Bitcoin Bros

expected to be very attractive to men looking to use online sports betting to perform technical masculinities.

The other type of gambling which attracts a disproportionate share of young men[5] is online casino gambling. Long before there were websites touting foolproof systems for how to make money off cryptocurrencies, there were guides to winning at blackjack and similar games that combine chance with skill. In theory, someone who can learn a system and calculate probabilities on the fly can have a small, but positive, expected return when playing these games. As such, winning at casino games is a test both of knowledge and skill, as well as perseverance: if a player is down, and the system is working, they just have to play through it, and trust that eventually they'll wind up winning. This is similar to how men talk about cryptocurrency and meme stocks, and the appeal is very similar. The fact that a system might be so complex that it is difficult or impossible to follow accurately simply makes it a better test of the individual's knowledge and skill.

Of course, not all of the popularity of gambling in the United States can be attributed to attempts to demonstrate technical masculinities. Older women, for instance, are more likely than other groups to engage in casino-based in-person gambling, an effect that gambling scholars attribute to a desire to socialize. Still, young men are more likely than other groups to both report problem gambling behaviors and to have scores on the PGSI that amount to a serious issue.

Men aged thirty and under aren't significantly more likely to report two or more problem gambling behaviors than men aged thirty-one to forty-four, but both of these cohorts are much more likely to report problem gambling behaviors than older men are, as shown in Table 7.3. However, the gap between the youngest cohort of men and other men is clear from the difference in the percent categorized as being problem gamblers because they've scored eight or higher on the PGSI.

Table 7.3 Number of Problem Behaviors Reported among Men, by Age, August 2024 Survey

Problem behaviors reported

	All	**Men 18–30**	**Men 31–44**	**Men 45–64**	**Men 65+**
No gambling reported	42%	29%	35%	41%	51%
No problem behaviors	37%	26%	27%	45%	42%
One problem behavior	9%	16%	12%	6%	4%
Two or more behaviors	12%	29%	26%	9%	3%

Table 7.4 Scores of Eight or above on the PGSI, by Age, August 2024 Survey

Meets or exceeds 8 on PGSI scale

	All	Men 18–30	Men 31–44	Men 45–64	Men 65+
No gambling reported	42%	30%	35%	41%	51%
Less than 8 on PGSI	55%	60%	60%	59%	49%
8 or above on PGSI	3%	10%	5%	1%	-

As shown in Table 7.4, the rates of problem gambling are just vastly higher for young men than for men in any other age bracket, largely driven by the differences in the types of gambling they're prone to: online sports and online casino games, both of which seem to be particularly linked to problem behaviors.

The fact that young men are more prone to these behaviors does not necessarily mean that they're tied to attempts to perform masculinity, but the circumstantial evidence is strong. First off, men who assert a "completely masculine" gender identity are *less* likely than other men to say that they engage in online sports betting. Five percent of completely masculine men say that they do so, compared with 13 percent of men who say that they're anything other than "completely masculine" on the masculinity-femininity scale.[6] As with crypto, though, the real gap comes when we include scores on the masculine role norms inventory.

Among men who say that they're "completely masculine," scores on the MRNI don't have any impact on the likelihood of engaging in online sports betting: 12 percent of "completely masculine" men with high MRNI scores do so, alongside 11 percent of those with low MRNI scores. Men who identify as anything other than "completely masculine" and have low MRNI scores are right there with them: 11 percent say that they've made an online sports bet in the last twelve months. But for men in the masculinity gap, with high MRNI scores, but not identifying as "completely masculine," the rate is 28 percent. Similar differences pertain for online casino games: "completely masculine" men aren't any more or less likely than women to engage with this kind of betting. Among "completely masculine" men, about 5 percent play them, regardless of MRNI scores, but among men in the masculinity gap, 18 percent do.

Just as important are the types of gambling for which there is no difference between men in, and outside of, the masculinity gap. Ten percent of men in the masculinity gap say that they've played online slot machines, a type of gambling that neither requires nor rewards skill or knowledge of any kind. And so that figure is not significantly higher than the 7 percent of other men or the 8 percent of women who play online slots. For in-person slots, the numbers are even closer: 21 percent for men in the trap, 19 percent for other men, and 20 percent for women. Forty-six percent of men in the masculinity gap, and 46 percent of men outside of it say that they've bought (non-scratch off) lottery tickets in the past twelve months.

Generally, men in the masculinity gap are more likely to engage in gambling and more likely to report problem gambling behaviors. Forty-four percent of women don't report any gambling at all in the past twelve months, as do 42 percent of men who aren't in the masculinity trap. But only 29 percent of men in the masculinity gap say that they haven't gambled in the past year. Men in the masculinity gap are also more likely to have a score of eight or above on the PGSI: for women, and for "completely masculine" men, the rate is just 2 percent. For men with a high MRNI who don't identify as "completely masculine," the rate is 8 percent. It's not just that men who value traditional masculinity but feel that they're falling short are engaging in gambling behaviors, it's that those men are really harming themselves in their attempts to do so. A PGSI score of eight or above means that gambling has gone well beyond a pastime, or a way to enjoy a sporting event, and is getting in the way of everyday life.

Just as there are forums for men to talk about their gains, losses, and strategies in investments, there are forums for men to talk about sports and sports betting, often centered around fantasy sports leagues, creating the communities necessary for these performances of gender to have an audience. The casinos and sportsbooks taking the bets also seem well aware of the masculinity-based appeal of their products, with ads stressing the male bonding elements, and the idea that the targeted of the ad might know more about the topic than the experts do. Young men may also be primed for this sort of display by videogames, which have long since incorporated random item drops and gambling mechanics into popular games. In the warfare simulator "Call of Duty," players can use real or in-game currency to buy draws that could get them rare weapons or outfits; in sports games, those draws can net high-end players, and even special versions of those players. Secondary markets built around the games—and sometimes incorporated into them—mean that these wins can have substantial retail value.[7]

Young men have also not been the only victims of the expansion of online gambling: problem gambling rates are also relatively high among young women (though not as high as for young men), though the selection of games is rather different for young women. But young men are still the target audience for these appeals, and as organized as cryptocurrency marketing is, and as big as those markets have become, casinos and sportsbooks seem much more effective at taking the money of young men looking to perform technical masculinities.

Conspiracy Theories

While data on masculinity-femininity and belief in conspiracy theories is not available, the same processes that lead men to buy cryptocurrency are also likely to lead them to embrace at least some kinds of conspiracy theories. As discussed in Chapters 3 and 4, conspiracy theories are very much at the heart of the narratives that have been built up around cryptocurrencies and meme stocks. Cryptocurrency only really makes sense in the context of believing that the existing financial markets are somehow a fraud propped up by colluding governments and business interests. The valuation of meme stocks is driven by the idea that the prices of these stocks are being artificially repressed by shadowy cabals of institutional investors.

But there are other reasons to believe that attempts to perform technical masculinities would lead men to be more likely to embrace at least certain kinds of conspiracy theories. To perform technical masculinities, men need to demonstrate knowledge and mastery of male-coded areas of expertise, and the more esoteric or complex the knowledge being demonstrated is, the better. Take, for example, a relatively benign but absolutely ludicrous theory that gained popularity online in the 2010s: the belief that the Earth is flat. In an April 2022 national FDU Poll, 4 percent of Americans said that it was "very likely" that the Earth is actually flat, with another 6 percent saying that it is "somewhat likely" to be true (most Americans, 72 percent, said that it was "not at all likely to be true").

The belief that the Earth is flat largely originates from Biblical literalism: since the authors of the Old Testament certainly believed the Earth to be flat, there are references in the Bible to the corners of the Earth, and to the Sun going around the Earth (and, in one instance, being stopped in that orbit). Most modern Christians would take such statements as metaphors, if they were to think about them at all, but they present a problem for individuals who believe in the inerrancy of the Bible, who have to somehow reconcile the Bible's clear statements on the issue with a modern understanding of cosmology. One way to do this is to hold that the Earth actually is flat, as is implied by the Biblical text, and that all of the clear evidence that the Earth is an oblate spheroid orbiting the Sun has been faked, probably for nefarious purposes.

So, the photographs taken of the Earth by NASA astronauts from space? Faked. International flights that cross the Pacific Ocean? Actually going the long way around. Telescopic observations of the phases of the other planets? Just observations of a shell surrounding the Earth that's thought to be something like an LED screen with infinite resolution. The centuries-old observation that ships on the horizon appear sails first? Just an issue of perspective.

Now, this is all plainly ridiculous. For one thing, a study of the times it takes to reach islands in the Pacific from both North America and Asia means that a flat earth would require that places like Hawaii and the continent of Australia not actually exist (or not be anywhere near where they actually are). The whole thing would require a giant conspiracy of silence or active deceit involving not just space agencies from around the world but also every astronomer, physicist, and airline pilot on Earth. So why would anyone—even just ten percent of Americans—think it's remotely plausible?

The answer comes from the opportunities that such a bizarre belief gives to demonstrate esoteric knowledge. The videos on YouTube that make the case for a flat Earth—or at least explain what are presented as holes in the observation that the Earth is (basically) spherical—almost universally take the form of lists of observations. For instance, the photographs presented by NASA of the Earth, as taken from space, are generally stitched together from multiple photos taken at different times (getting everything in one image would require spacecraft to be much farther away from Earth than they generally go). Or the observation that sufficiently large lakes couldn't be flat (as they appear to be) if the Earth was curving beneath them (the surfaces actually do curve, but subtly enough that it's hard to measure). The point isn't that these are reasonable objections, but rather that pointing out "101 reasons why the Earth must be flat" gives the individual 101 ways to demonstrate how much they know about something that the viewer, apparently, does not.

The assertion that the Earth is flat is an especially bizarre one, but the bizarreness is a plus, if the goal of the exercise is to demonstrate technical masculinities by knowing and explaining more than a real or imagined audience. A belief that's widely held is unlikely to require explanation, and so doesn't provide any opportunity to demonstrate esoteric or specialized knowledge. As such, it would be expected that demonstrations of technical masculinities through exposition about conspiracy theories would be biased toward more extreme or controversial theories: 9/11 truthers, alien visitation, even the various theories holding that hundreds of years in the Middle Ages didn't actually happen.[8] If someone is arguing that Viking explorers landed in North America before Columbus, the audience is likely to accept it, giving no opportunity to perform technical masculinities. If they instead say that no planes hit the World Trade Center, and it was really a cruise missile disguised as a hologram, well, that's going to require some explanation, which is, of course, the whole point of the exercise.

In order to be a credible demonstration of technical masculinities, such conspiracy beliefs should be tied to topic areas that are accepted as being masculine. Science, politics, and economics are certainly in that area, and all the better if those demonstrations can make use of scientific equipment. Flat Earthers, for instance, might use powerful laser pointers to attempt to demonstrate that a body of water is level over a long distance or sensitive thermometers to look at the temperature of the light coming off the moon.[9] At the extremes, it might be tied to amateur rocketry, with true believers putting cameras on rockets going high enough to theoretically observe the curvature of the Earth. Similarly, believers in alien visitation might make use of metallurgical experiments to try and show that samples purportedly from extraterrestrial artifacts could not have been manufactured on Earth. In all cases, the goal is the same: to show that the individual carrying out the performance knows more and has more technical prowess than the experts and scientists who hold conventional views.

Because these conspiracy beliefs are tied to masculine areas of expertise, give the individual the opportunity to demonstrate their knowledge of esoteric or technical topics, and generally feature an ill-defined overarching power that the individual is rebelling against, they can be used to perform technical masculinities. However, they're likely to remain a niche way of demonstrating technical masculinities because they're not linked to outcomes like wealth or sexual access to women. Cryptocurrency or meme stocks are better demonstrations of technical masculinities not necessarily because they better demonstrate knowledge over a masculinized subject area, but because they promise to get believers rich. Belief that the Earth is flat might be a way of performing technical masculinity, but it's never going to be a path toward dominant forms of masculinity in the way that other technical masculinities are.

Political Views

Generally, the link between technical masculinities and political views in the United States is obscured by the very strong relationship between dominant forms of masculinity and support for Republican candidates, especially Donald Trump. Generally, men who identify as being "completely masculine" on the

Table 7.5 Presidential Preference in 2024 by Sex and Gender, August 2024 National Survey

Who do you plan to support in November's Presidential Election?

	"Completely Masculine" Men	Other Men	"Completely Feminine" Women	Other Women
Kamala Harris, the Democrat	30%	55%	56%	58%
Donald Trump, The Republican	64%	35%	39%	36%
Someone else	6%	10%	5%	6%

unidimensional (or bidimensional) masculinit-femininity scale are much more likely to say that they support Republican candidates.

For instance, in an August 2024 US national poll of likely voters carried out by the FDU Poll, the Republican candidate[10] had the support of 64 percent of men who said that they were "completely masculine," compared to just 35 percent support among other men, as shown in Table 7.5. Given the embrace of technical masculinities among men who identify as being something other than "completely masculine" on this scale, it seems that the performance of technical masculinities should be linked with support for Democratic candidates.

The gender story here about political views is familiar: men who assert a traditionally masculine gender identity form the base of Republican support, with other groups leaning toward the Democratic side. Given that men who assert such a gender identity tend to be older, less educated, and higher on sexism scales, this isn't at all surprising.

However, a rather different story arises upon a deeper delve into the views of the men who do not identify as being "completely masculine." Men who do not assert a gender identity at the end of the masculinity scale but say that they value traditional masculinity (have a high score on the MRNI), support the Republican candidate by a wide margin, fifty-six to thirty-four over the Democrat. Men who are otherwise similar, but have low scores on the MRNI, support Harris by a sixty-nine to seventeen margin (there is also a gap based on MRNI among "completely masculine" men, but there just aren't enough men in the completely masculine but low MRNI group to allow for any conclusions about them).

As shown in Table 7.6, men who say that they're "completely masculine" may form the core of the Republican electorate in the United States, but men who aren't

Table 7.6 Presidential Preference in 2024 by the Masculinity Gap, August 2024 National Survey

Who do you plan to support in November's Presidential Election?				
	"Completely masculine" men, high MRNI	"Completely masculine" men, low MRNI	Other men, high MRNI	Other men, low MRNI
Kamala Harris	22%	50%	34%	73%
Donald Trump	72%	44%	56%	18%
Someone else	6%	6%	10%	9%

traditionally masculine, but say that they *value* traditional masculinity, are almost as likely as they are to support a Republican candidate in 2024. It's in this gap between asserted masculinity and valuing of traditional masculinity that we expect to see men who embrace technical masculinities, and these men are embracing Republican candidates at about the same rates as traditionally masculine men. There are lots of potential explanations for this. One line of research in political science has looked at this as being purely about gender role strain. As DiMuccio and Knowles (2025) argue, men who value traditional masculinity, but feel that they're falling short of it, are likely to embrace more aggressive—in the US context, conservative and Republican—policies in order to try and perform masculinity. In this view, these men are essentially doubling down, taking advantage of the fact that conservative and Republican policy positions are coded as masculine to use political views as a compensatory mechanism.

The lens of technical masculinities, though, provides an alternative explanation for these behaviors. Men who have traditionally masculine gender identities might well be embracing Republican or conservative politics as a performance of their gender. To the extent that the goal of hegemonic masculinity is to ensure the continued social and political dominance of heterosexual men over other groups, the policies promulgated by these parties may also be seen as favorable, absent any other appeal. But technical masculinities give an insight into why men who don't identify as traditionally masculine would embrace the same policies. It seems likely that US men who are embracing technical masculinities are using conservative or Republican policies because, and to the extent that, they're out of the mainstream of traditional political rhetoric.

Take, for example, the act of wearing the symbolic red MAGA hat. In much of the country, it may be accepted or welcomed, but in others, it's a provocation, guaranteed to generate disagreement. That disagreement creates an opportunity for men to demonstrate to others why controversial views are actually correct—showing knowledge and mastery over masculinized areas of expertise, like politics or economics. Holding mainstream views on politics is not likely to generate much in the way of disagreement and therefore doesn't give an opportunity to perform knowledge. But by claiming heterodox beliefs, men may be able to reliably give themselves a stage on which they can perform their masculinity.

It is difficult, and perhaps impossible, to sort out how much of the appeal of these candidates among men in the masculinity gap can be attributed to performance of a gender identity and how much is based on policy agreement— or even if that question is meaningful. For instance, in the 2024 US presidential election, people who said that they owned cryptocurrencies or related assets— dominantly young men—favored the Republican candidate by a wide margin. Is that because both the Republican candidate and these assets appealed to men looking to perform protest masculinities? Or because the Republican candidate had put some time and effort into making concrete appeals to crypto owners, talking about, for instance, a federal Bitcoin reserve? The causal story isn't easy to parse, but the outcome is clear.

From the perspective of the underlying model of crypto as a protest masculinity, it seems that the dominant force in the relationship between crypto and Republican support in 2024 was ideology, rather than specific issues. As unlikely a messenger as he was, the Republican candidate argued again and again that he was going to tear down existing power structures, drain the swamp of the corruption, and help people—especially white men—who feel that the system is biased against them. While the data to sort out this causation empirically just isn't available, the theoretical argument would make a case for crypto purchases and Republican support in 2024 to have been driven by the same underlying factors, rather than causing one another.[11]

Of course, many of the policies of recent Republican candidates unrelated to crypto might also appeal to men in the masculinity gap. In other countries studied by masculinity scholars, shifts in economic and societal power have led to upheavals in the gender hierarchy, and there's no reason to think that the United States is any different. While white heterosexual men are still dominant in many parts of public life in the United States, they aren't quite as dominant as they once were, and Republican rhetoric has provided reasons why this might be the case. Such rhetoric identifies reasons why these men don't have the lives that they imagine their fathers and grandfathers to have had. Free trade deals took away the good factory jobs that used to be available to men without a college degree. Diversity, equity, and inclusion and affirmative action policies that they believe discriminate against white men took what should have been theirs. Immigrants took the jobs that they should have had. Competition from China took what was left. Whether there's a concrete plan to reverse these shifts—if reversal is even possible—is beside the point: the airing of these grievances, which have been built up over decades, is enough. Part of the argument made around technical masculinities is that the traditional way of reaching prosperity (education, hard work, moving up the ladder) is a lie, a scam, that it can't really work in the modern economy. The shift in Republican rhetoric against immigrants, against diversity policies, and against free trade and globalization supports this contention.

In the 2024 US Presidential election, even as the voting gap between men and women overall narrowed relative to 2020, the gap between young men and young women expanded. In the 2024 exit polls, 56 percent of male voters under thirty supported the Republican candidate, compared with just 40 percent of women. In 2020, the gap was much smaller, when the Republican candidate had the support of 33 percent of women and 41 percent of men (the Democratic candidate got 65 percent of young women and 56 percent of young men). At the time of this writing, the sort of verified datasets that would allow for deeper analyses of this gap are not yet available, but it seems likely that the performance of technical masculinities plays some role in the shifting political preferences of young men. The fact that the movement seems to be relatively marge among young Black and Latino men, who are more likely to have high scores on the MRNI and face challenges in trying to meet the demands of currently hegemonic forms of masculinity, only adds to the case.

If men are looking to perform technical masculinities, they can go well outside of cryptocurrency and meme stocks. Even if performances that are linked to the rewards of dominant forms of masculinities—like money and sexual access to women—are likely to be favored, the fact that there are many audiences means that there are likely to be a variety of performances. The extent to which men embrace these performances is likely to be driven by the extent to which others see the field in which the performance is happening as masculine in nature, and how much disagreement it's likely to generate. Politics seems like a fertile ground for such performances, and the link to money means that gambling is likely to be widespread as well. The main takeaway here is that the performance of technical masculinities is far more widespread than investment behaviors, and the research agenda of scholars looking at masculinities must expand as well.

"Believers always win in the end." Technical Masculinities and the Future of Men

One of the first things I did when preparing to write this book was look into the bankruptcy case surrounding the collapse of Celsius, a major crypto trading platform. The details of why Celsius collapsed are contentious, but it's enough to know that hundreds of thousands of people had placed their crypto investments on the platform, and despite assurances from the company that their assets were safe and earning interest for them, they seemed to have lost everything.[1] Had Celsius been a bank, the depositors would likely have gotten their money back, but it wasn't a bank, wasn't regulated or secured at all, and the customers were treated in bankruptcy court as unsecured creditors, last in line to get any assets out of the failed business.

Most of the thousands of documents on the public docket for the Celsius bankruptcy are legal filings from one of the many parties to the case,[2] but a little less than a thousand of them are letters sent by Celsius' depositors to the bankruptcy judge. Nearly all these letters are written by men, and while most are from the United States, there are some from other English-speaking countries (Australia is especially well represented) and a smattering from other countries. Some of these letters concern narrow technical issues, but many of them are pleas to the judge, asking him to return the cryptocurrency that they had deposited—under what they say were false premises—into Celsius.

My plan was to carry out a content analysis on these letters, comparing the depositors pleas to get at least some of their money back to unsecured creditors of other bankruptcy cases to look for differences in how they talk about masculinity, knowledge, and gender. As it turned out, though, there just weren't any cases that had anything like the number of letters to the judge or the outpourings of grief that are in these letters. A comparative content analysis isn't possible, but that doesn't mean that there isn't anything to be learned from reading these letters. A sense of humiliation is pervasive; these men talk about priding themselves on how much they know about finance, talking friends and relatives into investing with Celsius, then losing everything. Discussions of suicide show up far too often.

A few excerpts make the tone of these letters clear.

> That was our life savings. It was our chance of having a baby, and funding medical expenses. It was our chance of taking care of our parents as they age. Since the halt of withdrawals, I have not been able to sleep or eat properly. I have been emotionally distressed which is impacting my marriage and my life. I feel like I just cannot get up each day and keep going

> Please return at least the 13.2 Bitcoins that were deposited after withdrawals were already halted, the alternative outcome will have me in default on my mortgage and lose my home, and it will cause me to spend the rest of my life fighting interest repayments … I have suicidal thoughts and the only reason I haven't already taken my life was the burden that would leave my family, and I have lost 15% of my body weight in 6 weeks from the stress of losing everything that I've spent my entire life building. Worst of all, my mother split my home with me so if I default on the home she'll be homeless at 60 years of age with no other savings

> Having my funds frozen has been devastating to me and my family both financially, mentally, and physically. I cannot sleep most nights and am overwhelmed with worry and dread for my family's future. I have two small children, a 3-year-old daughter and a 2-year-old son. I am the sole bread winner for my family, and I pride myself on making smart financial and parental decisions for them to provide a better life and a bright/positive future.

To me, these letters—and there are hundreds of them—serve as a reminder of the real human toll taken by the attempts of these men to find some way to do the things that they believe men need to do: provide for children, own a home, take care of their parents. In the abstract, it's easy to mock or caricature these guys, but they're also victims, in this case, twice over. Victims of what they believed to be misrepresentations from a platform that they trusted, despite all the warning signs that they were told were just haters spreading fear, uncertainty, and doubt. Victims, too, of internalized gender expectations that are harder and harder to meet in an increasingly unequal globalized world.

Summing Up

The story being told by the data is straightforward. Increasing economic inequality means that men who, in the past, might have seen a path for themselves into hegemonic forms of masculinity now feel shut out, knowing that they'll never be able to get to the rewards that go along with dominant forms of masculinity. Expectations about what men should be able to achieve just haven't kept up with the reality of what most men can realistically achieve, alienating men, especially middle-class men who look for alternative ways of performing their gender.

In the past, these alternate forms of masculinity—called protest masculinities—were mostly found among working-class men and were characterized by a rejection of authority figures and the proscribed ways that they were supposed to behave in order to achieve class mobility. Today, the protest masculinities adopted by some men still center on a rejection of authority figures and institutions, the belief that education and the stock market, and even dating rituals, are all scams, and that the only real way to get ahead is to understand how these systems "really" work in order to find secret paths forward.

This means that their performances of masculinity become centered on knowledge over topics that are perceived as being masculine in nature. The idea that knowledge and mastery of technical areas is a way to perform masculinity isn't new, nor is the idea of nerd masculinities, in which men perform gender by demonstrating how much they know over esoteric male-coded pursuits. What is new is the way in which the advent of cryptocurrencies (and, to a lesser extent, meme stocks) has linked these pursuits with money, and therefore with the traditional rewards that accompany hegemonic masculinity.

Cryptocurrency works well for this purpose because understanding, buying, and selling it typically requires a great deal of technical skill. Being able to spot the (many) scams and sticking with the asset even when it dips precipitously gives men the opportunity to demonstrate traits that they see as masculine. All of this is in service to a community of like-minded men who cheer each other on, aided by the underlying heroic narrative casting these men as the underdogs in an epic battle against nefarious forces, but one in which the tides of history are on their side, and they are guaranteed to eventually prevail.

This confluence of narratives also opened up all sorts of opportunities for scammers, selling men on systems that are guaranteed to work (and, if they don't, it's fault of the users, not the system), promising wealth, respect, and sexual access to women if they try *just one more time*. The opaque, technical nature of cryptocurrency makes it a better demonstration of men's mastery over financial matters, but it also means that scams and outright theft can be harder to spot. The community narrative underlying crypto—it's us against the world—means that attempts to call out scammers and thieves are often seen as spreading fear, uncertainty, and doubt, hurting the collective, rather than helping it. And, of course, since cryptocurrencies operate largely outside of traditional finance markets, there is little or no regulation to protect consumers or even rules that would make actions like pump and dump schemes illegal.

This sort of dynamic has played out before, across scandals like #gamergate, and while those movements have been destructive for many of the people receiving abuse from the online hordes, cryptocurrency is very different, because of that link with money and because it has become so widespread. If this were just some niche online occupation it might be fine to ignore it, but cryptocurrency is anything but. Almost 20 percent of voters in the United States own, or have owned, cryptocurrency or related assets (like NFTs). Among men under the age of thirty, that figure is more than 40 percent. The figures for meme stocks, which carry many of the same narrative elements and have similar communities, but a lower technical barrier to entry, are even higher.

After the first wave of crypto popularization faded, and Middle America was no longer seeing Super Bowl ads with celebrities telling men to seize their chance at wealth, or risk being left behind, it would be easy to think that it could be ignored, that it was a passing fad that had passed. By 2024, the markets for NFTs had collapsed: owners of even the most prominent NFTs couldn't find buyers for pennies on the dollar, and they moved from being a billion-dollar industry to a punchline. But even if crypto stopped being quite as visible, the 2024 US presidential election put any thoughts that it was over to rest. In that election, the Republican candidate reached out directly to crypto owners, and people who owned cryptocurrency responded, favoring him in the election by a wide margin. He soon put out his own memecoin, raising millions (while most investors lost, as is the case with nearly all memecoins). Crypto firms poured hundreds of millions of dollars into the coffers of both candidates, and rather than being consigned to the dustbin of history, crypto appeared poised to become part of the financial mainstream, opening it up to enormous amounts of new capital.

Crypto purchases provide men who feel—generally correctly!—that they can't get ahead through traditional means with a hypothetical path toward status, wealth, the ability to buy a house and raise a family, all the things that they believe men are supposed to do. For men who value traditional masculinity, who feel the pressure to achieve it, but know that they can't, that's powerful. If crypto was just a crutch, a way for men to express their gender identity to other men, it might not be great, but it would be something on the level of the men's gatherings of the 1980s or 1990s, an interesting cultural phenomenon, but one that could be ignored. If some men lose money, well, men spend money on worse things.

What makes crypto different, and of much greater concern to society, is that it represents a fundamentally different way for men to establish their masculinity. There have been plenty of performances of gender based around technical masculinities in the past, but they were marginalized, the province of nerds, video gamers, and niche interests who didn't quite put up signs reading, "No Girls Allowed," but weren't far from it. The combination of this way of performing masculinity with the promise of financial returns moved these from a marginalized performance of gender to one that is challenging existing dominant forms with the gender hierarchy, a shift seen and reinforced even in Hollywood blockbusters. The currently dominant forms arose in a social and economic structure that no longer exists, making it vulnerable to this sort of challenge. Other countries have seen their gender hierarchy shaken up by the globalizing economy, and there's no reason to think that the United States should be different.

Even this might not seem like such a big deal if the performance of technical masculinities were limited to buying crypto and meme stocks. But, as we've seen, the same dynamics that lead men to embrace these financial aspects also impact their likelihood of gambling, their political views, and the same web forums that cheer on these purchases and commiserate over losses are linked to the repellent misogyny and bizarre beliefs of the manosphere. Currently dominant forms of masculinity are not great for a lot of reasons, but the ideas and behaviors that have become part and parcel of the version of technical masculinities being promulgated online are arguably worse. And suppose the gender hierarchy is upended, that these technical masculinities become the version of masculinity that our sons and grandsons aspire to? At some point, the realignment of masculinities stops being a problem for young men and becomes a problem for everyone.

#NotAllMen

Whenever I talk about crypto and the manosphere, I can count on hearing one objection: "I (or my brother or my boyfriend or my uncle) buys cryptocurrency but doesn't have any of these other attitudes!" In some sense, these are the objections that every social scientist hears, as social science works not in absolutes, but in tendencies. Men in the masculinity gap are *more likely* to buy crypto, *more likely* to vote for a Republican candidate, and *more likely* to gamble. Men who are in online crypto forums are *more likely* to fall prey to masculinity influencers, *more likely* to buy into red pill pseudoscience. Humans are not automatons, and not everyone behaves in the same way. The fact that someone buys Bitcoin and uses the proceeds to support Planned Parenthood doesn't call the overall story into question. The fact that individuals are unpredictable doesn't mean that societal tendencies are. It's like Brownian motion: I don't have to know where each particle is going to end up in order to have some idea what the overall end state is going to be.

But even if they're not universal, these tendencies should be troubling. An eight-point increased likelihood of being a problem gambler corresponds to millions of men ruining their lives or at least making those lives a lot more difficult. Any increase in the number of men caught up in the misogynistic pseudoscience of the manosphere makes life worse for both them and the women around them. The belief that education isn't a real way to get ahead flies in the face of data showing the enormous return on investment from even a bachelor's degree, and men who don't get that degree are likely to find themselves disadvantaged for life. Money that goes into buying cryptocurrency and meme stocks is money that isn't saved for retirement, or to put toward a down payment on a house, or any number of other things that could make men's lives easier and more productive going forward. Believing that the system is a scam becomes, in essence, a self-fulfilling prophecy. Men who don't get a college degree are likely to be less prosperous. Men who eschew traditional investments are likely to end up poorer. Men who assert misogynistic views about women are likely to have harder time finding meaningful relationships. Opting out of the system because they believe that it won't work only makes it more likely that they won't be able to find happiness and success in it.

Just as the tendencies and trends explored in this book don't apply to everyone, the explanation for the appeal of cryptocurrencies and meme stocks doesn't apply to all buyers. Men under thirty are more likely than other groups to buy crypto, but men aged thirty-one to forty-five do so at relatively high rates as well. Across age groups, women are less likely than men to buy these assets, but there are still substantial numbers of women who do so. Of course, older men might still be in the masculinity gap, and women may seek to assert masculine gender identities, but it's also entirely possible that members of these groups who are buying crypto are doing so for very different reasons. Perhaps they did it on a lark; perhaps they think it's really a good investment; perhaps it was the pandemic, and they were bored; perhaps the Super Bowl ads worked and persuaded some people who otherwise wouldn't have bought into crypto to give it a try. There are plenty of reasons why someone might buy into these assets that have nothing to do with assertions of masculinity but not being able to explain the behavior of everyone doesn't mean that the dynamics discussed here don't do a good job of explaining the behavior of some people.

Why Isn't It Working?

If buying cryptocurrency and related assets serves as a way for men to perform masculinity, shouldn't men who buy cryptocurrency have gotten themselves out of the masculinity gap? Put another way, men are motivated, in part, to buy these assets in order to prove how masculine they are—so why isn't it working?

To some extent, the answer to this question is outside of the limitations of the available data. If buying up crypto allows men to meet their own internalized version of what it means to be a man, then there should be some sign of longitudinal effects, whereas men who are buying crypto rate themselves as more masculine after having done so, compared to similarly situated men who did not. The longitudinal data that would allow for that to be tested just doesn't yet exist.

However, attempts to prove masculinity through external achievements are almost necessarily doomed. Masculinity is necessarily tenuous: no matter how well they think they've established their masculinity, men are always just one failure away from losing their status. Masculinity isn't something that's achieved; it's something to be striven for. It's a process, not a goal. Certainly, some small number of men investing in crypto or meme stocks have made a great deal of money (at least on paper) and would now fall out of the masculinity gap in the measures that have been used here. But for most, buying these assets, showing off how much they know about them, shouting down naysayers, fighting the institutions, that's all part of the process. Were the final apocalyptic victory to come—and it never will—and these men were to find themselves validated and wealthy, perhaps then they would be secure enough to no longer be in the masculinity gap. Until then, though, the promise of that day will be enough to keep them striving.

The Future of Crypto

In the wake of the 2024 US presidential election, crypto advocates were jubilant, believing that the new administration would be relatively supportive of cryptocurrency. Due to criminal prosecutions and asset seizures, the US government already had a substantial portion of all of the Bitcoin in the world, which, crypto advocates hoped, could be used as the basis for a "strategic Bitcoin reserve," rather than sold off. While it's unclear what the governmental goal of such a reserve would be—generally, programs like the petroleum reserve are used by the federal government to even out price fluctuations, or to ensure access to important assets in the event of wars or other emergencies[3]—it would mean that the government would start buying and selling Bitcoin, potentially driving up demand (and the price), and moving us closer to the future predicted in the original narrative of cryptocurrency. If the idea is that digital, decentralized currencies are going to replace government-issued fiat currencies, getting the government that issues the world's reserve currency on board is an important step forward.

Even before 2024, there had been movement toward the mainstreaming of Bitcoin and other cryptocurrencies, with Wall Street firms starting to offer products derived from price fluctuations in cryptocurrencies, even if they weren't offering the assets directly. This meant that investors could start buying into crypto at the same place that they were making their other investments, making them just another part of a portfolio. Indeed, banks and investment firms had already been buying into cryptocurrencies (if not the seedy underbelly of memecoins): for them, the volatility in the prices represents profit potential as they do with any other asset.

While much of the narrative underlying and motivating cryptocurrencies is tied to the fact that it's outside of government regulation—courts don't have to enforce smart contracts!—crypto advocates and larger firms have been pushing for greater regulation, on the theory that it will make it more attractive as an investment for a larger swath of buyers. Regulating crypto markets would help to drive out some of the scams, and the presence of rules would also likely mean recourse from investors if they were to lose money because of bad behaviors that would be illegal in other markets. Since cryptocurrencies are rarely being used like currencies (for buying and selling of other goods), and because they're not based on any real underlying asset, increases in their prices are entirely driven by the belief that the price will go up. For the price to go up, one of two things has to happen: either individuals who already own cryptocurrencies have to buy more of them, or new people have to be brought into the market. The latter is, perhaps, why crypto markets have been so keen to get some kind of regulatory imprimatur, so that investors who are potentially interested in crypto, but have been put off by the complexity and risk of buying it, will be more willing to jump in. We have, after all, seen this kind of attempt at market expansion before, in the Super Bowl ads urging men not to be left behind, in hiring Kardashians to try and reach out to women.

There are limits to the extent to which this strategy can work. The more money that's tied up in crypto assets, the more money it takes to drive the price up even further: at a certain point, increased investment in crypto isn't going to do anything to increase the price, blunting the appeal of the currencies as a tool for generating returns.[4] At that point, believers in the system would argue that cryptocurrencies would continue to attract individuals looking for a safe place to store their money, without the possibility of devaluation due to inflation, and others would be more likely to use cryptocurrency for its original intended purpose of buying goods and services (if the expectation is that the price of currency is going to increase, making everything that might be bought relatively cheaper, it makes little sense to cash out to buy a pizza).

While all of this seems like it would be a good outcome for believers in cryptocurrency, this kind of mainstreaming is also likely to blunt its appeal. As we've seen, much of the reason why men buy cryptocurrency is because it serves as a credible marker of technical prowess: the fact that the markets are difficult and risky, the fact that they are the underdogs struggling against what they see as an oppressive system of fiat currencies, these are part of the appeal. If anyone can easily buy into crypto, if the regulation smooths the edges off the market, if people are just holding it their 401(k)s, it loses much of its symbolic appeal. That might not matter so long as the price continues to rise, but as the example of meme stocks shows, there's nothing magic about cryptocurrencies that makes them the only way in which technical masculinities can be harnessed to increase the price of an asset. As crypto becomes less exciting, there's no reason to think that the people currently holding it will move on to some other asset or behavior that allows them to perform masculinities.

It's hard to imagine that the seediest elements in cryptocurrency markets—the sketchy slot machines that are meme coins—will achieve this level of acceptance and integration into financial markets. If regulation suffers them to exist, they might well remain a way for men to demonstrate technical masculinities, but the appeal of these assets has always been limited, with the big money always having gone into the bigger currencies like Bitcoin and Ethereum. Bitcoin and similar currencies matter not just because they demonstrate how men can use finance to perform some kinds of masculinities, but because they're owned by tens of millions of people, because they've become somewhat integrated into financial markets, and because they're simply too big to ignore. A small group of mostly men buying dubious assets online because they think they're funny, or because Andrew Tate told them to, is more akin to men's performances around craft beer or videogames: something people outside of the group can safely put out of their minds.

Are LLMs the Next Frontier?

In recent days, the furor over cryptocurrency has been replaced, in part, by the widespread adoption of generative large language models (LLMs), often referred to as AI. While it is far too early to know how the current spate of LLMs will shake out, there are some indications that they may be serving much the same function as cryptocurrency and meme stocks have. Individuals who come up with novel or interesting ways to get the LLMs to produce imagery or text have taken to calling themselves "prompt engineers" and sell their services online. Message boards fill up with people—mostly men—sharing their tips for how to get the LLMs to produce what they want, and sharing their best results (as well as, less often, their failures).

Like cryptocurrency and meme stocks, the nascent narrative underlying AI is about individuals being able to seize power from institutions and the powerful. In the past, the ability to create the sort of imagery outputted by the LLMs was restricted to a small group of people with years of training and experience. Now, individuals can use their mastery of computers and coding to get similar results. This narrative also excuses the widespread problems with copyright violations: corporations and rich content creators[5] want to keep their content locked up and force others to pay for it, while LLMs want to make it free and accessible to everyone.

Just as the narrative of cryptocurrencies holds that current adopters are part of the march toward an inevitable future where they'll be validated, and their technology will be dominant over existing institutions, LLM users look for a future dominated by general artificial intelligence. In such a future— seemingly always a few years down the line—the models will solve problems like hallucinations,[6] and computers will outstrip human intelligence and creativity. Other problems—like the use of energy and water for the servers powering LLMs, which outstrip the sizeable demands of crypto processing—will be solved by new technologies invented by the LLMs themselves.

A heroic narrative, plus a way to display mastery in an online community, plus the potential to make money from the products generated by the LLMs, together, would seem to indicate that LLMs could appeal to the same audience using crypto as a way of performing masculinity. However, there are some reasons to think that LLMs are unlikely to take over for crypto as a dominant means of displaying technical masculinities. One is that the use of LLMs is just not as complicated: people with strong coding or prompt engineering skills can get marginally better outputs, but not that much better than those provided to people with minimal skills. As such, it's harder to give a clear demonstration of skill. In addition, the stakes are relatively lower: subscriptions to current LLMs can be expensive, but not terribly so, meaning the buying into them is less of a credible commitment to a community than buying crypto or meme stocks is. While there is a path to making money through LLMs, it comes from using them to generate valuable content. In some cases, this might be a valid business model, but any business model is more complex than watching the price of a memecoin or stock go up or down.

The use of LLMs also doesn't provide any way for men to demonstrate other masculine traits like tenacity or fortitude. The volatility of crypto and meme stocks provides ample opportunity to commiserate over downturns and highlight rationality and endurance by staying put, or even buying more. With LLMs, there just isn't any such opportunity, making them less valuable as a masculinity display than crypto, meme stocks, or even other activities, like sports betting.

What Does a Reordering Look Like?

In earlier chapters, I talked about how the gender hierarchy had been upset in other countries: corporate, knowledge-based masculinities supplanting traditional rural masculinities in Ireland, for example. If it has happened in other countries, it can certainly happen here as well, but what would such a reordering of the gender hierarchy look like?

I would not expect men who base their performance of gender around currently hegemonic forms of masculinity to suddenly change. Rather, I'd expect something like a secular realignment, happening gradually through differential socialization patterns among young men and boys. Much of the work of adolescence for boys is to try out different performances of gender to see what works for them, a process that is driven in great part by feedback from their peers (Rogers, Nielson, & Santos 2021). What would be expected, then, is for boys to get more positive feedback and acceptance from their peers when they make use of technical masculinities than when they perform traits associated with currently hegemonic forms. Being good at coding, for instance, might get more positive feedback than joining a sports team. Even these sorts of outcomes are unlikely to be experienced evenly across a society, and the dynamics could look very different across regions, or even across schools.

As these boys age, it creates positive feedback loops, such that more men are performing technical masculinities, making them more acceptable to boys looking for guidance on how to be a man, creating greater pressure among peer groups to carry out this kind of performance. Data on the habits of minors is hard to come by, but what research has been done on how and why boys engage with crypto (Boumas-Sims et al. 2024, for instance) indicates that this process may already be underway.

While it's reasonable to be skeptical about cryptocurrency and meme stock trading in general, there are ways in which gender performances built around technical masculinities might be a positive for young men. While boys have started to lag behind girls in education in the United States, researchers have argued that this gap is less about sex than it is about gender, with different performances of masculinity and femininity leading to very different educational outcomes (Yu, McLellan, & Winter 2021; Van Houtte 2023). Privileging performances of masculinity that are more aligned with success in school could push boys to do better, especially in areas that can be plausibly linked with technical masculinities. Put another way, if nerds are seen as masculine, more boys are going to try to be nerdy.

However, such pressure to do better in school has to contend with the anti-institutional views that are currently part of crypto communities. While the online forums that are the dominant source of information about crypto meme stocks and the like privilege knowledge and mastery, they also contend that existing institutions—corporations, governments, and schools—are hopelessly corrupt or outdated. Being smart may be good, but being a smart dropout, like Mark Zuckerberg or Bill Gates, is even better. Attempts to leverage aspirations toward technical masculinities with education will have to somehow cope with this disconnect.

Another potential downside for this comes from how it impacts girls. Despite years of effort on the part of educational institutions, girls still lag in their interest and engagement in science, engineering, and math. Linking these fields with dominant forms of masculinity is likely to make them less attractive to some girls and increase the likelihood that men will police their entry into these fields (even more than they currently do). As with craft beer, once an area is defined as being masculine, men in that area will be motivated to enforce a norm of "no girls allowed."

To the extent that technical masculinities seriously challenge currently dominant performances of masculinity, I would also expect some pushback. This sort of pushback commonly takes the form of incorporating important aspects of the upstart performances into hegemonic performances, in much the same way that hegemonic forms of masculinity borrow behaviors from marginalized masculinities. Given the corporate flavor of dominant forms of masculinity, some elements of technical masculinities can likely be incorporated without too much trouble. For instance, linking technical skills to success in the sorts of institutions that the manosphere is suspicious of, like banks, hedge funds, and corporations, rather than opposition to these institutions, would serve to incorporate technical performances into hegemonic forms, rather than into opposition to them. This might mean decentralizing the traits that are currently seen as useful for success in these institutions, like aggression and instincts, but there's enough crossover to make for a plausible case.

In addition, the pushback could take the form of arguments as to why technical masculinities fail to demonstrate why men should hold a dominant role in society: pointing out that most owners of crypto or meme stocks don't actually make money, that they're being duped, could serve this end. If the ways in which men performing technical masculinities aren't really displaying desirable traits, and are just being taken advantage of, it's hard to argue that these performances should be aspirational. Women, or men from marginalized groups, becoming more visible in these markets could serve much the same function: it's hard to make the case that technical masculinities explain dominance over groups who are carrying out the same performances.

Just as the rise of technical masculinities was prefigured by media representations, we'd expect the backlash to be visible in the same way. The trend in recent years has been for the Tony Starks and Mark Zuckerbergs to be the heroes of the story, triumphing against bigger, stronger, more traditionally masculine opponents by virtue of their technical prowess. A backlash would likely see a reversal, with the Thors and Winklevosses of the world being shown as the role models because of their superior masculine traits.

A society in which boys are competing to see who's better in math because they believe that will get them money or sexual access to women doesn't seem that bad, but there are real concerns associated with it. Primary among these is the association of technical masculinity displays with the broader manosphere. The displays of technical masculinities discussed here are very much built to appeal to other men in online forums, and the entanglement of these forums means that discussions of crypto or meme stocks are linked with the overt misogyny of pick-up artists or problematic influencers like Jordan Peterson or Joe Rogan. Even if individual elements of these performances aren't that problematic, the overall package is rather more troubling. The anti-institutional nature of that package—part of the legacy of current technical masculinities as a form of protest masculinity—also tends to discourage young men from activities that are likely to be much more useful to them, like higher education and prudent investments. A pure form of technical masculinities, one that eschewed the misogyny of the manosphere and the self-defeating anti-institutionalism of crypto and meme stocks wouldn't necessarily be a bad thing, but that's not the form that seems likely to become dominant.

What Is To Be Done?

It's easy to look at research like this and decide that the goal should be to change men. After all, young men's attempts to perform the types of masculinities being defined by the manosphere are leading them to all sorts of maladaptive behaviors. As reprehensible as some of the rhetoric that comes out of these websites is, we can see these young men as victims, people who are flailing about looking for any way that they can meet the increasingly unrealistic demands of societally dominant forms of masculinity. At the same time, they're often engaging in sexist behaviors that make others the victims of the toxic soup they're swimming in. All of these problems could be fixed if men were to stop worrying about performing masculinities, to stop worrying about where they are in the gender hierarchy. The goal, it seems, should be for men to just stop caring about this gendered hierarchy.

However, the leading scholars of masculinities argue that it isn't nearly this simple (Connell 1995, 220–4; Messerschmidt 2018). Gender is deeply ingrained in human social behaviors, in the way that people are raised and socialized, and even if gender is entirely learned, and not driven at all by biological factors like genes and hormones (a straw man that few today would seriously contend), gender performances are not going to go away. At best, efforts like this are likely to lead to what Messerschmidt calls "exit politics," as men performatively claim to divest themselves of male privilege, but as the work on hybrid masculinities has shown, such divestments often just serve to reinforce the existing hierarchies.

It doesn't seem likely that men will stop performing masculinities, but it may be possible to even out the gender hierarchy, such that the gap between dominant performances and other performances isn't so big, making the stakes lower.

A world in which the masculinities performed by marginalized groups aren't valued much less than those performed by dominant ones is one in which men feel that they have more options, that they can be successful without meeting demands that range from unrealistic to impossible. It isn't enough to replace male role models in media with a new type of role model, replace one form of dominant masculinity with another. Rather, the best outcome is a world in which there are a variety of acceptable role models and masculinity performances available to boys and have all of those be seen as viable ways of being a man.

In some ways, a society in which there is conflict over the dominant form of masculinity is one that is more friendly to men in general. If the dominant form of masculinity is being contested, then there are necessarily more ways to be a man in a way that is socially valued (at least in some circles). This could reduce the stakes for boys and men trying to perform their gender identity, opening up new ways for them to embrace their gender identities, similar to how some scholars argue that women have more avenues for performing femininity now than they did in the past. If there are lower stakes, there's less call for protest masculinities, and perhaps the opportunity to split off performances of technical masculinities from the problematic elements brought into them by the association with protest masculinity.

Masculinity is not monolithic, and contrary to the claims that masculine traits have been stable throughout history—that the ones valued now are the same ones valued by the Spartans, or the Romans, or the generation that fought the Second World War—masculinity is fantastically adaptable. Research I coauthored on cooking (Besen-Cassino & Cassino 2014), for example, showed how a change in the way cooking was presented in pop culture, from a feminine activity to a risky, skill-based masculine one involving technical skills and fire, transformed the relationship between men and cooking in the United States over the course of just a few years. In that time, cooking went from something men would avoid when they felt their masculinity was threatened to something that they would embrace as a way to perform masculinity. If *Iron Chef* and Gordon Ramsay can change the way American men think about cooking, society can change the way that men construct technical masculinities, stripping out misogyny and gambling, and keeping the parts that can actually help men thrive. It's possible to reduce the stakes, make men happier and more secure, and, in doing so, make the world safer and more welcoming to all kinds of people: only by taking men and their masculinities seriously.

Methodological Appendix

Required notice: Data for this publication is derived from surveys administered by the Understanding America Study, which is maintained by the Center for Economic and Social Research (CESR) at the University of Southern California. Funding for this data collection was provided by the Social Security Administration and the National Institute on Aging through the grant U01AG054580 "Toward Next Generation Data on Health and Life Changes at Older Ages" (Kapteyn, PI). The project was reviewed and approved by BRANY IRB (22-030-1044). The content of this paper is solely the responsibility of the authors and does not necessarily represent the official views of USC or CESR.

The text makes repeated references to a number of surveys; details of each can be found in Table M1.

Chapter 1

The five-item version of the Masculine Role Norms Inventory (MRNI-VB) used in the book are presented here, along with the introduction to them used in the survey.

Gender roles in the United States have been changing rapidly, and we'd like to hear what you think about how men should act today. For each of the following statements, tell me whether you strongly agree or disagree, agree or disagree but not strongly, or have no opinion.

Men should watch football games instead of soap operas.
Boys should prefer to play with trucks rather than dolls.
A man should always be the boss.
I think a young man should try to be physically tough, even if he's not big.
Men should not be too quick to tell others that they care about them.
Overall responses to the MRNI-VB in the August 2024 survey can be found in Table M2.

Table M1 List of Surveys Referenced in Text

Study	Chapters used	Modality	Sample size	Population	Notes
August 2024 national survey	1, 4, 5	Live Caller + TTW	806	US Residents	Includes PGSI
December 2022 Survey of young men	3, 5	Online – multistream	1,681	Men 18–30 in US	Random assignment to modules
February 2023 poll	3	Live caller + TTW	801	New Jersey residents	Includes order experiment
March 2024 newark survey	3	TTW	1,100	Newark residents	Includes Black oversample
August 2023 national survey	3	live caller + TTW	806	US Likely primary voters	Includes priming experiment
UAS 278 (Jan–Feb 2021)	6	Online panel	6,301	US residents	
UAS 287 (Dec 2020–Feb 2021)	6	Online panel	1,001	US residents	Risk taking experiment
UAS 378 (May–June 2021)	6	Online panel	2,510	US residents	Financial literacy questions

Table M2 Overall Responses to MRNI-VB, August 2024 Survey

	Strongly agree	Agree	No opinion	Disagree	Strongly disagree
Men should watch football	9%	12%	32%	28%	20%
Boys should prefer trucks	17%	19%	24%	22%	19%
A man should be the boss	4%	5%	12%	35%	45%
Young men should be tough	11%	23%	19%	27%	20%
Should not be too quick to care	5%	11%	20%	35%	29%

Table M3 Percent Agree or Strongly Agree to MRNI-VB Items by Sex and Age, August 2024 Survey

	Men 18–30	Men 31–44	Men 45–64	Men 65+	Women
Men should watch football	15%	26%	29%	36%	15%
Boys should prefer trucks	44%	48%	46%	45%	26%
A man should be the boss	23%	19%	4%	11%	5%
Young men should be tough	59%	54%	40%	35%	25%
Should not be too quick to care	21%	25%	11%	23%	13%

These results indicate the extent to which gender role norms among men are strongest with regard to child rearing (the toughness and play items), but there is substantial variance on all of them, even those that seem very outdated.

The age dynamics, as shown among men in Table M3, are also telling: on some of these items, young men have rates of agreement very similar to those of older men, with middle-aged men being the least likely to endorse traditional masculinity norms.

The same dynamic is clear in the mean MRNI scores, as shown in Table M4. Also interesting is the shift in variance: among younger men, the high standard error is driven by big gaps between groups of men holding more traditional attitudes and everyone else. These young men endorsing traditional views of masculinity drive many of the results in this book.

Table M4 Mean MRNI Score by Sex and Age, August 2024 Survey

	Mean MRNI score	Std error
Men 18–30	9.1	0.6
Men 31–44	9.2	0.6
Men 45–64	8.0	0.3
Men 65+	9.4	0.5
Women	6.5	0.2

Chapter 3

Details of Regression Analysis of Survey of Young men

The logit model predicting crypto ownership in the December 2022 survey of young men has a sample size of 526 (respondents were randomly assigned to modules, so not all respondents got the cryptocurrency questions; this also limits the use of some non-demographic controls, like party identification).

In the survey overall, 43 percent of respondents said that they had "ever owned any cryptocurrency, NFTs, or other similar digital products." Forty-nine percent said that they had not, 8 percent said that they didn't know what those were, and one respondent refused to answer the question.

Note that in these models—as in most of the later regressions—the Masculinity Gap variable represents the interaction of MRNI scores and masculinity (though masculinity scores are generally brought in as a dichotomous completely masculine or not completely masculine variable, rather than in a continuous form, as in this analysis, due to data availability).

These results, as presented in Table M5, are robust to the addition or removal of control variables. For instance, if the femininity self-placement is removed from the model, the gap variable has a coefficient of 0.86 (std error 0.35), and the masculinity variable has a coefficient of 0.011 (std error 0.005). The inclusion of the Gap variable and the Masculinity variable means that MRNI measure cannot be included in this model, as it is collinear with the combination of Masculinity and the Gap. If the Gap variable is not included, and both MRNI score and Masculinity self-placement are, both Masculinity and MRNI score are significant, in the expected direction (higher values mean greater likelihood of owning crypto).

Table M5 Regression Results for Crypto Ownership, Survey of Young Men

	Coef	Std error	Z
MRNI/masculinity gap	0.78*	0.35	2.19
Masculinity	0.02*	0.01	3.51
Femininity	0.01*	0.00	3.49
Age Category (18–21 baseline)			
22 to 25	0.63*	0.24	2.69
26 to 30	0.91*	0.24	3.86
White?	0.37	0.32	1.13
Black	0.31	0.34	0.90
Hispanic	0.02	0.37	0.05
Constant	–2.75	0.60	–4.62

Chapter 4

In addition to the results presented in the text, regression analysis was used to confirm the results of the effects of men's gender identities on their likelihood of buying individual stocks (with the outcome being the reported purchases, a dichotomous outcome, and therefore modelled with logit). The first such analysis uses the respondent's asserted gender identity (in categorical form, as elsewhere) and their MRNI score in a logit model.

Controls in this model, shown in Table M6, include age (four categories, from eighteen to twenty-nine at one, to sixty-five and above at four), education (whether the respondent has a four-year college degree or not: 39 percent do), race or ethnicity (with non-Hispanic white as the baseline category) and MRNI score (total score included as a scalar). The model has a sample size of 732 (out of the 801 total in the sample; missing data comes largely from the MRNI, as anyone who refused to answer any of the MRNI items lacks an overall score) and a pseudo r^2 of 0.11.

In this model, men who say that they're something other than completely masculine are more likely to say that they have bought individual stocks than "completely masculine" men, with an expected gap of 13 percentage points (32 percent vs 19 percent). There is no significant gap based on gender among women. Both categories of women are expected to have about a 13 percent chance of buying individual stocks, on the border of being significantly different from "completely masculine" men, but not different from each other. At the

Table M6 Regression Results for Buying Individual Stocks, August 2024 survey, Model One

	Buying individual stocks		
	Coef	Std error	Z
Other man	0.707*	0.264	2.68
Feminine woman	−0.553	0.310	−1.78
Other woman	−0.439	0.321	−1.37
Age	−0.481*	0.105	−4.59
Education	0.696*	0.212	3.29
Black	−0.295	0.357	−0.83
Hispanic/Latino	0.126	0.292	0.43
Other Race/Ethnic	0.850	0.603	1.41
MRNI	0.069*	0.024	2.88
Constant	−1.766	0.536	−3.30

same time, MRNI scores have a significant effect on the probability of buying individual stocks, moving from an expected probability of 13 percent at the low end of the scale to 33 percent at the high end of the scale, controlling for other factors. The expected gap between the 25th percentile (an MRNI of four) and the 75th percentile (ten) is about six points (15 percent vs 21 percent).

Of course, we are more concerned with the interaction of asserted gender identity and MRNI scores, so an additional model was used to look at the effects of being in the masculinity gap on the probability of trading individual stocks. This model, presented in Table M7, had the same sample size as the previous model and a pseudo r^2 of 0.11.

In this model, controlling for other factors (including MRNI score), men are more likely than women to report buying individual stocks, but men in the gender gap are more likely to do so than other men. Controlling for other factors, 33 percent of men in the gender gap say that they've bought individual stocks, compared with 24 percent of men not in the gender gap and just 14 percent of women. Age and education also prove to be important factors: only 10 percent of respondents 65 and over are expected to have traded individual stocks, compared with 32 percent of those aged thirty and younger. Respondents with a college degree are about ten points more likely than other respondents to report having traded individual stocks. These results support the argument in the main text that stock buying activities are driven by the gap between valuing of masculinity and asserted masculinity among men.

Table M7 Regression Results for Buying Individual Stocks, August 2024 survey, Model Two

	Buying individual stocks		
	Coef	**Std error**	**Z**
Men in gap	1.510*	0.453	3.33
Men not in gap	1.001*	0.383	2.61
Women	0.291	0.394	0.74
Age	−0.509*	0.102	−4.98
Education	0.679*	0.209	3.25
Black	−0.340	0.355	−0.96
Hispanic/Latino	0.104	0.289	0.36
Other Race/Ethnic	0.809	0.604	1.34
MRNI	0.037	0.024	1.50
Constant	−2.137	0.525	−4.07

Chapter 5

Survey of Young Men

The 2022 survey of men aged eighteen to thirty and under was carried out in December 2022 using a multi-stream online survey in which respondents were recruited from various online survey platforms and given a small reward (about $2, depending on the platform) for their participation. Overall, 1,681 men completed the survey. Respondents were randomly assigned to complete various modules within the survey, so not everyone answered questions about stocks, meme stocks, or gender identity. The sample was divided equally between respondents aged 18 to 21 (558), 22 to 25 (572), and 26 to 30 (551), and was 40 percent white, 27 percent Black, and 19 percent Hispanic or Latino. Eighteen percent said that they had completed a four-year college degree, and 8 percent said that they had completed an advanced degree, with a substantial number still in school. Forty percent of respondents who answered the MRNI and masculinity-femininity items were in the masculinity gap.

To confirm the results of the crosstabs shown in the main text, logit regressions, shown in Table M8, were used to look at the effect of being in the masculinity gap on men's likelihood of buying stocks and buying meme stocks. Controls included age (with eighteen- to twenty-one year olds as the excluded baseline), education level, and dummies for race.

Table M8 Regression Results for Stock Buying Behaviors, 2022 Survey of Young men

	Buying individual stocks			Buying meme stocks		
	Coef	Std error	Z	Coef	Std error	Z
Men not in gap	−0.385*	0.148	−2.60	−0.593*	0.175	−3.39
Age 21–25	0.165	0.183	0.90	0.443*	0.225	1.97
Age 26–30	0.347	0.189	1.84	0.529*	0.231	2.29
Education	0.233*	0.042	5.49	0.109*	0.050	2.19
White	0.405	0.241	1.68	0.482	0.295	1.63
Black	0.574*	0.253	2.27	0.569	0.308	1.85
Hispanic/Latino	0.399	0.273	1.46	0.566	0.335	1.69
Constant	−1.260	0.279	−4.52	−1.191	0.336	−3.54

In the regression models, men in the masculinity gap are significantly more likely to report buying individual stocks and buying meme stocks than men who are not in the masculinity gap. With the controls included, men in the masculinity gap are expected to be about nine points more likely to say that they have bought stocks than men not in the gap (55 vs 46 percent), and fourteen points more likely to say that they have bought a meme stock (51 vs 37 percent). Including asserted masculinity or MRNI scores as controls do not make a substantial difference in the results.

August 2024 Survey

Data from the August 2024 National survey was used to analyze the effect of being in the masculinity gap on the likelihood that an individual reported buying individual stocks. As shown in Table M9, MRNI is included in one of the models as a continuous variable to show how its inclusion does not substantially change the effects of being in the gender gap on the reported behavior.

Chapter 6

Financial Knowledge and Preferences Analysis

The data for the financial knowledge and preferences analysis comes from the Understanding America Study, survey 378, carried out May 13, 2021, through

Table M9 Regression Results for Stock Buying Behaviors, August 2024 National Survey, with and without MRNI Included as Control

	Buying individual stocks			Buying individual stocks		
	Coef	Std error	Z	Coef	Std error	Z
Men in gap	1.870*	0.411	4.55	1.510*	0.453	3.33
Men not in gap	1.328*	0.364	3.65	1.001*	0.383	2.61
Women	0.499	0.381	1.31	0.291	0.394	0.74
Age	−0.484*	0.100	−4.86	−0.509*	0.102	−4.98
Education	0.582*	0.200	2.90	0.679*	0.209	3.25
Black	−0.229	0.342	−0.67	−0.340	0.355	−0.96
Hispanic/Latino	0.133	0.279	0.48	0.104	0.289	0.36
Other Race/Ethnic	0.794	0.598	1.33	0.809	0.604	1.34
MRNI	–	–	–	0.037	0.024	1.50
Constant	−2.010	0.498	−4.03	−2.137	0.525	−4.07

June 20, 2021. As in the risk study, this data was merged with UAS survey 287 (December 21, 2020–February 1, 2021): a total of 2,282 respondents answered both surveys, out of the 2,470 who completed survey 287. Non-randomness in survey attrition is always a potential concern, but the relatively close field dates of these surveys, combined with a greater than 90 percent crossover, indicates that it is probably not a serious concern in this analysis. Respondents were paid $12 for completing UAS 378.

UAS 378 included five scenarios in which respondents were asked to answer questions about finance: the data used here are from one leg of an experiment embedded in the survey. The experiment assigned respondents to answer the questions after receiving a short narrative that was designed to teach them some of the concepts included in the questions (e.g., about compound interest). To see the effects of these instructional narratives, the experimenters also included control conditions, in which the respondents answered without first seeing the instructional narratives: it's these control conditions that the analysis here is drawn from, as the sample size is large enough (more than 2,000) that adding more data wouldn't be particularly useful, and the contamination from the instructional narrative effects isn't worth it.

Three of them (discussed in the main text) were asked of all respondents. The other three were asked of half of the respondents. Of these three questions, one (a scenario about buying power decreasing when inflation outstrips investment returns) had an objectively correct answer. This scenario had answers very similar to the other scenarios: 55 percent gave the correct answer, and other men were 5 percentage points more likely than "completely masculine" men to answer correctly.

Of the other two scenarios, one did not have an objectively correct answer. The scenario asked whether a bonus should be invested for retirement in the stock of the employer, a sector-based stock index fund, or a diversified index fund. While the last of these choices is certainly the safest, the question is multidimensional, especially since the option to invest in the company that the individual in the scenario works for is said to give them a stake in the success of their employer. If we were to assume that the reference to retirement savings means that respondents should pick the safest investment, the diversified portfolio option is correct, and other men were four points more likely than "completely masculine" men to pick it (70 percent vs 66 percent; 59 percent for women with no gender differences).

The final scenario asked respondents to calculate the return of a $1,000 investment, earning 7 percent annual returns over twenty years, and asked if the investment would go up by 2x, 3x, or 10x. Given that the correct answer is 7.6x, 10x is probably the best answer, but none of them are correct, and it's much harder than the other questions: 3x was the most popular choice (33 percent), but 18 percent chose 10x, and 20 percent chose 2x. Twenty-nine percent picked the "don't know" option, much higher than in any of the other scenarios. On this item, Other Men were 4 percentage points more likely than other groups to pick the 3x answer than Completely Masculine Men, and four points *less* likely to pick the Don't Know option.

The unclear correct answers and smaller sample sizes on these items lead me to set them aside from the main analysis, but the results from them are consistent with the results presented in the main text.

Day-to-Day Financial Matters

As with the other analyses, I check the results of the crosstabs on interest in quotidian financial matters, using regression analysis—in this case, ordered logit—to control for potential confounding factors, as shown in Table M10.

In both models, respondents who gave "don't know" or refused responses were omitted from the analysis. Sample size of the first model is 2,355, with a pseudo r^2 of 0.04. In the first model, looking at stated interest in day-to-day financial matters, Other Men are significantly less likely to say that they "Strongly Agree"

Table M10 Regression Results for Interest in Day-to-Day Financial Matters

	Day-to-day matters			Tracks household spending		
	Coef	**Std error**	**Z**	**Coef**	**Std error**	**Z**
Other man	−0.269*	0.134	−2.00	0.247	0.137	1.80
Feminine woman	0.296*	0.096	3.09	−0.058	0.096	−0.61
Other woman	0.099	0.118	0.84	0.169	0.119	1.42
Age	0.023*	0.006	4.11	−0.015*	0.006	−2.67
Education	0.154*	0.020	7.71	−0.046*	0.020	−2.29
White	0.212	0.169	1.25	0.029	0.173	0.17
Black	−0.090	0.202	−0.45	0.111	0.209	0.53
Hispanic/Latino	−0.094	0.165	−0.57	0.143	0.174	0.82
Working?	−0.045*	0.095	−0.47	0.050	0.095	0.53
HH Income	0.092*	0.012	7.47	−0.003	0.013	−0.26

that they're good at dealing with day-to-day financial matters, with a predicted gap of about six points (37 percent vs 43 percent). "Completely feminine" women are more likely than any other sex or gender group to "Strongly Agree," with 50 percent expected to do so controlling for other factors. These gaps are very much in line with those seen in the crosstabs.

The second model looks at responses to how often the respondent tracks their household spending. The sample size of this model is 2,227, with a pseudo r^2 of 0.01. Older people and more educated people are more likely to say that they track their spending frequently (are less likely to be on the high, or "never" side of the scale), but there are no significant effects of sex or gender.

In the survey, there are two other items that are close to measuring interest in day-to-day finances but were not included in the main text. The first asks if respondents have ever taken part in a financial education class: 28 percent of respondents said that they had, with men being more likely to do so than women, but no difference in either the crosstabs or the regressions between "completely masculine" men and other men. Results for this item are questionable, as 62 percent of respondents (including 66 percent of women and 57 percent of men) say that they have never been offered such a class: among those who have been offered a class, men and women are about equally likely to have taken it.

The other item asks if respondents find that thinking about finances makes them anxious. Responses are on a seven-point strongly agree to strongly disagree scale, with 5 percent strongly agreeing and 15 percent strongly disagreeing. This item was not used because (1) it is not clearly about day-to-day financial matters, and (2) the issue of anxiety comes too close to the construct of gender role strain. In the crosstabs, women are much more likely than men to agree that thinking about finances makes them anxious, and less likely to disagree. Respondents in the Other Women category are the most likely to agree, with 20 percent in the agree/strongly agree categories, compared with 11 percent among men (across gender categories). These differences hold up in the regression analysis (using the same model as above), with women (in both gender categories) being significantly higher on the agree scale than the baseline category of Completely Masculine men, and Other men not being significantly different. As might be expected, household income and age are the biggest predictors of this kind of anxiety. So, while it doesn't fit in well enough to be included in the main analysis, there's nothing in either of the questions not used there that are at odds with the narrative presented in the text.

Risk Experiment

The coin-flip risk-taking experiment is from the Understanding America Study, survey 287 (December 21, 2020–February 1, 2021). For the analysis here, it was merged with UAS survey 278 (January 6, 2021–February 2, 2021) because of the overlap in the survey frames (which was entirely coincidental), nearly all of the respondents who answered one of these surveys also answered the other: nearly 90 percent (88.6 percent) of respondents to survey 278 also responses to survey 287, mitigating potential concerns about bias due to respondent mortality in longitudinal studies. Because of some missing data, the analyses have a total sample size of 868.

Overall, respondents took the risky side of the bet 48.8 percent of the time, with a standard deviation of 11.2 points. Results cluster around the 50 percent mark: only 10 percent of respondents took the risky bet more than 60 percent of the time, and only 16 percent took it less than 40 percent of the time.

The safe bet in these questions has a base amount of $3.40, with a variance of $0.25 (so only a quarter of offers were less than $3.15 and only a quarter were offered more than $3.65). The payoffs for the risky option had a baseline level that averaged out to $3.40, but were similarly moved up or down by a random value with a variance of $0.25. The options were not designed to be precisely equivalent but are close to it. Responses were grouped according to when in the study they were taken. Even though respondents were required to answer

Table M11 Base Payoffs of Risky Bets by Round

Choices	Base low payoff	Base high payoff	Expected value
1–4	$ 2.00	$ 4.80	$ 3.40
5–8	$ 2.25	$ 4.65	$ 3.45
9–12	$ 2.45	$ 4.65	$ 3.55
13–16	$ 2.30	$ 4.90	$ 3.60
17–20	$ 2.50	$ 4.50	$ 3.50

questions showing that they understood the questions, I expect some degree of a learning curve (hence the focus on the last ten choices they made, rather than the first ten). The stakes changed within the course of the study, with the gap between the good and bad outcomes of the risky bet moving up or down in blocks, and unevenly increasing as the rounds went on, lowest in the first eight rounds, and highest in rounds nine through sixteen. Overall, the expected payoff in the second half of the game is 10 cents higher than in the first half ($3.55 vs $3.45). Expected payoffs by round are shown in Table M11.

As in other analyses, the responses to sex (male or female, called "gender" in the dataset) were merged with the responses to the unidimensional masculinity-femininity item to create four categories: Completely Masculine Men, Other Men, Completely Feminine Women, and Other Women.

In the basic descriptive analysis, the difference between the overall percentage of risky bets taken by Other Men (50.2 percent) is significantly higher than that of Completely Masculine Men (47.9 percent; p<.05), but there is no such difference between Completely Feminine Women (49.0 percent) and Other Women (49.1 percent). However, the differences within sex groups by gender are not different within the first half of the study, which includes the lower expected value rounds: Other Men have a higher propensity to take the risky side of the bet (49.4 percent) than Completely Masculine Men (48.1 percent), but the gap is not significant (nor is it among women, where Other Women are just slightly higher than Completely Feminine Women). The biggest difference comes from the analysis of the second half of the study, which includes the higher expected value rounds. There, Other Men are 3.4 percentage points more likely to take the risky bet than Completely Masculine Men (51.0 percent vs 47.6 percent, p<.05). Again, there is no similar difference to be found among women, where Completely Feminine Women are actually slightly higher (by 0.5 percentage points) than Other Women.

Table M12 Percent Risky Bets Taken by Sex

	Percent risky	First half	Second half	Lower risk	Higher risk
Men	48.5%	48.4%	48.5%	48.4%	48.3%
Women	49.0%	48.8%	49.3%	49.3%	48.0%

There are no significant differences in any of the rounds or combinations of them based on the sex of the respondent. There are no significant gaps between men or women, overall, between the first and second halves of the experiment, or in the high versus low expected value rounds. The fact that we don't see sex differences even where the gender differences are substantial provides greater confidence that the behavior is being driven by gender, and masculinity in particular, rather than sex, as shown in Table M12.

For the regression analyses, a number of demographic controls were included, drawn from the characteristics recorded by the UAS, and updated annually by them (so, not asked in either of the particular surveys that the data was drawn from). These variables included age in years (with very little missing or refused data, which was dropped; mean of 53.6, std 15.4), education (16 point scale where HS graduate is 9, BA is 13, mean is 11.3), race (included as a series of dummy variables, white 86 percent, Black 9 percent, Hispanic/Latino 6 percent), whether the respondent is currently working or not (58 percent were), and household income (16 point scale, mean 11.5, std 3.9).

Full regression results for the three models (all bets, the lower stakes rounds and higher stakes rounds) are presented in Table M13 (with "completely masculine" men used as the baseline category for the sex-gender variable). Results presented make use of the survey weights, as recommended by UAS (but the results are not substantially different without the weights).

Including all of the listed controls, across all of the rounds, men who identify as anything other than "completely masculine" are 3.2 percentage points more likely to take the risky bet than "completely masculine" men, and if we focus on the riskiest rounds (nine through sixteen), the difference is 5.9 percentage points. In the low-risk rounds, there are no significant effects of masculinity-femininity by sex.

The coefficient of determination on all of these models is relatively low, as evidenced by the lack of significant control variables. Of the included variables, on whether or not the respondent is working has any effect, with employed respondents being more likely to take a risky bet (as might be expected). In light

Table M13 Regression Results for Percent Risky Bets Taken

	Overall			Low risk			High risk		
	Coef	Std error	T	Coef	Std error	T	Coef	Std error	T
Other man	0.032*	0.016	2.01	−0.001	0.025	−0.05	0.059*	0.026	2.30
Feminine Woman	0.018	0.013	1.36	0.012	0.020	0.63	0.031	0.021	1.51
Other woman	0.024	0.016	1.54	0.024	0.022	1.09	0.020	0.023	0.87
Age	0.000	0.000	1.21	0.000	0.001	−0.32	0.001	0.001	1.34
Education	0.000	0.003	0.07	0.001	0.004	0.39	−0.001	0.004	−0.27
White	0.013	0.016	0.8	−0.009	0.024	−0.39	0.033	0.029	1.17
Black	0.021	0.019	1.12	0.025	0.028	0.88	0.030	0.033	0.89
Hispanic/Latino	−0.008	0.016	−0.51	−0.035	0.023	−1.48	0.009	0.026	0.33
Working?	0.033*	0.011	3.12	0.030*	0.017	1.76	0.031*	0.018	1.75
HH Income?	−0.001	0.001	−0.91	−0.001	0.002	−0.37	−0.002	0.003	−0.82
Constant	0.435	0.038	11.4	0.477	0.055	8.73	0.414	0.061	6.80

of this, the strong and consistent effects of being in the other man category are even more notable. The fact that the coefficients mirror the results of the crosstabs fairly closely is a good indication that the effects of the masculinity-femininity by sex category are not being driven by variables that might correlate with them.

There are some concerns about the representativeness of the study: it is, after all, a longitudinal online panel. The mean age is rather higher than I would normally like to see, and the racial composition of the sample does not look much like that of the Unites States overall. However, since the purpose of this analysis is to look at the relationship between variables, rather than try and use the sample to establish facts about the population from which the sample is drawn, it is acceptable.

Chapter 6

The content analysis discussed in this chapter was carried out by my three fantastic undergraduate research assistants at Fairleigh Dickinson University in 2024: (in alphabetical order) Madalyn McEvoy, Deborah Solanke, and Ashley Sperduto.

They began by identifying web forums with discussions of cryptocurrency, with sources including Twitter/X, Instagram, TikTok, various subreddits discussed elsewhere in the text, and 4Chan. From these sites, they identified posts that had substantive discussion of cryptocurrencies and saved both the original posts and all substantive replies to those posts. They then used this initial batch of 100 posts to create fourteen preliminary coding categories.

Next, they threw out the initial batch of data (some of which is used for illustrative purposes in the text) and gathered a second batch of substantive posts and responses. They then worked to code each of these posts according to the preliminary categories, modifying the categories and definitions of them as they went in order to ensure that placement into the categories was clear to all of the coders and that the functional definitions were fully fleshed out. They continued this process until they hit a saturation point, where the posts being coded could be clearly identified as fitting into the categories without need for further alterations to those categories. After categories were combined or separated as necessary, this resulted in a final list of nineteen categories. Note that some of these categories— all relatively rare ones—were absent in the final round of coding.

In the third step, they threw out the data from the previous step (in order to ensure that the posts being coded fit into the categories, rather than having the categories modified to fit the posts, as in the first and second steps). They then began going through the forums listed on separate days, searching for posts about cryptocurrencies, then coding all of the responses to all posts that had substantive responses. The idea is to look not at what individuals initially post, but to look at how people responded to those posts, creating a back-and-forth discussion, rather than just a statement. The algorithms on these sites also ensure that posts which generate responses are given greater prominence, so the content being analyzed is more representative of what users would be likely to see than it would be if all posts were analyzed. For instance, a post on Reddit that is ignored is likely to fall out of the top of a sub-Reddit very quickly, while one that receives many responses is likely to be seen, and engaged with, by many more users in the forum, making it much more representative of the overall experience of users.

In the course of their work, the coders were able to identify patterns in postings that led them to believe that they were seeing posts made by bots, rather than authentic users. Most often, these took the form of posts urging users to look at content by a finance expert, and providing links to their work, without any real substantive engagement with the initial post. When the coders were confident that this content was from a bot, they left it out of the content analysis; when in doubt, they included it.

Each of the posts was independently coded by two of the research assistants, with the process continuing until they again hit a saturation point, at 485 posts coded. I did spot checking, independent coding 150 of the posts. Diagnostics for this final stage of coding show strong inter-rater reliability, with a percent agreement score of 83 percent and a Cohen's Kappa of 0.60 (representing a 60 percent increase in accuracy over that which would be expected by chance). Both of these figures are on the high end of the range considered acceptable for content analysis research.

I thank Madalyn, Deborah, and Ashley for their hard and careful work; this chapter would not have been possible without their efforts.

Coding Categories

1. Assertion of knowledge: instances where op or commenters share their knowledge or opinion and explain their methods or reasoning or back it up with "facts."

2. Unsupported assertions of knowledge: instances where op or commenters share their knowledge or opinion without explaining their methods and reasoning or backing it up with "facts."
3. Emasculating speech: op or commenters use language that attacks the perceived masculinity of another—including by way of homophobic or transphobic speech.
4. Community support: instances where commenters show support, understanding, and appreciation for op and each other.
5. Loyalty in crypto: instances where people support and defend specific companies, strategies, and crypto "idols" or "influencers" (i.e., Elon Musk, specific content creators).
6. "Bro" speech: instances where op or commenters use language indicating brotherhood.
7. Government and politics: instances mentioning government and politics in its relation to or impact on crypto or meme stock.
8. White supremacy: statements demeaning members of other races or ethnicities, or positive traits of whites.
9. Objectification, sexualization, and masculinization of women: instances putting women down by sexualizing them, disregarding their intelligence, or using feminine language in a derogatory way.
10. Questioning or demeaning intelligence: instances using verbiage demeaning questioning the intelligence of op or another poster.
11. Gambling/Taking Risks/Metaphor for Randomness: instances where investment is discussed in terms of playing a game, taking risks, or talked about like gambling. Also includes statements that crypto is a risk and investing is like playing at a casino; it's a game of chance.
12. Systematicity of gambling: falls more into the idea of playing the game and outsmarting the risks (like how people count cards to beat casinos) and showing off their rewards.
13. Negativity towards crypto: instances talking about the downfall or downsides of crypto.
14. Dissuading outsiders from investing: warning "normies" from getting involved or gatekeeping the community.
15. Suicidal or self-harm ideation or encouragement.
16. Economic disdain: where the current economy or traditional stocks or Wall Street is displayed as broken or rigid, typically by or because of older generations, the wealthy, and the banks—"rich get richer" mentality or underdogs fighting the system mentality.

Table M14 Frequency of Each Coding Category in the Overall Corpus

Supported assertions of knowledge	1	56	5%
Unsupported assertions of knowledge	2	121	10%
Emasculating speech	3	33	3%
Community support	4	167	14%
Loyalty in crypto	5	28	2%
"Bro" speech	6	21	2%
Government and politics	7	88	8%
White supremacy	8	2	0%
Objectification, sexualization, and masculinization of women	9	4	0%
Questioning or demeaning intelligence:	10	192	16%
Gambling/taking risks/metaphor for randomness	11	50	4%
Systematicity of gambling	12	16	1%
Negativity towards crypto	13	124	11%
Dissuading outsiders from investing	14	9	1%
Suicidal/self-harm ideation or encouragement	15	0	0%
Disdain for institutions	16	122	10%
Age aggression	17	7	1%
Scams/ warnings about scams	18	53	5%
Bragging about gains	19	74	6%

17. Age aggression: instances where speech targets age—typically anti-boomer and sometimes attacking people "too young" to understand.
18. Scams and warnings about scams: instances calling out certain cryptocurrencies or information as scams.
19. Bragging about gains: bragging about experience in crypto and wealth accumulation from crypto.

Chapter Seven

The questions used for the Problem Gambling Severity Index included in the August 2024 national FDU Survey were as follows:

In the last 12 months, how often …

… have you bet more than you could really afford to lose?

… have you needed to gamble with larger amounts of money to get the same feeling of excitement?

… have you gone back to try to win back the money you'd lost?

… have you borrowed money or sold anything to get money to gamble?

… have you felt that you might have a problem with gambling?

… have you felt that gambling has caused you any health problems, including stress or anxiety?

… have people criticized your betting, or told you that you have a gambling problem, whether or not you thought it is true?

… have you felt your gambling has caused financial problems for you or your household?

… have you felt guilty about the way you gamble or what happens when you gamble?

Responses for each of the items were Almost Always, Most of the Time, Sometimes, and Never. One point is awarded for each "sometimes" response, two points for a "most of the time," and three for an "almost always." The points are then totaled across all of the questions for the PGSI score. An individual who scores eight or above is said to be suffering gambling harm (or having a gambling problem).

Notes

1 "Do you even lift, bro?" Cryptocurrency and Technical Masculinities

1. Much of the research uses the term "hegemonic," rather than "dominant," but there is a distinction between the two that I'll talk about in Chapter 2.
2. "Rug pulls" are common crypto scams in which the founders of a coin abandon it, pocketing the money that's been put into it by others.
3. This is also, bizarrely, how the term is generally used in major surveys in political science and sociology.
4. Similar conceptions of masculinity have been referred to previously in the literature as "nerd masculinity" for reasons that will become apparent later.
5. Posters on both of these subreddits are also about 2.5 times as likely as the average Reddit user to post in forums supporting Bernie Sanders for President.
6. Users of the leading meme stock subreddit, r/wallstreetbets, are about four times as likely as the average user to post in major crypto forums, making them closely connected to this network as well.
7. Ging (2019b) lists five major content areas in the online manosphere: Men's Rights Activists, Men Going Their Own Way (anti-feminist, arguing for social separation between men and women), Pick-up Artists, Traditional Christian Conservatives, and Geek/Gamer Culture.
8. Posters on r/theredpill are six times as likely as the average Reddit user to post on subreddits for crypto markets, car sales, day trading and watches, and three times as likely to post on forums about the military shooter videogame "Call of Duty."
9. The film "Fight Club" also released in 1999, also comes up frequently in these forums, with users seeing it as a dramatization of the transition from a beta male (in the form of Ed Norton) to an alpha male (Brad Pitt).
10. Yes, in the later movies he has superpowers in the world outside of the Matrix as well, but, as a society, we've decided not to think too much about "The Matrix Revolutions."
11. The less said about the understanding of consent promulgated in these forums, the better.
12. This argument is also useful for explaining away failures of a purportedly unbeatable system: the individual failed because they stopped playing the game too early (perhaps even treating the woman in question as a human being).

13. Of course, it would be better to get direct measures of cryptocurrency ownership and activities, but the whole structure of cryptocurrency and related assets is designed to obfuscate who actually controls particular assets, making this nearly impossible.

14. Or, in the case of the BSRI, were seen as desirable traits for men or for women by Stanford undergraduates in the 1970s.

15. The two items asked about attitudes toward the Equal Rights Amendment and whether men wanted their wives to be virgins upon marriage. These questions didn't load neatly onto any of the identified dimensions in the factor analysis, leading the authors to conclude that men can hold traditional attitudes toward men's roles while also adopting more modern attitudes toward women.

16. This represents a slight simplification of the original form of the scale, which makes use of a seven-item response scale. This means that overall scores on the scales used here are not directly comparable with those that use the larger response scale, but also reduces the amount of time needed to complete the scales, an important consideration in non-dedicated telephone surveys.

17. The full scale is presented in the Methodological Appendix.

18. As his X/Twitter bio promises: "I unplug men from comforting lies, with cold, hard, uncomfortable truths about life & women."

2 "Have fun staying poor." Technical Masculinities and the Gender Hierarchy

1. This distinction between dominant masculinities and hegemonic masculinities is discussed in greater detail later in the chapter.

2. Howson (2006) offers an overlapping triad of breadwinning, heterosexuality, and aggression, though Messerschmidt (2018) argues that this set of traits might be better considered dominant without being hegemonic.

3. This represents a major split between forums like r/TRP and incel groups. Incels are much more likely to push for the system to be torn down completely, often by violent means. While others have been "red-pilled," incels talk about the "black pill": despair and acceptance that they'll never have a satisfying romantic relationship.

4. This is a very 1950s way to try and understand teenage delinquency, and this sort of phrasing is one of the unexpected joys of going this far back in the literature.

5. Anyone questioning how complex it could really be should ask a player how to resolve the order of instants and interrupts in the stack.

6. Proponents of inclusive masculinity theory might argue that the use of homophobic language isn't necessarily itself homophobic, if that language doesn't specifically

target gay people. However, the use of such language as derogatory, regardless of the target, certainly makes a prima facie case against the purported inclusivity of the people using it.

3 "Buy the dip!" Men and Cryptocurrencies

1. To be technical, he was downloading chances to buy the coin at the presale rate, something like a slot machine pull, or a loot box in an online game, adding an additional level of complexity to the whole enterprise. This has been referred to as "shitcoin roulette."
2. This is actually a subgenre of online discussions of crypto: men starting with a small amount of money, and documenting how they build their portfolios in order to reach some preset outcome, often a million dollars.
3. This isn't to say that governments on the gold standard didn't have to take steps akin to devaluing their currency in order to resolve trade deficits: they just did so by cutting wages and prices.
4. Bitcoin will never hit the cap of 21 million that would otherwise be reached in the year 2140, as a large number of coins, somewhere around four million, have been lost: for instance, the codes that would allow access to hundreds of millions of dollars worth of Bitcoin previously owned by James Howells is somewhere in a landfill in Wales (Max 2021). Generally, this means that the password that would allow someone to access them has been lost. There is also expected to be some gap between the total number minted and 21 million because of issues with the way that rounding is handled by the system.
5. In reality, Bitcoin and other cryptocurrencies have proven to be remarkably unstable, suffering chronic bouts of inflation and deflation.
6. When and if the maximum number of Bitcoins has been minted, the bounty system for paying accounts that process transactions will necessarily go away as well, replaced by a system in which users pay a transaction fee to have the transactions processed.
7. Some cryptocurrencies, often called stablecoins, are pegged to real assets, most commonly currencies like the dollar, with the groups running the currencies promising to alter the supply of the coins or bring in more currency in order to ensure a stable exchange rate between the cryptocurrency and the actual currency. This makes them vulnerable to the same type of speculative attacks that bedeviled currencies backed by precious metals in the past. Other stablecoins are, confusingly, pegged to the value of other cryptocurrencies.
8. Yes, even the Funko Pops, loath as I am to admit it.

9. Yes, that is how her name is spelled. I don't understand either, and I already know way more than I would care to about this particular young woman, so I'd prefer not to dig into it.

10. If anyone reading this doesn't already know, they might be wise to do themselves a favor and not look it up.

11. If false statements were made to entice buyers, that could be illegal, but we are very much in a gray area overall. Welch has denied that she, or any of the team behind the coin offering had any part in the price fluctuations.

12. It has since fallen dramatically from these highs, but as of this writing has a market capitalization of $15B (down from around $90B at the peak). If meme coin market capitalization meant the same thing that stock market capitalization means, that $15 billion would be about the same market cap as Williams Sonoma, Best Buy, or Domino's Pizza.

13. The bigger cost comes from having a medical team on standby to gather up the remains and get the body frozen and transported to the center, where the remains will be kept within the proscribed time frame.

14. About 80 percent say that they have never, and about 4 percent say that they have no idea what in the world the question is talking about. The distinction between "have owned cryptocurrencies" and "say that they have owned cryptocurrencies" comes up later.

15. Figures here are from the August 2024 US national survey carried out by the FDU Poll.

16. After the standard party identification question, respondents were asked, "In addition, which of the following terms would you use to describe your political views? You can choose as many as you like" (the order of the response options randomly was determined): Liberal, Moderate, Conservative, Socialist, Progressive, Libertarian, Make American Great Again or MAGA, Nationalist.

17. Figures for self-described libertarians should be taken cautiously, as there are only a small number (sixty-one, or about 8 percent) in the sample, and two-thirds of them are men.

18. Self-reported crypto owners who are considered likely voters: 50 percent Trump, 38 percent Harris. Non-owners: 53 percent Harris, 41 percent Trump. At the time of the survey, Trump had recently made headlines for embracing cryptocurrencies and promising to establish a federal "strategic Bitcoin reserve."

19. Slightly more than half (50.4 percent) of men in the August 2024 poll are being referenced here.

20. There are some indications that at least with regard to crypto ownership, the online sample of young men is pretty good: the proportion who say that they own crypto is very similar to the August 2024 survey, for instance.

21. There aren't enough women who report owning cryptocurrency in the sample to draw any valid conclusions about the effect of the experimental condition on women who own crypto versus those who don't.

4 "Hodl to the Moon!" Men, Meme Stocks, and the MOASS

1. Often even packaging the download codes in game boxes that can be bought in stores.
2. Such consoles don't have an external drive to play physical copies of games and are sold at a discount to standard versions of the consoles that have a physical drive.
3. Many within the meme stock community believe that the shares were not borrowed as part of a short sale, but were rather "naked shorts," in which someone agrees to buy back shares at a future time (shorting the stock) without actually owning any shares in the first place. This practice is generally banned by SEC regulations in the United States.
4. Given what happened to those Spartans, you'd think they'd find a different movie to cite.
5. The frequent references to "Planet of the Apes" and investors referring to themselves as "apes" probably emerged from the popular NFT Bored Ape Yacht Club, and as an ironic embrace of being seen as foolish, but has also been turned into a backronym for "All People Equal."
6. Bradley et al. (2024) pay particular attention to Due Diligence posts, which are structured around new information or analysis about a stock.
7. This is after excluding respondents who failed the attention check, as well as those who were moving through the survey implausibly quickly.
8. See the Methodological Appendix for regression results supporting these findings.

5 "It's all about winning." Masculinity and Finance

1. Sample characteristics like these are likely what drives the difference between many of the past lab findings on these topics and the findings presented here. I would argue that these studies are, generally, picking up endorsement of masculine norms of behavior (measured in this book with MRNI scores) among a sample population that's disproportionately likely to believe that they're falling short of that standard— basically, men in the gender gap. More on this later in the chapter.
2. Gambling behaviors do turn out to be related to the same factors that drive crypto buying; see Chapter 7.

3. Lusardi also makes the argument that the gap in measured financial knowledge might be driven, in part, by men's greater propensity to guess on multiple-choice tests when they don't know an answer. I would argue that such behaviors are likely to be conditional on the perceived gendering of the issue area being discussed, with finance being seen as a masculine area of interest and is another example of men's behavior being driven by an attempt to assert a masculine gender identity.

4. This paradigm also has the advantage, to the author at least, of being fun.

5. A full description of the study is found in the Methodological Appendix.

6. See the Methodological appendix for a discussion of the fourth item: results follow the same pattern, but since none of the options were exactly correct, it is excluded from the analysis.

7. Note that the figures for the sex differences and those for the sex–gender differences are drawing from slightly different groups, as the former includes respondents who did not answer, or were not asked, the masculinity-femininity items.

8. See the Methodological Appendix for the regression analyses supporting all of these results.

9. The length of the index finger, relative to the length of the ring finger, is used as a rough proxy for in utero testosterone exposure. Men tend to have a longer ring finger. This ratio has been tied to a number of behaviors, but the exact mechanism by which this occurs is not clear.

10. This isn't always possible, but the two studies referenced here were carried out simultaneously and thus have a very high crossover; additional details are found in the Methodological Appendix.

11. Even aside from the amount of research funding it would require to hold high stakes experiments, there are real ethical problems that would arise from such designs: if someone could win thousands of dollars for taking part in a study, there's no way that they're not going to do so, even if they're uncomfortable with the study. Some researchers have tried to get around this by using smaller amounts of money in very poor countries (as in Marlowe 2004), but that's not better.

12. There has been limited work on foreign exchange investments (forex), in which day traders try to leverage changes in the value of one currency against another for profit, but given the risk and complexity of such investments, they would likely follow the same patterns as the crypto and meme stock investments dealt with here.

6 "Bro. You don't realize how ignorant this comment is." How Men Talk about Crypto

1. This step is necessary to ensure that the posts fit into the categories, rather than vice versa. If the categories have been created or modified to fit specific posts, finding

that the post fits the category simply doesn't tell us anything. As such, best practices (when possible) are to discard all of the data that was used to create the coding categories before applying those categories to a fresh set of posts.

2. Of course, we don't know the actual sexual identity of any of these posters, but they nearly universally refer to each as male (except when they're insulting someone by calling them a girl), and the coding team reported that they didn't see any of the posters in the statements coded claiming to be a woman.

3. "Paper hands" is an insult meaning that someone is too quick to give up on an investment when it drops, often contrasted with someone who holds on through losses, demonstrating perseverance, who might be said to have "diamond hands."

4. The content analysis coding protocol allowed individual statements to get multiple codes: this statement was coded as questioning or demeaning intelligence, and as a supported assertion of knowledge.

5. There it is again. People love that word.

7 "Put it all on black." Other Performances of Technical Masculinities

1. This change was not due to legislation, but rather to a lawsuit from the State of New Jersey, which was attempting to legalize sports betting in order to avoid having to bail out casinos in Atlantic City.

2. The full scale is reproduced in the Methodological Appendix.

3. Though there have been indications that sportsbooks do their best to avoid paying out when gamblers actually manage to pull off such a coup: see Funt (2024). Other reports (Funt 2022) indicate that online sportsbooks also actively throttle or ban anyone who is too successful at picking winners.

4. Of course, cautioning that only knowledgeable and experienced players should make these kinds of bets would itself be attractive for players looking to demonstrate knowledge and mastery.

5. Young people (men and women) in the United States are also disproportionately likely to gamble via online slot machines, which involve no skill, and seem about as close to being a pigeon in a Skinner box as late capitalism has been able to achieve.

6. Among women, there's no significant gap based on gender traditionalism: 4 percent among "completely feminine" women, 7 percent among all other women.

7. A pink diamond Kobe Bryant in NBA 2K24, for instance, might sell for several hundred dollars.

8. Namely, 614–911 CE, because the Catholic Church wanted the year 1000 to arrive sooner.

9. The idea here being that since the moon can't be reflecting the light of the sun, the light generated by the moon doesn't carry heat as it would if it were reflected sunlight, and I, too, know how many problems there are with that whole line of reasoning.

10. It is unclear to what extent this relationship existed before Trump's candidacies, as political scientists in the United States were not commonly gathering data on masculinity-femininity and political views before 2015, though it seems likely that the relationship between asserted masculinity and Republican support has grown stronger in recent years.

11. The Republican candidate's own memecoin was marketed directly at his supporters and was easy to buy with a credit card in a way that would make most crypto investors wince, leading to the possibility that for some people, support for a candidate could have led to crypto ownership.

8 "Believers always win in the end." Technical Masculinities and the Future of Men

1. Celsius eventually was reorganized, and starting in 2024—about two years after freezing withdrawals—gave most depositors back about half of what they had put in, along with stock in a new publicly traded company that proposed to earn money through Bitcoin mining and validating blockchain transfers.

2. If anyone feels like reading the eight pages of "Certificate of No Objection Pursuant to LR 9075-2 / Certificate of No Objection Regarding the Debtors' Motion for Entry of an Order Authorizing the Debtors to Redact and File Under Seal Certain Confidential Terms of the Coinbase Distribution Services Agreement," it's there.

3. If the US government were to use a Bitcoin reserve to stabilize the price, it would potentially make Bitcoin more useful as a currency, but would run contrary to what most people holding Bitcoin want it to do, which is increase in price.

4. Given the size of world financial markets, we are likely nowhere near this point, nor would we expect to be there any time soon.

5. The narrative works better if they're rich, regardless of the facts about most content creators, whose royalty checks look more like mine than like Stephen King's.

6. The preferred LLM term for "making things up."

Works Cited

Abraham, J., Sutiksno, D. U., Kurniasih, N., & Warokka, A. (2019). Acceptance and penetration of bitcoin: The role of psychological distance and national culture. *SAGE Open*, *9*(3), 2158244019865813.

Acker, J. (2004). Gender, capitalism and globalization. *Critical Sociology*, *30*(1), 17–41.

Almog, R., & Kaplan, D. (2017). The nerd and his discontent: The seduction community and the logic of the game as a geeky solution to the challenges of young masculinity. *Men and Masculinities*, *20*(1), 27–48.

Amato, F. J. (2012). The relationship of violence to gender role conflict and conformity to masculine norms in a forensic sample. *The Journal of Men's Studies*, *20*(3), 187–208.

Anderson, E. (2010). *Inclusive masculinity: The changing nature of masculinities*. Routledge.

Anghel, E., Mahalik, J. R., & Harris, M. P. (2023). Examining the measurement invariance of the conformity to masculine norms inventory (CMNI-30) by sexual orientation. *Assessment*, *30*(7), 2318–31.

Archer, M. S. (2007). *Making our way through the world: Human reflexivity and social mobility*. Cambridge University Press.

Austin, J. L. (1962). *How to do things with words*. Harvard University Press.

Bajtelsmit, V. L., & Bernasek, A. (1996). Why do women invest differently than men? *Financial Counseling and Planning*, *7*(1): 1–10.

Baldwin, J. (2018). In digital we trust: Bitcoin discourse, digital currencies, and decentralized network fetishism. *Palgrave Communications*, *4*(1).

Barber, B. M., & Odean, T. (2001). Boys will be boys: Gender, overconfidence, and common stock investment. *The Quarterly Journal of Economics*, *116*(1), 261–92.

Barber, K. (2016). *Styling masculinity: Gender, class, and inequality in the men's grooming industry*. Rutgers University Press.

Bauer, N. M., & Santia, M. (2022). Going feminine: Identifying how and when female candidates emphasize feminine and masculine traits on the campaign trail. *Political Research Quarterly*, *75*(3), 691–705.

Bauer, N. M., & Santia, M. (2023). Gendered times: How gendered contexts shape campaign messages of female candidates. *Journal of Communication*, *73*(4), 329–41.

Baumeister, R. F., & Vohs, K. D. (2004). Sexual economics: Sex as female resource for social exchange in heterosexual interactions. *Personality and Social Psychology Review*, *8*(4), 339–63.

BBC (August 7, 2020). *The Matrix is a "trans metaphor," Lilly Wachowski says*. BBC News. https://www.bbc.com/news/newsbeat-53692435 (accessed October 1, 2024).

BBC (November 2, 2021). *Squid game crypto token collapses in apparent scam*. BBC News. https://www.bbc.com/news/business-59129466 (accessed July 3, 2024).

Beasley, C. (2008). Rethinking hegemonic masculinity in a globalizing world. *Men and Masculinities, 11*(1), 86–103.

Bem, S. L. (1974). The measurement of psychological androgyny. *Journal of Consulting and Clinical Psychology, 42*(2), 155–62.

Besen-Cassino, Y., & Cassino, D. (2014). Division of house chores and the curious case of cooking: The effects of earning inequality on house chores among dual-earner couples. *AG About Gender-International Journal of Gender Studies, 3*(6): 25–53.

Black Unicorn (1994). DigiCash Announcement. Post on Cypherpunks Forum, May 10, 1994. https://cypherpunks.venona.com/date/1994/05/msg00616.html (accessed November 5, 2024).

Blalock, G., Just, D. R., & Simon, D. H. (2007). Hitting the jackpot or hitting the skids: Entertainment, poverty, and the demand for state lotteries. *American Journal of Economics and Sociology, 66*(3), 545–70.

Bosson, J. K., Vandello, J. A., & Caswell, T. A. Precarious manhood. In M. Ryan & N. R. Branscombe (Eds.) *The sage handbook of gender and psychology* (pp. 115–30). Sage.

Bottazzi, L., & Lusardi, A. (2021). Stereotypes in financial literacy: Evidence from PISA. *Journal of Corporate Finance, 71*, 101831.

Bouma-Sims, E., Hassan, H., Nisenoff, A., Cranor, L. F., & Christin, N. (2024). "It was honestly just gambling": Investigating the experiences of teenage cryptocurrency users on Reddit. In *Twentieth symposium on usable privacy and security* (*SOUPS 2024*), pp. 333–52.

Bradley, D., Hanousek Jr, J., Jame, R., & Xiao, Z. (2024). Place your bets? The value of investment research on Reddit's Wallstreetbets. *The Review of Financial Studies, 37*(5), 1409–59.

Brannon, R. (1976). The male sex role: Our culture's blueprint for manhood, what it's done for us lately. In D. David & R. Brannon (Eds.), *The forty-nine percent majority: The male sex role*. Addison-Wesley.

Brannon, R., & Juni, S. (1984). A scale for measuring attitudes about masculinity. *Psychological Documents, 14*(Doc.# 2612).

Bridges, T. F. (2010). Men just weren't made to do this: Performances of drag at "Walk a Mile in Her Shoes" marches. *Gender & Society, 24*(1), 5–30.

Bridges, T. F. (2014). A very "gay" straight? Hybrid masculinities, sexual aesthetics, and the changing relationship between masculinity and homophobia. *Gender & Society, 28*(1), 58–82.

Bridges, T. F., & Pascoe, C. J. (2014). Hybrid masculinities: New directions in the sociology of men and masculinities. *Sociology Compass, 8*(3), 246–58.

Bridges, T. F., & Pascoe, C. J. (2018). In the elasticity of gender hegemony: Why hybrid masculinities fail to undermine gender and sexual inequality. In *Gender reckonings*, pp. 254–74. New York University Press.

Brunton, F. (2020). *Digital cash: The unknown history of the anarchists, utopians, and technologists who created cryptocurrency*. Princeton University Press.

Bucher-Koenen, T., Lusardi, A., Alessie, R., & Van Rooij, M. (2017). How financially literate are women? An overview and new insights. *Journal of Consumer Affairs*, *51*(2), 255–83.

Bujalka, E., Rich, B., & Bender, S. (2022). The manosphere as an online protection racket: How the red pill monetizes male need for security in modern society. *Fast Capitalism*, *19*(1), 1–16.

Burton, R. V., & Whiting, J. W. (1961). The absent father and cross-sex identity. *Merrill-Palmer Quarterly of Behavior and Development*, *7*(2), 85–95.

Carian, E. K., & Sobotka, T. C. (2018). Playing the Trump card: Masculinity threat and the US 2016 presidential election. *Socius*, *4*, 2378023117740699.

Carlson, J. (2015). Mourning Mayberry: Guns, masculinity, and socioeconomic decline. *Gender & Society*, *29*(3), 386–409.

Cassino, D. (2018). Emasculation, conservatism, and the 2016 election. *Contexts*, *17*(1), 48–53.

Cassino, D., & Besen-Cassino, Y. (March 2020). Sometimes (but not this time), a gun is just a gun: Masculinity threat and guns in the United States, 1999–2018. *Sociological Forum*, *35*(1), 5–23.

Cassino, D., & Besen-Cassino, Y. (2021). *Gender threat: American masculinity in the face of change*. Stanford University Press.

Cheah, E. T., & Fry, J. (2015). Speculative bubbles in Bitcoin markets? An empirical investigation into the fundamental value of Bitcoin. *Economics Letters*, *130*, 32–6.

Chen, H., & Volpe, R. P. (2002). Gender differences in personal financial literacy among college students. *Financial Services Review*, *11*(3), 289–307.

Cheng, C. (1999). Marginalized masculinities and hegemonic masculinity: An introduction. *The Journal of Men's Studies*, *7*(3), 295–315.

Chiu, T. N., & Yahya, M. A. (2022). The meme stock paradox. *Corporate and Business Law Journal*, *3*, 1.

Chong, K. H., & Kim, N. Y. (2022). "The model man": Shifting perceptions of Asian American masculinity and the renegotiation of a racial hierarchy of desire. *Men and Masculinities*, *25*(5), 674–97.

Connell, R. (2010). Lives of the businessmen. Reflections on life-history method and contemporary hegemonic masculinity. *Österreichische Zeitschrift für Soziologie*, *35*(2), 54–71.

Connell, R. (2016). Masculinities in global perspective: Hegemony, contestation, and changing structures of power. *Theory and Society*, *45*, 303–18.

Connell, R. W. (1982). *Making the difference: Schools, families and social division*. Routledge.

Connell, R. W. (1989). Cool guys, swots and wimps: The interplay of masculinity and education. *Oxford Review of Education, 15*(3), 291–303.

Connell, R. W. (1995). *Masculinities.* University of California Press.

Connell, R. W. (1998). Masculinities and globalization. *Men and Masculinities, 1*(1), 3–23.

Connell, R. W. (2005). Globalization, imperialism, and masculinities. In M. Kimmel & J. Hearn (Eds.), *Handbook of studies on men and masculinities* (pp. 71–89). Sage.

Connell, R. W., & Messerschmidt, J. W. (2005). Hegemonic masculinity: Rethinking the concept. *Gender & Society, 19*(6), 829–59.

Connell, R. W., & Wood, J. (2005). Globalization and business masculinities. *Men and Masculinities, 7*(4), 347–64.

Coston, B. M., & Kimmel, M. (2012). Seeing privilege where it isn't: Marginalized masculinities and the intersectionality of Privilege. *Journal of Social Issues, 68*(1), 97–111.

Cuthbertson, A. (2021). Bitcoin creator Satoshi Nakamoto now 15th richest person in the world. *The Independent* (November 15, 2021).

Dasgupta, R. (2005). Creating corporate warriors: The "salaryman" and masculinity in Japan. In *Asian masculinities* (pp. 118–34). Routledge.

Davison, C. (2016). The retail FX trader: Random trading and the negative sum game. Available at SSRN 2711214.

De Boise, S. (2015). I'm not homophobic, "I've got gay friends" evaluating the validity of inclusive masculinity. *Men and Masculinities, 18*(3), 318–39.

Demetriou, D. Z. (2001). Connell's concept of hegemonic masculinity: A critique. *Theory and Society, 30*(3), 337–61.

Dimuccio, S. H., & E. D. Knowles. (2025). Understanding the role of precarious manhood in politics. In M. McDermott & D. Cassino (Eds.), *Masculinity in American politics* (pp. 140–54). New York University Press.

Driessen, S., Jones, B., & Litherland, B. (2024). From fan citizenship to "fanspiracies": Politics and participatory cultures in times of crisis? *Convergence, 30*(1), 304–12.

Eckert, P., & McConnell-Ginet, S. (2013). *Language and gender.* Cambridge University Press.

Eisen, D. B., & Yamashita, L. (2019). Borrowing from femininity: The caring man, hybrid masculinities, and maintaining male dominance. *Men and Masculinities, 22*(5), 801–20.

Eisler, R. M., & J. R. Skidmore. (1987). Masculine gender role stress: Scale development and component factors in the appraisal of stressful situations. *Behavior Modification, 11*, 123–36.

Elias, J., & Beasley, C. (2009). Hegemonic masculinity and globalization: "Transnational business masculinities" and beyond. *Globalizations, 6*(2), 281–96.

Farrell, M. (November 27, 2015). The KaloBios Short Squeeze. *The Wall Street Journal.* http://blogs.wsj.com/moneybeat/2015/11/27/the-kalobios-short-squeeze.

Federal Reserve. (2023). Report on the economic well-being of U.S. households in 2022—May 2023. *Federal Reserve Publications*. https://www.federalreserve.gov/publications/2023-economic-well-being-of-us-households-in-2022-banking-credit.htm (accessed August 12, 2024).

Ferguson, H. (2001). Men and masculinities in late modern Ireland. In B. Pease & K. Pringle (Eds.), *A man's world? Changing men's practices in a globalized world* (pp. 118–34). Zed Books.

Funt, D. (November 17, 2022). Sportsbooks say you can win big. Then they try to limit winners. *The Washington Post*. https://www.washingtonpost.com/sports/2022/11/17/betting-limits-draft-kings-betmgm-caesars-circa/ (accessed January 13, 2025).

Funt, D. (January 17, 2024). He hit three monster bets—and then the sportsbook wouldn't pay. *The Washington Post*. https://www.washingtonpost.com/sports/2024/01/17/sports-bets-errors-payouts/ (accessed December 11, 2024).

Garcia, D., Tessone, C. J., Mavrodiev, P., & Perony, N. (2014). The digital traces of bubbles: Feedback cycles between socio-economic signals in the Bitcoin economy. *Journal of the Royal Society Interface*, *11*(99), 20140623.

Gater, R. (2024). Amalgamated masculinities: The masculine identity of contemporary marginalised working-class young men. *Sociology*, *58*(2), 312–29.

Ging, D. (2019a). Alphas, betas, and incels: Theorizing the masculinities of the manosphere. *Men and Masculinities*, *22*(4), 638–57.

Ging, D. (2019b). Bros v. Hos: Postfeminism, anti-feminism and the toxic turn in digital gender politics. In D. Ging & E. Siapara (Eds.), *Gender Hate Online* (pp. 45–67). Palgrave MacMillan.

Goldstein, M. (October 3, 2022). Kim Kardashian to pay $1.26 million to settle S.E.C. charges over crypto promotion. *The New York Times*. https://www.nytimes.com/2022/10/03/business/kim-kardashian-sec-crypto.html (accessed April 11, 2024).

Grable, J. E. (2000). Financial risk tolerance and additional factors that affect risk taking in everyday money matters. *Journal of Business and Psychology*, *14*, 625–30.

Greenebaum, J., & Dexter, B. (2018). Vegan men and hybrid masculinity. *Journal of Gender Studies*, *27*(6), 637–48.

Hanson, K. R., Pascoe, C. J., & Light, R. (2023). "It's getting difficult to be a straight White man": Bundled masculinity grievances on reddit. *Sex Roles*, *88*(3), 169–86.

Harris Poll. (February 9, 2021). Going viral: "Meme stocks" win over 1 in 4 Americans. https://theharrispoll.com/briefs/viral-stocks-gamestop/ (accessed August 16, 2024).

Hartley, R. E. (1959). Sex-role pressures and the socialization of the male child. *Psychological Reports*, *5*(2), 457–68.

Hirsch, D., & Kachtan, D. G. (2018). Is "hegemonic masculinity" hegemonic as masculinity? Two Israeli case studies. *Men and Masculinities*, *21*(5), 687–708.

Howson, R. (2006). *Challenging hegemonic masculinity*. Routledge.

Itzkowitz, J., Itzkowitz, J., & Schwartz, A. (2023). The gender gap in stock market participation: Evidence from stock gifting. Available at SSRN 4539694.

James, H., & Agunsoye, A. (2023). The gendered construction of risk in asset accumulation for retirement. *New political economy*, *28*(4), 574–91.

Jefferson, T. (2017). Subordinating hegemonic masculinity. In *Crime, Criminal Justice and Masculinities* (pp. 31–56). Routledge.

Kaplan, D., & Offer, S. (2022). Masculinity ideologies, sensitivity to masculinity threats, and fathers' involvement in housework and childcare among US employed fathers. *Psychology of Men & Masculinities*, *23*(4), 399.

Kaustia, M., Conlin, A., & Luotonen, N. (2023). What drives stock market participation? The role of institutional, traditional, and behavioral factors. *Journal of Banking & Finance*, *148*, 106743.

Kaya, A., Iwamoto, D. K., Brady, J., Clinton, L., & Grivel, M. (2019). The role of masculine norms and gender role conflict on prospective well-being among men. *Psychology of Men & Masculinities*, *20*(1), 142.

Kelly, A. (2023). Alpha and nerd masculinities: Anti-feminism in the digital sphere. In N. van der Gagg, A. Massoumian, & D. Nightingale (Eds.), *Patriarchy in practice: Ethnographies of everyday masculinities* (pp. 25–40). Bloomsbury.

Kendall, L. (1999). "The nerd within": Mass media and the negotiation of identity among computer-using men. *The Journal of Men's Studies*, *7*(3), 353–69.

Kendall, L. (2000). "Oh no! I'm a nerd!" Hegemonic masculinity on an online forum. *Gender & Society*, *14*(2), 256–74.

Kessler, S., Ashenden, D. J., Connell, R. W., & Dowsett, G. W. (1985). Gender relations in secondary schooling. *Sociology of Education*, *58*(1), 34–48.

Keynes, J. M. 1936. *The general theory of employment, interest and money*. Palgrave-Macmillan.

Klapper, L., & Lusardi, A. (2020). Financial literacy and financial resilience: Evidence from around the world. *Financial Management*, *49*(3), 589–614.

Komarovsky, M. ([1976] 2004). *Dilemmas of masculinity: A study of college youth* (Vol. 7). Rowman Altamira.

Lemaster, P., & Strough, J. (2014). Beyond mars and venus: Understanding gender differences in financial risk tolerance. *Journal of Economic Psychology*, *42*, 148–60.

Levant, R. F., Hirsch, L. S., Celentano, E., & Cozza, T. M. (1992). The male role: An investigation of contemporary norms. *Journal of Mental Health Counseling*, *14*(3), 325–37.

Levant, R. F., Smalley, K. B., Aupont, M., House, A. T., Richmond, K., & Noronha, D. (2007). Initial validation of the male role norms inventory-revised (MRNI-R). *The Journal of Men's Studies*, *15*(1), 83–100.

Longtermtrends.net. (2025). Home price to income ratio. https://www.longtermtrends.net/home-price-median-annual-income-ratio/ (accessed January 22, 2025).

Lopez-Gonzalez, H., Estévez, A., & Griffiths, M. D. (2018). Controlling the illusion of control: A grounded theory of sports betting advertising in the UK. *International Gambling Studies*, *18*(1), 39–55.

Lu, A., & Wong, Y. J. (2013). Stressful experiences of masculinity among US-born and immigrant Asian American men. *Gender & Society, 27*(3), 345–71.

Markstedt, E., Wängnerud, L., Solevid, M., & Djerf-Pierre, M. (2021). The subjective meaning of gender: How survey designs affect perceptions of femininity and masculinity. *European Journal of Politics and Gender, 4*(1), 51–70.

Marlowe, F. W. (2004). Dictators and ultimatums in an egalitarian society of hunter-gatherers: The Hadza of Tanzania. In J. Henrich, R. Boyd, S Bowles, C. Camerer, E. Fehr & H Gintis (Eds.) *Foundations of human sociality: Economic experiments and ethnographic evidence from fifteen small-scale societies* (pp. 168–93). Oxford.

Max, B. T. (2021). Half a Billion in Bitcoin, Lost in the Dump. *The New Yorker*, December 6.

McDermott, M. L. (2016). *Masculinity, femininity, and American political behavior*. Oxford University Press.

McDermott, R. C., Levant, R. F., Hammer, J. H., Borgogna, N. C., & McKelvey, D. K. (2019). Development and validation of a five-item male role norms inventory using bifactor modeling. *Psychology of Men & Masculinities, 20*(4), 467.

McKenzie, B., & Silverman, J. (2023). *Easy money: Cryptocurrency, casino capitalism, and the golden age of fraud*. Abrams.

Meier-Pesti, K., & Penz, E. (2008). Sex or gender? Expanding the sex-based view by introducing masculinity and femininity as predictors of financial risk taking. *Journal of Economic Psychology, 29*(2), 180–96.

Mendick, H., Ottemo, A., Berge, M., & Silfver, E. (2023). Geek entrepreneurs: The social network, Iron Man and the reconfiguration of hegemonic masculinity. *Journal of Gender Studies, 32*(3), 283–95.

Messerschmidt, J. W. (2015). *Masculinities in the making: From the local to the global*. Rowman & Littlefield.

Messerschmidt, J. W. (2018). *Hegemonic masculinity: Formulation, reformulation, and amplification*. Rowman & Littlefield.

Messerschmidt, J. W. (2019). The salience of "hegemonic masculinity." *Men and Masculinities, 22*(1), 85–91.

Messerschmidt, J. W., & Messner, M. A. (2018). Hegemonic, nonhegemonic, and "new" masculinities. In J. W. Messerschmidt, M. A. Messner, R. Connell & P. Y. Martin (Eds.). Gender reckonings: New social theory and research (pp. 35–56). New York University Press.

Morrell, R. (1998). Of boys and men: Masculinity and gender in Southern African studies. *Journal of Southern African Studies, 24*(4), 605–30.

Morrell, R. (2002). Men, movements, and gender transformation in South Africa. *The Journal of Men's Studies, 10*(3), 309–27.

Munsch, C. L., & Gruys, K. (2018). What threatens, defines: Tracing the symbolic boundaries of contemporary masculinity. *Sex Roles, 79*(7), 375–92.

Nanney, M., Chapman, N. G., Lellock, J. S., & Mikles-Schluterman, J. (2020). Gendered expectations, gatekeeping, and consumption in craft beer spaces. *Humanity & Society, 44*(4), 449–68.

Neelakantan, U., & Chang, Y. (2010). Gender differences in wealth at retirement. *American Economic Review, 100*(2), 362–7.

Nelson, J. (2020). Petro-masculinity and climate change denial among white, politically conservative American males. *International Journal of Applied Psychoanalytic Studies, 17*(4), 282–95.

Neuman, N., Gottzén, L., & Fjellström, C. (2017). Masculinity and the sociality of cooking in men's everyday lives. *The Sociological Review, 65*(4), 816–31.

Newman, N. F. (2023). GameStopped: How Robinhood's GameStop trading halt reveals the complexities of retail investor protection. *Fordham Journal of Corporate & Financial Law, 28*, 395.

Oeppen, C. (2023). Misogyny, fear or boundary maintenance? Responses to brand activism on gender diversity amongst players of Magic: The Gathering. In N. van der Gagg, A. Massoumian, & D. Nightingale (Eds.), *Patriarchy in practice: Ethnographies of everyday masculinities* (pp. 133–51). Bloomsbury.

O'Neill, R. (2018). *Seduction: Men, masculinity and mediated intimacy.* John Wiley.

Ozbay, C., & Soybakis, O. (2020). Political masculinities: Gender, power, and change in Turkey. *Social Politics: International Studies in Gender, State & Society, 27*(1), 27–50.

Parent, M. C., Kalenkoski, C. M., & Cardella, E. (2018). Risky business: Precarious manhood and investment portfolio decisions. *Psychology of Men & Masculinity, 19*(2), 195.

Parsons, T. ([1954] 2010). *Essays in sociological theory.* Simon and Schuster.

Phillips, R. C., &Gorse, D. (2018). Cryptocurrency price drivers: Wavelet coherence analysis revisited. *PloS One, 13*(4), e0195200.

Pleck, J. H. & Sawyer, J. (1974). *Men and masculinity.* Prentice-Hall.

Post, T., Van den Assem, M. J., Baltussen, G., & Thaler, R. H. (2008). Deal or no deal? Decision making under risk in a large-payoff game show. *American Economic Review, 98*(1), 38–71.

Quam, S., VanHook, C., Szoko, N., Passarello, A., Miller, E., & Culyba, A. J. (2020). Racial identity, masculinities, and violence exposure: Perspectives from male adolescents in marginalized neighborhoods. *Journal of Adolescent Health, 67*(5), 638–44.

Randles, J. M. (2020). *Essential dads: The inequalities and politics of fathering.* University of California Press.

Reidy, D. E., Berke, D. S., Gentile, B., & Zeichner, A. (2014). Man enough? Masculine discrepancy stress and intimate partner violence. *Personality and Individual Differences, 68*, 160–4.

Rogers, A. A., Nielson, M. G., & Santos, C. E. (2021). Manning up while growing up: A developmental-contextual perspective on masculine gender-role socialization in adolescence. *Psychology of Men & Masculinities, 22*(2), 354.

Ronson, Jon (February 12, 2015). How one stupid tweet blew up Justine Sacco's life. *The New York Times Magazine* (accessed September 18, 2015).

Rosenberg, B. G., Sutton-Smith, B., & Morgan, E. (1961). The use of opposite sex scales as a measure of psychosexual deviancy. *Journal of Consulting Psychology*, *25*(3), 221.

Schippers, M. (2007). Recovering the feminine other: Masculinity, femininity, and gender hegemony. *Theory and Society*, *36*, 85–102.

Schmitz, R. M., & Haltom, T. M. (2017). "I wanted to raise my hand and say I'm not a feminist": College men's use of hybrid masculinities to negotiate attachments to feminism and gender studies. *The Journal of Men's Studies*, *25*(3), 278–97.

Serada, A. (2023). Happier than ever: The role of public sentiment in cryptocurrencies, meme stocks, and NFTs. In *Activist retail investors and the future of financial markets* (pp. 35–53). Routledge.

Serviss, G. P. (1900). *The moon metal.* Harper and Brothers.

Siapara, E. (2019). Online misogyny as witch hunt: Primitive accumulation in the age of techno-capitalism. In D. Ging and E. Siapara (Eds.), *Gender hate online* (pp. 22–44). Palgrave MacMillan.

Sims, C., & Cereno, B. (July 2, 2018). The dude hates wizards: The gospel of Luke. In *Apocrypals.* https://apocrypals.libsyn.com/10-the-dude-hates-wizards-the-gos pel-of-luke (accessed August 4, 2025).

Tash, M. S., Kolesnikova, O., Ahani, Z., & Sidorov, G. (2024). Psycholinguistic and emotion analysis of cryptocurrency discourse on X platform. *Scientific Reports*, *14*(1), 8585.

Terman, L. M., & Miles, C. C. (1936). *Sex and personality: Studies in masculinity and femininity.* McGraw-Hill.

Thébaud, S. (2010). Masculinity, bargaining, and breadwinning: Understanding men's housework in the cultural context of paid work. *Gender & Society*, *24*(3), 330–54.

Thompson, A. (2024). The beginner's guide to prop bets. Bookies.com. Retrieved January 16, 2025 from https://bookies.com/guides/prop-bets.

Thompson Jr, E. H., & Pleck, J. H. (1986). The structure of male role norms. *American Behavioral Scientist*, *29*(5), 531–43.

Tinghög, G., Ahmed, A., Barrafrem, K., Lind, T., Skagerlund, K., & Västfjäll, D. (2021). Gender differences in financial literacy: The role of stereotype threat. *Journal of Economic Behavior & Organization*, *192*, 405–16.

Van Houtte, M. (2023). Understanding the gender gap in school (dis) engagement from three gender dimensions: The individual, the interactional and the institutional. *Educational Studies*, *49*(2), 260–78.

Van Valkenburgh, S. P. (2021). Digesting the red pill: Masculinity and neoliberalism in the manosphere. *Men and Masculinities*, *24*(1), 84–103.

Vandello, J. A., & Bosson, J. K. 2013. Hard won and easily lost: A review and synthesis of theory and research on precarious manhood. *Psychology of Men & Masculinity*, *14*, 101–13.

Verlaine, J., & Banjeri, G. (2021). Keith Gill drove the GameStop Reddit mania. He talked to the journal. *Wall Street Journal*, January 29.

Vescio, T. K., & Schermerhorn, N. E. (2021). Hegemonic masculinity predicts 2016 and 2020 voting and candidate evaluations. *Proceedings of the National Academy of Sciences, 118*(2), e2020589118.

Walker, G. J., Hinch, T. D., & Weighill, A. J. (2005). Inter- and intra-gender similarities and differences in motivations for casino gambling. *Leisure Sciences, 27*(2), 111–30.

Walker, G. W. (2006). Disciplining protest masculinity. *Men and Masculinities, 9*(1), 5–22.

Watson, J., & McNaughton, M. (2007). Gender differences in risk aversion and expected retirement benefits. *Financial Analysts Journal, 63*(4), 52–62.

Wetherell, M., & Edley, N. (1999). Negotiating hegemonic masculinity: Imaginary positions and psycho-discursive practices. *Feminism & Psychology, 9*(3), 335–56.

Weaver, J. R., Vandello, J. A., & Bosson, J. K. (2013). Intrepid, imprudent, or impetuous? The effects of gender threats on men's financial decisions. *Psychology of Men & Masculinities, 14*, 184–91.

Wedgwood, N., Connell, R., & Wood, J. (2023). Deploying hegemonic masculinity: A study of uses of the concept in the journal *Psychology of Men & Masculinities, 24*(2), 83.

Wesley, L. (2015). The intersection of race and gender: Teaching reformed gender ideologies to black males in the context of hegemonic masculinity. *Journal of Black Sexuality and Relationships, 1*(4), 63–84.

West, C., & Zimmerman, D. H. (1987). Doing gender. *Gender & society, 1*(2), 125–51.

Whiting, B. B. (1965). Sex identity conflict and physical violence: A comparative study. *American Anthropologist, 67*(6), 123–40.

Whybrow, A., Andrade, M., Torrance, J., & Newall, P. W. S. (2024). "Are you struggling to keep it up?": Problematic content in day-trading adverts targeted at men on Instagram. https://doi.org/10.31219/osf.io/4t2as.

Williams, C. (Writer), Rees, P. (Writer), Christiansen, S. (Director), & Williams, L. G. (Director) (August 7, 2014). Traffic tricks (Season 12, Episode 14) [TV series episode]. In *Mythbusters*. Beyond Productions.

Willis, P. ([1977] 2017). *Learning to labour: How working class kids get working class jobs*. Routledge.

Wolkomir, M. (2012). "You fold like a little girl": (Hetero) gender framing and competitive strategies of men and women in no limit Texas hold em poker games. *Qualitative Sociology, 35*, 407–26.

Yaffee-Bellamy, D. (2024). Bitcoin hits a milestone: $100,000. *The New York Times*, December 4.

Yang, Y. (2020). What's hegemonic about hegemonic masculinity? Legitimation and beyond. *Sociological Theory, 38*(4), 318–33.

Yermack, D. ([2013] 2024). Is Bitcoin a real currency? An economic appraisal. In *Handbook of digital currency* (pp. 29–40). Academic Press.

Yousaf, I., Pham, L., & Goodell, J. W. (2023). The connectedness between meme tokens, meme stocks, and other asset classes: Evidence from a quantile connectedness approach. *Journal of International Financial Markets, Institutions and Money, 82,* 101694.

Yu, J., McLellan, R., & Winter, L. (2021). Which boys and which girls are falling behind? Linking adolescents' gender role profiles to motivation, engagement, and achievement. *Journal of Youth and Adolescence, 50*(2), 336–52.

Index